Praise for Saints

'Wonderful . . . Each lifestory is a gem . . . It's beautifully
written, evocative, informative, compulsive reading'
Scottish Field Magazine

'A rewarding and beguiling collection of legends that
are little known, a wide-ranging introduction to
medieval saints' lives'
Literary Review

'The legends are beautifully told and illustrated . . .
The writer's approach is both imaginative and scholarly'
The Tablet

Praise for *Wild*

'Marries words and images to create a special echo of this country's rich past'
The Times

'Across seven themed chapters the *Storyland* author presents an inspiring excavation of the British countryside through diverse medieval texts'
Waterstones
(Best History Books of 2022)

'Suffused with portent and otherworldliness. Listeners gain a series of folk songs, written and performed by Jeffs, each of which adds a thrilling new dimension to these ancient fables'
Guardian
(Audiobook of the Week)

Praise for Storyland

'This gorgeous book should live on the bookshelves in every house that cares about the idea of Britain, what it was and where it came from'
The Times

'A beautiful retelling of British myths and exquisitely illustrated too'
James Holland, Daily Express

'It's hugely original, and starkly lovely: I've never come across anything quite like it'
Katherine Rundell

Also by Amy Jeffs

STORYLAND

WILD

Saints

Medieval Legends of Heroes, Humans and Magic

AMY JEFFS

❖

riverrun

First published in Great Britain in 2024 by riverrun
This paperback edition published in 2025 by

r

riverrun

An imprint of

Quercus Editions Ltd
Carmelite House
50 Victoria Embankment
London EC4Y 0DZ

An Hachette UK company

The authorised representative in the EEA is Hachette Ireland,
8 Castlecourt Centre, Dublin 15, D15 XTP3, Ireland (email: info@hbgi.ie)

Copyright © 2024 Amy Jeffs
Illustrations copyright © 2024 Amy Jeffs

The moral right of Amy Jeffs to be identified as the author
of this work has been asserted in accordance with the
Copyright, Designs and Patents Act, 1988.

All rights reserved. No part of this publication may be reproduced or
transmitted in any form or by any means, electronic or mechanical, including
photocopy, recording, or any information storage and retrieval system,
without permission in writing from the publisher.

Quercus Editions Ltd hereby exclude all liability to the extent
permitted by law for any errors or omissions in this book and for any
loss, damage or expense (whether direct or indirect) suffered by a
third party relying on any information contained in this book.

A CIP catalogue record for this book is available from the British Library.

Paperback ISBN 978 1 52941 662 6
Ebook ISBN 978 1 52941 663 3

1

Designed and typeset by EM&EN
Printed and bound in Great Britain by Clays Ltd, Elcograf S.p.A.

MIX
Paper | Supporting responsible forestry
FSC® C104740

Papers used by Quercus are from well-managed forests
and other responsible sources.

For Christine and Christopher,

my parents.

Contents

Foreword: Legenda *xv*

Quikening 1

JANUARY 3

Scoithín: The Sailor on the Plain 5

Edward the Confessor: An Eye for an Eye 12

Mungo: The Broken Bird 23

Smaragdus: The Lost Child 32

Agnes: Death in Aquarius 39

FEBRUARY 47

Brigid: Virgin, Again 49

Werburgh: The Goose Princess 57

Ia: The Impossible Boat 67

MARCH 73

David: Shifting Ground 75

Patrick: The Dreadful Door 83

Cuthbert: Otters in the Cold 93

William of Norwich: The Body in the Woods 102

Outsending 111

APRIL 113

George: The Princess and the Dragon 114

Mellitus: Sacred Salmon 126

Erkenwald: A Secret under St Paul's 136

MAY 145

Brendan: The Skull 146

Mary: Cherry Time 152

JUNE 163

Boniface: The Fallen Oak 165

Columba: The Wind Whisperer 175

Alban: The Unfortunate Executioner 181

Mightsomeness 191

JULY 193

Veronica: The True Image 195

Uncumber: The Golden Shoe 202

Margaret: A Strange Gestation 211

Christopher: The Wandering Giant 220

James: The Unthinkable Penance 233

The Seven Sleepers: Into the Cave 243

AUGUST 253

Germanus: The Resurrection 255

Lawrence: 'Turn Me over and Eat' 259

Bartholomew: Skin on Skin 265

SEPTEMBER 271

Marymas: From Eden to Golgotha 272

Ailbhe: Wolf Child 282

Cosmas and Damian: Spiritual Surgery 288

Michael the Archangel: A Hole in the Head 294

Clensing 303

OCTOBER 305

Frideswide: The Hiding Place 306

Ursula and Cordula: 11,000 Dead 314

NOVEMBER 323

Martin: Four Wishes 325

Edmund: Aelwine the Hairdresser 335

Catherine: The Scholar and the Wheel 345

DECEMBER 355

Nicholas: The Mistake 357

Thomas Becket: The Rose and the Lily 364

TESTAMENT 381

Epilogue 383

Acknowledgements 393
Further Reading 397
Timeline of Feast Days 413
Index 417

Who has not wondered in what mysterious forests our ancestors discovered the models for the beasts and birds upon their tapestries; and on what planet were enacted the scenes they have portrayed? It is in vain that the dead fingers have stitched beneath them – and can picture the mocking smile with which these crafty cozeners of posterity accompanied the action – the words 'February', or 'Hawking', or 'Harvest', having us believe that they are but illustrations of the activities proper to the different months. We know better. These are not the normal activities of proper men. What kind of beings peopled the earth four or five centuries ago, what strange lore they had acquired, and what were their sinister doings, we shall never know. Our ancestors kept their secret well.

Hope Mirrlees, *Lud-in-the-Mist* (1926)

Foreword: Legenda

There's a giant so strong and so holy, just seeing him will prevent sudden death. Or so it was said. On the walls of medieval churches, his spectre yet paddles ankle-deep in a fading river, an infant on his shoulder; the moment before the rising flood, the growing weight of the child and the first of the achievements for which the giant, Scoundrel, will earn a new title and name. Saint Christopher.

This book sets out to enchant you, to appal you, to transport you to another world, and, by the end, to declare with you that we should be as drawn to medieval saints' legends as we are to myth, folklore and fairy-tale. And that is hopefully to say, hauled by our collars and cuffs. But this book does not expect you to find these stories moral or believe them. It takes them for the crafted creatures they are.

Saints transcend a single religion. They are found globally; characters who renounce the world and live in spiritual ecstasy. In the words of the *Bhagavad Gita*, a Hindu text from the second half of the first millennium BCE, 'forsaking conceit and power, pride and lust, wrath and possessions, tranquil in heart, and free from ego, [the saint or ascetic] becomes worthy of becoming one with the

Foreword: Legenda

imperishable'. Here we will meet legends born, unless biblical, from around the fourth century and set in territories within and sometimes beyond the late Roman Empire. Thus the tales' heroes originate from as far east as Turkey and North Africa and as far west as Britain and Ireland (by medieval European reckoning, the very ends of the world). And their readers' world view, inherent to the stories themselves, is of an orb divided into Asia, Africa and Europe, with East at the top, Jerusalem in the centre, and the Mediterranean, as the cosmic drama unfolds and as its name proclaims, ebbing and flowing over the more-or-less middle of the earth.

All saints' legends are human episodes in a divine history that begins with the world's creation by God. Lucifer's expulsion to Hell follows and the fall of the rebel angels, along with the Fall of Adam and Eve after consuming the forbidden fruit in the Garden of Eden. Humanity's loss to infernal forces remains absolute for several thousand years, during which time every dead soul goes to Hell. Then, the Archangel Gabriel appears to Mary and she agrees to carry and deliver the very Son of God. His later Crucifixion and Resurrection redeem the sins of humanity and release the good souls from Hell to Heaven. After this, humans must follow Christ's teachings and cleanse themselves of sin through Church sacraments; here begins the struggle to escape the determined, relentless, seductive solicitations of the Devil and achieve Salvation. In the end, the Apocalypse

Foreword: Legenda

will see Christ returning in glory, the Archangel Michael defeating Lucifer forever, and all the dead leaping from their coffins and rising from the depths of the ocean to join the living for the Final Judgement. Then, Michael will weigh the souls of each human who has ever lived, casting those unfit for Heaven into the slathering mouth of Hell.

Within the context of this urgent spectacle, saints were humans living between the Resurrection and the Second Coming of Christ, and their superhuman faith had set them apart, winning for them a place beside the throne of God and special access to the divine ear. In it they would advocate for the pious living who had made pilgrimages to the saint's earthly remains and offered candles at their shrines. There these faithful souls would look to images of high and low craftsmanship for protection, drink from phials, wear amulets and say ritual words on special days in ways that we might now call religious 'magic'. Later, when religious Reformation swept through sixteenth-century north-western Europe, the folk beliefs of the medieval age were labelled 'heathen' and the rituals were recorded and exaggerated to condemn the Catholic faith. Now, we often read the folk aspects of medieval Christianity as subversive relics of earlier faiths. But this is an over-simplification of a much more complex and interesting history.

The Christian medieval year had three parallel timelines. It had the seasonal cycle of manual occupations and leisure activities, like ploughing, making hay and enjoying the spring; then there was the 'liturgical cycle' of Church masses and rituals based around the life of Christ; and the third was the *sanctorale*: an achronological cycle of saintly feasts celebrated throughout the year and serving as markers on the circular annual road: St Brigid's Day, St Swithun's Day, Michaelmas, the feast of St Nicholas, St Stephen's Day and more besides. Cycles of feast days were written into calendars at the start of prayer books and Psalters (books of the Psalms). Their pantheon of saints varied depending on the interests of the makers and patrons, but the supersaints, like the disciples of Christ and the early martyrs, feature everywhere. When a saint's feast came around, it was customary for their life or *Vita* to be read aloud. These texts were also known as legends; some are historical, by our reckoning, some much less so. Some are written in dense Latin prose, full of learned allegories, some in accessible vernacular verse. Whatever the style, the word *legenda* was born with the cult of saints. In its original context, it does not mean a work of pseudo-history, but, quite simply, 'a thing to be read'.

I have structured this book according to the months of the year, retelling saints' legends as fictional narratives in the month in which their feast fell and following each story with a non-fiction commentary. Along the way, I will refer repeatedly to medieval liturgical calendars featuring the *sanctorale*.

Foreword: Legenda

Medieval calendar pages also commonly have accompanying illustrations of the associated Labours of the Months and sign of the Zodiac. For a fuller understanding, these are relevant too. The Labours of the Months reflect the seasonal timeline mentioned above. They are made up of a traditional catalogue of activities such as feasting, digging, reaping and threshing. The labours do not necessarily represent the lives of medieval people, but they were a widespread convention. While their exact subject and order varied with time and place, their connection to the seasons reminds us to feel a January chill as we read about St Mungo and to sweat in the putative July sun when we come to St Veronica.

Zodiac symbols often accompany illustrations of the labours, each symbol having a whole month to itself by medieval reckoning. And at this time, the symbols' significance was less to do with prognostication and more to do with the body. Medieval Europe received much Classical medical learning through Arabic scholars such as Abu Ma'shar al-Balkhi (died 886). The prevailing theory was that, just as four elements (earth, water, air and fire) governed the earth and its atmosphere, so the four humours (black bile, yellow bile, phlegm and blood) governed the body. The moon's relationship to the supercelestial bodies not only affected such earthly phenomena as the tides, but also how these humours flowed and how they could be managed through treatments like bloodletting. Given how implicated the medieval cult of saints was with the body and the passing seasons, I will return to the Labours of the Months and the Zodiac at the start of each new month.

Most of the research for this book happened in my twenties, which were spent in a pinch-myself haze at Cambridge studying for a PhD, as well as behind the scenes in the British Museum and the British Library. In academia, I studied medieval illuminated English manuscripts. At the Library, I interned for a collaborative project with the Bibliothèque nationale de France, which digitised hundreds of manuscripts from England and France, dating from between 700 and 1200 CE. At the British Museum, I spent every Friday making images of and rewriting catalogue entries for its vast collection of medieval pilgrim souvenirs and secular badges. These were mostly coin-sized lead alloy images, cheap as chips in the Middle Ages and enormously popular between the twelfth and sixteenth centuries. And those at the Museum had, for the most part, been found in the Thames by Victorian mudlarks, just as the collections in King's Lynn Museum, Salisbury Museum and Bristol's M-Shed had come from the mud of the River Purfleet, the old medieval sewers and the harbour respectively. Medieval badges introduced me to a wealth of legends, cultures of visual storytelling and folk belief. All this revealed to me both how much heritage the Protestant Reformation had destroyed, not just in terms of buildings and objects, but in terms of what remained in the collective memory.

Foreword: Legenda

No medieval calendar would have had the exact list of saints I am presenting here. I have chosen them for their legends' interest individually and as a group, alongside their potential as jumping-off points for telling a history of the medieval cult of saints and its demise in countries affected by the Protestant Reformation. To give myself some parameters (within which there is still an embarrassment of riches), I have chosen not to include mendicant and mystic saints or, apart from Uncumber, also known as Wilgefortis, whom we'll meet in July, any saints whose legends are set after 1200. This is the date when the papacy took full control of the 'canonisation' (saint-making) process and when saints are more likely to have existed in real life. Indeed, many of the saints included here have shady if not fictional origins and are no longer, or never were, recognised officially by the Catholic Church, which is probably one of the reasons I enjoy them so much. Inevitably, the picture is large and complicated and extends well beyond the scope of this book. Other writers specialising in medieval Cornwall, Wales, Ireland, Brittany, France, the Netherlands, Germany, Scandinavia, Spain, Italy, Armenia, Egypt, Turkey and Ethiopia (the list could go on) have tales and histories in their publications and up their sleeves that could (and do) fill a thousand or more books besides this one. I therefore encourage readers to go complement this text with their own explorations, perhaps with the help of the list of Further Reading at the end. I have tried, where possible, to

Foreword: Legenda

highlight which books and articles can be freely accessed online.

It is almost time to begin, but first I would like to give some background to the illustrations. Inspired by the beautiful children's book *Mama, Is it Summer Yet?* by Nikki McClure, I have illustrated these stories with paper cut-out. The whole image is connected to itself and, being made from black paper, demands thinking in light. Paper cut-out is also a joy to perform; I have relished the surgical quality of the process, somehow in keeping with the tales of gruesome martyrdoms, which, for all they were designed to horrify their readers, surely thrilled them too. In the same vein, skin-tones and textures have been underlaid using detailed images of parchment from William Cowley's.

When we speak of folklore, fairy-tale and myth, we should be speaking of saints' legends. They are not the property of a single creed. They are ours, whatever our beliefs. By the glimmer of words written in gold and the intrigue of letters in blood, I hope this book makes normality seem strange. I hope it brings the marvellous closer. *Saints* is a compendium of tales from another age that looked, as we do, for forces equal to the darkness: powers that would bind it and crush it each time it threatened to overwhelm. The pages of this new legendary contain old ideas quite different from our own, though, as you will read, they remain a witness to the immense antiquity of wonder and the longing to say, 'we are safe'.

Part One

Quikening

❖

January

On the medieval calendar page for January, a man of gold and pigment sits down to a Christmas banquet. He has two heads, their backs fused like a double mushroom. To the first of his open mouths, he lifts a strip of bread; to the second, a goblet of wine.

He is Janus, January's namesake, and the Roman god of thresholds. In medieval calendars, he always eats for two, looking forward and back. He reflects on the year just gone and anticipates the year to come and, by now, he has done so seven hundred times.

January's labour, 'Feasting', is a tribute to labours already complete. And for the super-rich, the groaning table was no artistic fantasy. In 1424, the funeral feast of Nicholas Bubwith, Bishop of Bath and Wells, included blancmange (not a sweet dish, at this time, but one of rice, blanched almonds and white meat), pork shins, roast heron, swan, larks, snipe, plover and woodcock, with swan's neck pudding and baked custard.

At New Year's feasts, gifts would have passed from hand to hand. There are surviving medieval gold rings bearing the words *en bon an* ('a good year'): presents, or 'handsels', to bestow fortune on the receiver.

Physically speaking, January implicates ailments of the calves and ankles, but it also concerns melancholy. No wonder, then, that it is the month for gathering at the table, for storytelling, and for giving gifts in hope of future fortunes. Here you will meet Scoithín (pronounced *Skuh-heen*), Edward the Confessor, Mungo, Smaragdus and Agnes: an Irish monk, an English king, a British bishop, an Egyptian hermit and a Roman virgin martyr. And maybe it's just my imagination, but there seems to me a wintry yearning for January's invisible sun. Our eyes cannot be trusted: reality is just out of sight.

Scoithín: The Sailor on the Plain

Died 6th century
Feast Day: 2 January

The nameless man walked, kicking the seeding grasses and sending up clouds of pollen that would have made him sneeze had he been in an ordinary meadow. It was very large and very flat. There were no hills or mounds or trees, no other people or animals to distract his mind. He felt carefree and let his gaze fly off and away, as far as it could reach into the blue-grey distance.

Then something came into view, disturbing the expanse before him. It was growing apace, and it couldn't be part of the meadow; its shape was too sharp. And as it came closer, he saw that it had a sail full of a wind he could not feel. Then he saw, by this and by the point of its prow ploughing through the meadow, slicing the green, making it roll like black waves, that it was a boat, the turf it had parted collapsing back in a cloud of pollen, butterflies and bees.

The nameless man stopped walking and watched in amazement. Then he leapt out of the way to let the long vessel pass by without crashing into him. As he rolled onto his back in the damp stems of the grasses, he saw people on the boat craning at him in return, their hair and clothes whipping about them, as if they stood in high winds, though all around the air was still. They wore thick, warming coats, despite the mellow sunshine.

'Stop the boat!' cried a man onboard with billowing blond hair and a coat of brown wool. His companions hurried to obey. They furled the sails and tossed an anchor over the side of the boat. It plunged into the meadow with a ripping noise, driving through the grass, the roots and the sod, until the anchor found purchase on some hidden rock and brought the vessel to a stop.

It swayed a little as the blond man in the woollen coat leaned out, his hair still whipping this way and that, as he called back to the nameless man:

'How are you walking on the water?'

The nameless man approached the boat. 'I'm not walking on water,' he said, 'I'm walking on earth.'

Then he bent down and looked for something he could give the man to show what he was saying was true. He saw a red flower and picked it, straightened up and walked through the long grasses to the boat where the man stood.

'Here,' the nameless man said.

Their hands touched as the flower passed from one to the other, and, as soon as it left the nameless man's grasp, the bloom began bending and flapping in the wind.

Scoithín: The Sailor on the Plain

The man on the boat cupped a hand around the flower and looked at it, frowning and shaking his head. His companions, brethren by the look of their carefully shaved heads, gathered round and all seemed just as bewildered. Then the nameless man called up from the ground, nudging them out of their wonder. He had a question in return.

'How are you sailing on a field?'

The other man said, 'I'm not.'

Then he gave the flower to one his brothers, and said to him:

'Help me reach the sea.'

The brother kept him from falling as he leaned out of the boat, stretching his hand down to the turf, pale hair and woollen clothes still blustering, though the grass hardly moved at all.

Then the man snatched at the grasses. All at once, he was holding a salmon, glittering silver against green. He tossed the fish to the nameless man, who caught it with both hands and cried out.

The salmon was cold as snow. He struggled to keep hold of it as it thrashed and gaped. When he let it go, it waggled through the air, disappearing into the grass in a cloud of yellow dust.

Already the men on the boat were raising the anchor and unfurling the sails, which filled with wind that the nameless man couldn't feel. But the other man called back as the vessel moved away, hugging his cloak around him.

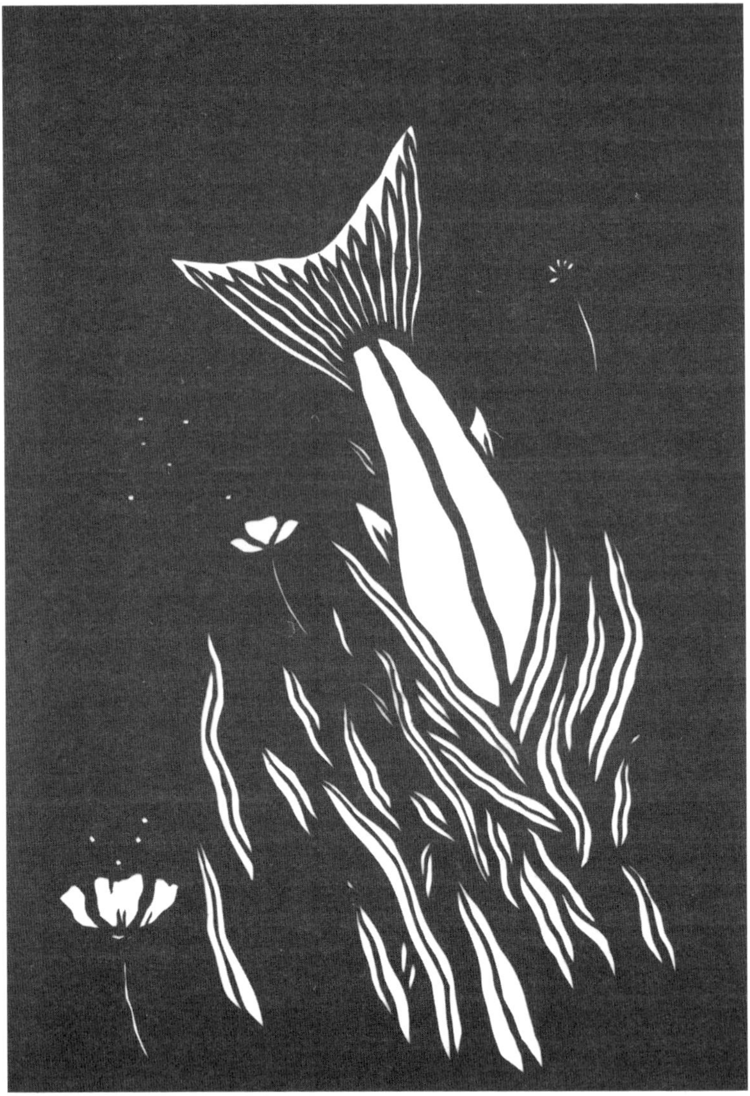

Scoithín: The Sailor on the Plain

'I am Barra of Cork. And from this day forward your name will be Flower.'

The Irish word for flower is *scoth*, so the nameless man whispered his new name to himself in his own language:

'Scoithín.'

And as he watched the blond-haired Barra sail away, shrinking until he and his boat were no bigger than the bees that pitched and dived around him, Scoithín remembered that he had heard stories of Barra, whom some called Finbarra because of his blond hair. Hadn't his mother been put in a fire for conceiving him? Hadn't the unborn Barra called out from his mother's belly, telling her persecutors that they would go to hell? Scoithín breathed long and slow and turned to continue his journey. The sun was warm on his face and the ground was firm beneath his dew-flecked feet.

❖

With the story of St Scoithín we meet a paradox fundamental to the medieval cult of saints. There are only one or two saints' legends that completely lose their grip on history (see Uncumber in July) and most are at least loosely rooted in the soil of earthly time. They begin with the lives of saints who appear in the Bible as the family and disciples of Christ. Some of these figures go on to become the first missionaries, taking the Gospel into Armenia and India and other territories to the north-east. Some of those figures become among the early martyrs, killed abroad or within the Roman Empire. Later martyrs die during the successive swathes of Christian persecution. In 313, Emperor Constantine converted to Christianity and the first monastic communities in the deserts of Egypt followed, as well as another raft of missionaries. With the latter, we come to Patrick, Hilary and Martin of Tours, as well as itinerant bones evangelising from beyond the grave, like those of James and Andrew. And the story of Scoithín and Barra plays out just after that, against the backdrop of early monasticism in Britain and Ireland.

However, the story retold here, from an anonymous Irish text in an eleventh-century manuscript, is reminiscent of early Irish *Immrama*, or 'voyage tales'. These contain Otherworlds that the characters encounter on their journeys. In the *Immraim Brain* (or 'Voyage of Bran'), Bran and his companions are at sea when they meet Manannân Mac Lir, the pre-Christian Irish sea god, riding over the water in a chariot. To Manannân, the bitter sea and its leaping salmon are a pleasant field full of gambolling lambs where the god and his family live in bliss. The saint, or god in the *Immrama*, inhabits two worlds at once. While not all saints' legends are as lyrical in their expression of the earthly within the eternal, you will see that all contend with it.

St Scoithín is held to have died in the sixth century. In the *Life of St David*, which we will come back to in March,

Scoithín: The Sailor on the Plain

Scoithín sails across the Irish Sea on the back of a marine monster to warn David of an assassination attempt. In this text, he has two names, although both are given in a Latin form: 'Scutinus, who has also another name, Scolanus'.

The name 'Scolanus' reappears as Yscolan in the Welsh poem *Gwerz Skolan* from the mid-thirteenth-century *Llyfr Du Caerfyrddin* (known as the Black Book of Carmarthen), as well as in a related Breton ballad. 'Yscolan' means, not 'flower', but 'the phantom'. He has committed terrible crimes. He has raped his sisters and killed the resulting children. Not only that, but Yscolan has lost his mother's most treasured book in the sea. In the poem he assures her that the book, at least, is safe. A small fish guards it and only three pages are damaged, one by his tears, one by fire and one by blood. We may never know how to reconcile Yscolan the rapist with Scoithín the Paradise-wandering saint, but it makes for a suitable story with which to begin January, the month of the two-faced god and the conundrum of forever-ness and time.

Edward the Confessor: An Eye for an Eye

Died 1066
Feast Day: 5 January

Edward often wished, as he washed the eyes of each hopeful face, that they were his brother's eyes and his brother's now half-remembered face. Alfred had been brave, beautiful and wholly undeserving of death. But he had put his faith in a traitor.

Edward bathed the supplicants' eyelids – some glued shut with mucus, some scarred, some with no outward sign of damage – and prayed. Did God restore sight through him because of how Alfred had died? Or might Edward, had he been there, have been able to save his brother? He would wonder who had betrayed Alfred to Harthacnut and abandoned him in the torturing dens of Ely. Had his deceiver been English, Danish or French?

When Edward had been crowned, he had met his court. Edith had arrived with her father and brothers, Godwin, Harold and Tostig. Pale-faced, she had presented Edward with a cloak that she had embroidered herself with a delicate pattern of birds and flowers, offering her prayers for his reign and standing out from the sycophants like a wild rose in a tangle of thorns.

As time passed, Edward realised that her father, Earl Godwin, intended Edith to become Edward's wife. Having been a courtier since the days of the Danish kings, Godwin was a cunning diplomat, forever winding among the courtiers, laying an arm across their shoulders and speaking softly, smilingly, in their ears. Almost by chance, it seemed, Edith often ended up sitting closest to Edward in the hall, though she rarely ate more than a mouthful and blushed if he spoke to her. But it was not due to her father that Edward married her. He had loved her from their first meeting.

After the wedding, Edward and Edith agreed to live in chastity. Miracles followed. Edward received a vision of the drowning of the Danish King even before the news had reached England. Then Edward had healed the legs of a man who couldn't walk. Hundreds began coming to Edward's palace for healing. Mostly, his prayers would help the blind to see.

He had wanted to make a pilgrimage to Jerusalem, but when his royal duties prevented him, he resolved to restore the church on Thorney that St Peter himself had appeared to consecrate long ago, in the days of Mellitus, the very first Bishop of London.

Edith supported him as they organised for stonemasons, carpenters, metalsmiths, glaziers and embroiderers to beautify the old building. He found perfect companionship in her, and she in him. She prayed with him, advised him and loved him. But sometimes he wondered if she had a secret. He couldn't say quite why, but it came to him now and then in her silences and on those rare moments when she seemed to avoid his gaze. He did not press her. He trusted her too much and did not want to cause her any pain.

She revealed her secret on Easter Sunday, when the court was feasting in the hall. A young servant stepped onto the dais with a ewer of wine. One of his feet slipped and he nearly fell, but he steadied himself on the other foot. A few seats away from Edward, Edith's father, Earl Godwin, laughed loudly, saying:

'So, it is true: brothers do care for each other!'

Edward caught the strange words. Had Earl Godwin likened the young man's feet to a pair of brothers? It was a strange notion, one that snagged like a thorn in cloth. Then Edith's veil brushed his cheek. He heard her voice in his ear.

'He's mocking you.'

Edward looked back at her father, who was watching him in return, his eyes sharp with malice. Edward thought about the man's history. Godwin had stepped lightly from court to court, never falling foul of whichever king held the throne.

The King saw it like leaves opening on a vine. Godwin had welcomed his brother to England, and it was Godwin whom Alfred had trusted enough to be led into the hands of Harthacnut. Godwin had caused Alfred to be taken to Ely and blinded with the point of a knife.

Edward took Edith's hand under the table. He spoke up, his voice carrying over the lyre and the other noises of the feast.

'And so might I have cared for my brother, Godwin, had you let him live.'

Silence followed.

'How you offend me,' Earl Godwin said, laughing again. Then he gazed round at the others at the table, who had paused, their knives and glasses still in their hands.

Earl Godwin spoke again. 'I'm innocent and I'll prove it.'

He tore a shred from a bread roll.

'If I'm able to enjoy this morsel of bread without choking, then you'll know I am telling the truth.'

Edward raised his hand and drew a cross in the air, blessing the piece of bread. Then he said, 'May God make the proof be sure.'

All eyes were on Godwin as he put the bread in his mouth and chewed. Almost at once, his face twisted grotesquely and people began to laugh. But then his mouth gaped and his eyes widened. As his face turned blue, the laughter faltered. Then it seemed as though his eyes were going to burst from their sockets; they were bulging, reddening at the edges, and his pupils great dark holes.

Edward made to rise, but Edith's grip tightened on his hand, making him stay where he was. It was the only order she would ever give him. When Godwin had stopped moving and thudded forward onto the table, Edith's hand relaxed, releasing her husband. He got to his feet, gesturing to the guards.

'Take this dog away.'

Earl Godwin's corpse was removed and little more was eaten before the King finally rose and left the room with his wife. Later it would be said that he received a vision of the Seven Sleepers of Ephesus, those portentous young men, rolling from their right sides to their left. He would say it boded ill.

One day, Earl Godwin's son Harold would sit on Edward's throne. But a rival would cross the sea from Normandy and meet Harold on the fields of Hastings. In that battle, an arrow would arc over the fray. It was one of thousands, criss-crossing like the threads on a loom, not loosed by a trained archer, but by one of the peasant mercenaries picking up fallen arrows from the field edge and shooting them back into the melee. The arrow, directed not by skill but by chance, by God, found a path towards Harold and, when he looked up, drove deep into his pupil. In an instant Harold would realise what had happened and perhaps he knew that he was paying for the sin of his father. But before he could speak a word, the Norman soldiers seized him and slaughtered him with their swords.

❖

Edward the Confessor: An Eye for an Eye

In the late sixth century, around the time of St Scoithín, Irish and Italian monks were converting the English in a two-pronged mission. It was successful. By the eleventh century, when the historical Edward the Confessor was alive, Christianity was well and truly established. It is this religion and its holy representatives that shape the narrative of the Norman Conquest of England. Born in around 1003, Edward was King of England from 1042 to his death in 1066. His lack of an heir led to the invasion of England by William the Conqueror in the same year. Between Edward's death and the accession of William the Conqueror, the throne was held by Harold Godwinson, son of Earl Godwin, an English courtier on whom tradition pins the death of Edward the Confessor's brother, Alfred Atheling (whose epithet is the Old English for 'prince'). As most of the texts that survive from the aftermath of the Conquest were written for Norman readers, the men of the English Godwin family might not have been as villainous as all that. The chronicles show favour only for Edith, Earl Godwin's daughter, who married Edward the Confessor and who was also remembered as a saint.

The Edward story retold above comes from a thirteenth-century *estoire* (or 'history') of Edward's life that is so consciously rooted in real events that you'd be forgiven for forgetting just what a literary work it is. It was written and illustrated by a St Albans monk called Matthew Paris just under a century after Edward the Confessor's canonisation in 1161. Matthew's original manuscript doesn't survive, but a copy does. In the latter half of the thirteenth century, a team of scribes and illuminators at the royal court at Westminster reproduced the original, including the illustrations. However, in the decades after its production, deliberate holes were made in the eyes of two pictures of Earl Godwin.

I noticed this damage on the digital facsimile when I was a postgraduate student. It motivated me to visit the book in the flesh in the Manuscripts Reading Room of Cambridge University Library, which happens to be the sweetest-smelling place on earth. A librarian brought over the manuscript on a trolley, and I took it from the other books and laid it on a supportive cushion, opening it to discover fine sheets of vellum (calf-skin parchment) and drawings and text, all much finer than the image on the screen had implied. I turned to folio 11v (the 'v' standing for 'verso' according to the convention for numbering the pages of medieval manuscripts), the words and images of which concern the reception and coronation of Queen Edith. Someone had stabbed out the eyes on the image of a man in a blue cap presenting her as she receives the royal sceptre. He was blinded again in the neighbouring scene, where he whispers in the ear of another courtier. A red image caption identifies Edith in Anglo-Norman French as *fille Godwin*, or 'Godwin's daughter', while the opening two words of the main text on that page read *Godwin fu traitre ateint*, or 'Godwin was a proven traitor'. From all this, I inferred that a past reader, presumably medieval given their understanding of the Anglo-Norman text and investment in the story, had blinded the image of Earl Godwin for his treachery against Edward the Confessor's brother. They had done this by poking out his eyes with a sharp object. Judging from the singed edges of the tiny holes and the fact that one hole in each pair is smaller than the other, perhaps due to the cooling of conductive material, the damage was inflicted using a needle or pin heated in a flame. I ordered some parchment scraps and sat in my Lambeth flat heating a safety pin in a candle and burning pairs of holes that looked just like those in the medieval page.

In this fascinating manuscript, the damage is too sensitive to the story, too invested in its politics, to be modern. It is, I believe, a response to the theme of blindness *versus* sight that snakes through the text like a divinely directed arrow. At the start of the narrative, the young Edward the Confessor and his older brother Alfred are in exile in Normandy, and England is in the hands of the Danes. In 1035, Earl Godwin pretends to welcome Alfred Atheling to England, with the implied promise that he will help him reclaim the throne from the incumbent Danish king. Instead, Godwin hands him over to King Harthacnut, who has Alfred's eyes put out at Ely. The young claimant then dies. This blinding is the paternal sin for which Godwin's son later atones at Hastings.

Once Edward the Confessor comes to the throne, he has a vision of a devil sitting on a heap of tribute to the Danes, and he then begins healing supplicants suffering from physical maladies, especially to the eyes. Throughout the course of his reign, the healings proliferate, with troops of blind subjects visiting Edward to have their sight restored. He rebuilds and magnifies St Peter's Abbey, Westminster, and, on his deathbed, he has a vision of the English royal line as a fallen tree, which will graft back onto its stump and sprout afresh in, the text insinuates, the reign of Henry I. When Edward dies, childless, Earl Godwin's son, Harold, takes the throne, only to be killed at the Battle of Hastings with an arrow to the eye. Throughout the story, Edward is associated with spiritual and physical sightedness, while the men of the Godwin family are described as thorns and briars and linked to violent ocular injuries.

What the singed holes in Earl Godwin's illustrated face tell us is that someone cared enough about Edward to torture his nemesis with a miniature red-hot poker. The damage also reflects a wider belief that, of all the parts of the body, the eyes were especially dangerous. In an age that believed in 'extramission' theory – namely, that we see by sending beams of light from our eyes onto the objects before them – the gaze of a sinner was palpably threatening.

Therefore, while this is not a unique instance of painted eyes being damaged to disempower an image, as we will see later on, it is uniquely subtle in relation to the world of the text.

In around 1250, Isabel, Countess of Arundel, and Sanchia of Provence, Countess of Cornwall, each borrowed Matthew Paris' Edward manuscript, along with his retellings of the lives of Thomas Becket, Alban and Edmund. Equal parts word and image, the pages cajoled the reader from left to right, through tales of defiance and sedition, chastity, martyrdom and divine retribution, all set in Britain. Matthew Paris dedicated his *Life of Edmund* to Isabel. He also put a note in his life of Alban permitting Sanchia to borrow it, along with the rest of the collection, until the feast of Pentecost. The Westminster copy of his Edward history is thought to have been made for Eleanor of Castile after her marriage to the saint's namesake, the future Edward I. All this suggests a lively circulation of legends about British and English saints among the wealthy women of Plantagenet England. It hints, perhaps, at the use of these volumes in the historical and religious education of their children, which fell within the responsibilities of a noble mother. Perhaps one of Eleanor's children performed the pseudo-blinding of the illustrated Earl Godwin. Or perhaps she did it herself. Either way, the damage shows how saints' legends were not just pious tales inflicted on reluctant pupils; they could inspire indignation, could encourage readers to discern which characters were 'good' and which were 'bad', and could send a hand reaching for a pin to drive into the painted face of a villain.

Mungo: The Broken Bird

Died 614
Feast Day: 13 January

Teneu wished she was back in the cottage with her swineherd, delivering her God-given child onto soft blankets, with herbs for the pain, and someone to hold her hand. But instead, here she was, kneeling on hard stones, sand on her face and in her hair. There was nothing to lessen the agony, and no voices but the cawing of the gulls, until, with a final cry, she pushed her baby onto the beach. Teneu was too tired to see that she was no longer alone. To her it was as if the voices of the men were merely the shrieks of more gannets and the hands that cradled her head and back were figments of a dream. Unconsciousness overtook her.

The next morning shepherds had found the girl, clothes tangled and bloody. With the skills they knew from their work, they wrapped the baby in their garments, cut the cord and buried the afterbirth. They stoked the dying fire, heated water and gave the mother a drink. When she was warm, one shepherd carried her, and another carried the baby to a missionary called Serf, whose monastery was in

Culross. Serf was rumoured to be of noble birth and to have come from a far-off land and to be wise from his many travels and deep learning. He would know what to do.

The buildings they sought were the largest of cut stone in that wide landscape, and though the walk took all morning and the mist came and went, they found them easily; Teneu slept and the baby fed, wrapped in their cloaks. The shepherds knocked on the great wooden door, and when it opened, Serf accepted them without hesitation. Mother and child were carried to a small room with a welcoming fire and comfortable bed, almost as if the old priest had been expecting them.

When the shepherds had returned to their flocks, Serf sat beside the girl.

'It would be an honour to know your name,' he said.

'Teneu.'

'And the child's?'

The girl looked down. 'Kentigern. My dearest friend.'

Teneu spoke the British tongue, and so for 'dearest friend' she said, '*Mungo*'.

Then Serf said words in his mother tongue, because he had seen visions of angels in the night and believed the child would be holy.

'I am so happy you have come!' he said, so Teneu would understand his language and the reason for his delight.

*

In the years that followed, Teneu grew evermore grateful to Serf, who protected her without question. She learned that he was the son of the King of Canaan and a princess of Arabia; that he had been Pope before travelling to Alba to teach the Britons about Christ; and that, not far away, in a cave in Dunning, he had vanquished a dragon using just his staff and the power of prayer. There was nowhere Teneu would rather be than at Culross, under the protection of Serf.

They raised Mungo in the monastery, and as he prayed and fasted with the older monks, his holiness was plain. But the other boys who lived in the monastery mocked him and none of it escaped Teneu.

One morning, ten years after their rescue, Teneu was laying out the wax tablets for the boys' lessons. Serf was outside, feeding a robin he had tamed. Beyond the window, she could see it hopping onto his aged hand and pecking at crumbs on his palm. The old man was laughing softly and muttering affectionate words to the robin in his own language. Then he called over his shoulder to Teneu.

'With his colourful chest, he reminds me of the birds of my childhood.'

She nodded, smiling. 'You'd better go to prayer now, before the lessons begin.'

Serf let the crumbs fall from his palm to the windowsill. Then, leaning on his stick, he crossed the cloister gardens to the chapel. It was his custom to pray before beginning lessons, but already the boys were filing from the refectory and lining up outside, Mungo among them.

As Teneu put the last tablet in its place and the bell for lessons started to ring, she heard a commotion. She saw the boys scuffling and laughing. Her own Mungo was looking on in dismay.

'What is going on?' she called out.

They hushed each other and sidled back to their places in the line, though the corners of their mouths twitched with mirth. It was then that Teneu saw a spatter of blood on the windowsill.

Dread seized her. Where was the robin? *No*, she told herself, *it must have flown away*.

Serf had come out of the chapel, his stick tapping on the stone path, and then Teneu heard his hoarse shout. And now she was rushing across the classroom, leaning out of the window, looking down at the ground. There in the dirt, its wings outstretched, lay the robin. Its head lay a little way off and the white plumage of its belly and rump were stained with blood. For a moment, she was back on the forest floor with the taste of blood in her mouth.

The boys had shuffled back. As Teneu lifted her eyes to their faces, she saw Mungo pushing his way to the front and kneeling down beside the tiny bird. Serf, his crooked hands resting on his walking stick, only stared in misery. It was hard to believe that he had, in his youth, slain a dragon.

Mungo: The Broken Bird

'It was Mungo,' one of the other boys said.

'Yes,' said some of the others, nodding. 'Mungo did it.'

Serf and Teneu watched as her son scooped up the body of the robin in one hand and its head in the other. As he bowed his own head, his hair hid Teneu's view of the bird.

Suddenly one of the boys stepped back in fright, another cried out, his voice breaking. Then Mungo raised his head and looked her full in the face.

That was how she would remember him later, when, as a man, he had left Culross and built his own monastery. In her imagination, she would see him as he knelt before her now, his eyes all wonder, his smile wide, lifting the miracle for her to see. The robin was standing on his open palm, whole and clean and alive as it had been before the bell.

❖

Jocelyn of Furness wrote a *Life of Kentigern* for the Bishop of Glasgow in around 1200. He based his narrative, or so he says, on an old book in the Scotic tongue, which he elevated with Latin prose to the version that survives today. He may have been telling the truth, though he wouldn't be the first medieval author to claim authority from a lost original shrouded in the vernacular tongue of a mythic age.

In the legendary record, Kentigern, more popularly known by his nickname 'Mungo', founds Glasgow by building a monastery there. He also travels from Culross, on the east coast of modern-day Scotland, to the west coast, where he converts thousands to the Christian faith, then south from Strathclyde to South Wales. On his journeys he meets David, Asaph, Columba and a host of other saints, performing miracles all the while.

Miracles fill saints' legends. Different hagiographic traditions from different regions inherited wonder motifs from their pre-Christian ancestors. Stories of the early Irish saints, for instance, share a singularly dreamlike quality. Stories of Mungo draw on Classical and biblical models. But what was the difference between something unheard of or wondrous and something definitively 'miraculous', when 'miracle' only means 'an object of wonder'?

Mungo: The Broken Bird

In the thirteenth century, Caesarius of Heisterbach wrote of two men travelling around Besançon in France, variously walking on water, standing in fire and performing other miracles for appreciative crowds. The local bishop and priest, however, were suspicious of the source of their power. They had the men arrested and discovered thin scars in the men's armpits. Opening up the scars, they drew out folded contracts with the Devil.

Conscious, perhaps, of stories like this, the contemporary theologian Albertus Magnus defined a miracle as an event 'raised above the order of nature'. Miracles were not an illusion, nor an acceleration of natural processes, and they should not, for instance, be the result of pronouncing special words: that was the method of magicians and witches. Those non-miracles, those magic tricks, were 'wonders' and nothing more. Some wonders could even be, as with the men from Besançon, the work of the Devil. In his study of the medieval natural and supernatural, Robert Bartlett notes Albertus Magnus' 'intellectual discomfort' when it came to defining miracles, stressing that, even for faithful medieval Christians, 'the natural and supernatural were fluid, potentially contradictory, and often indeed unexamined'. Saying God did anything contrary to 'nature' could risk suggesting God was in some way unnatural, but to say that miracles did not exist, no matter how much wonder they inspired, defied the stories of Christ's miracle-working in the Bible. It was a thorny issue.

Today, some medieval saintly miracles leave a bad taste in the mouth. Jocelyn of Furness writes of Mungo railing at a visiting priest ('of graceful form, great eloquence, and much learning') whom he suspects is homosexual:

> If the sacred canons forbid women [from becoming priests] by how much more ought those men be shut out from so sacred an order and duty who are perverters of their own sex and abusers of nature . . . and clothe themselves as female. Nowhere do we read of a more grave vengeance being selected or censure than against that monstrous race of men.

Another man accused by Mungo later drowns in a river, his soul, the narrator explains, descending at once to Tartarus. This Mungo 'miracle' is absent – little wonder – from those alluded to by the fish, bird, bell and tree on modern-day Glasgow's coat of arms, accompanied by the lines:

> Here is the tree that never grew,
> Here is the bird that never flew,
> Here is the fish that never swam,
> Here is the bell that never rang.

Returning to the medieval texts from which we draw our occasional modern references to saints reminds us how strange – or troublingly familiar – the past can be. And while the nature of the miraculous sparked debates and intellectual treatises, a more straightforward belief in miracles underpinned the medieval cult of saints for the thousand-year sweep of its history. Miracles serve to demonstrate the saint's power, also known as their *virtus*, to which we will now turn.

Smaragdus: The Lost Child

DIED 470
FEAST DAY: 16 JANUARY

Smaragdus' name meant 'precious stone of green hue'. In ancient days, such a stone had glowed in the breastplate of the high priest of the Israelites. At the end of time, it would gleam under the New Jerusalem. He had chosen the name when he entered the monastery. He had worn it in the cool of his cell for his whole life as a monk. Now, he was dying, labouring to breathe the homely smells of stone and incense as a spider tiptoed across the ceiling. Beyond the walls of his hermitage, the wind skittered on the sand, and a long way away, the sound as muted as if he were listening underwater, the city of Alexandria screamed.

Paphnutius' name meant 'man of God'. It described him well. The grieving old man was devout as any monk and a generous benefactor to the community. After Euphrosyne's disappearance, the Abbot had instructed the brothers to pray for a revelation, but none had come. The Abbot told Paphnutius that God must have a reason to withhold the

Smaragdus: The Lost Child

truth. Smaragdus took God's silence as permission to be silent too.

But Paphnutius had never stopped hoping he would find his daughter, nor grieved less with time. When he visited Smaragdus each week, fresh tears had fallen into his beard and tracked between the tangle of greying hairs. *My beloved Euphrosyne*, he would say. *What if she's asking for me? What if, for all these thirty-eight years, she has been in the caves beyond the city, thinking I've lost hope?* Smaragdus had prayed and listened. One day soon he would share his secret, then everything would change.

Smaragdus was used to hiding: himself as well as his secrets. Long ago, when he had first entered the monastery, he had told the monks he had been a eunuch for the King. But then, in chapel, when they stood in facing lines to say the antiphonal Psalms, he noticed the brothers' eyes roaming from his fine features to his habit, then to what they could make out of his body underneath. He began hiding his face with his hood, but the monks went on watching, for all their embarrassment and shame.

In time, the Abbot noticed and for his own good sent Smaragdus into the desert, where there was a lonely stone cell. He had lived there alone for three decades, so that the scratch of sand between fingers and toes, long fasts and endless hours of prayer replaced his old life as an ornamented object of men's desires. Smaragdus became known for his sanctity and drew outsiders to his hermitage, asking for prayer and guidance. When Paphnutius had first visited, Smaragdus had been frightened. But the years had passed and his fears had been allayed.

Two taps on the hermitage door caused Smaragdus, weak but no less cautious, to drag his hood further down his face. His visitor stepped inside.

'Father Smaragdus?'

From under his hood, Smaragdus could see Paphnutius' feet. He imagined him looking at the untouched bread on the chair and the bowl of bloodied vomit on the floor.

'You're ill.'

'Stay with me?' Smaragdus asked.

'If you wish.'

And he did. For three days Paphnutius tended Smaragdus. He read to him, bathed his feet and hands, and took his bowl to be emptied. Smaragdus tried not to give in to the mounting pain. But, by the end of the third day, he knew he could not wait. Through the weave of his hood, he saw how the light of the oil lamp pooled on the side of Paphnutius' face, sending a shadow of a great nostril against his cheek. Smaragdus summoned the strength to speak.

'I know what happened to your daughter.'

The old man's gaze lifted, bright, unsure.

'To Euphrosyne?' he asked.

Smaragdus nodded, lowering his hood. He looked into Paphnutius' eyes and waited.

'What do you know about my girl?' Paphnutius said.

Smaragdus: The Lost Child

'It's me, Táta,' Smaragdus replied. 'It's me.'

Euphrosyne. *She who bestows beauty*. That beauty was faded. Perhaps it had gone altogether and left no trace of the person Smaragdus had once been. But when recognition fell, the shock was so great that the old man slid to his knees.

'Euphrosyne?' Paphnutius said. 'My girl?'

Smaragdus leaned forward, touching another human for the first time in thirty-eight years. Then the old man's hands lifted to Smaragdus' back and hovered, unsure. A feeling of betrayal dwelled within the relief. When Paphnutius had told Smaragdus, then Euphrosyne, to marry, his disobedient child had taken vows, donned the habit of a monk, chosen a new name, and had run away to the brotherhood, living there as Smaragdus ever since. Paphnutius had looked in the convents, from Alexandria to Cairo, but he had neglected to search in the very monastery closest to his home.

Smaragdus smelled the balsam oil in Paphnutius' beard and felt many years away from the cell in the desert. The dying monk was a child again, comforted by his father. When Paphnutius' arms finally enclosed him, Smaragdus said:

'I want no one but you to prepare my body. Keep my secret, Táta.'

When Smaragdus died, the wind blew his father's cries across the desert to the monastery. Hearing in them the truth of their hermit's earlier life, the monks shared the news far and wide. And they remembered the name Euphrosyne in their readings and their songs.

❖

Strength has many guises. In the Old English life, *St Euphrosyne*, written in the eleventh century, the saint's pronouns change from *heo* (she) to *he* (he) with his change of name. At first glance, this detail suggests an unexpected attitude to gender presentation, but it is contradicted by the reversion to the saint's pre-monastic name after death.

Medieval readers did not understand the transition from womanhood to manhood in terms we would immediately recognise. That *even a woman* could achieve such heroic holiness might well have been the dramatic crux of Smaragdus' story. It is, perhaps, better understood as a defiant rejection of morally frail femininity in favour of morally strong masculinity. The writings of the Church Fathers describe a woman's choice to leave the domestic and maternal life and embrace holy virginity as, to all intents and purposes, a transition to manhood.

The double standard at the heart of the stories of 'transvestite virgin saints' is further evinced by the (almost) complete lack of men doing the same thing in the opposite direction. For a woman to wish to dress as a man was both reasonable and virtuous. For a man to wish to dress as a woman was dangerous: an immoral travesty. One rare example of a monk dressing in feminine clothes appears in a twelfth-century legend about St Jerome, illustrated in the luxurious *Belles Heures* of Jean, Duc de Berry. It shows a malicious fellow monk sneaking into Jerome's cell in the middle of the night and exchanging his habit for a noblewoman's blue dress. Early the next morning, a bleary Jerome rises for matins, puts on the dress by mistake and wanders into chapel. His fellow monks whisper to each other from a choir stall as the bearded and tonsured Jerome approaches, his shoulders bare, his torso hugged by the rich blue cloth, his forearm flatteringly displayed by a slash in a close-fitting sleeve. Some pages later, the text explains that he was mocked so shamefully for his mistake, he was forced to flee. The story may have been inspired by that of a humiliated Hercules, tricked by Omphale, Queen of Lydia, into wearing feminine dress.

Smaragdus' transition to manhood shows his *virtus*, a word that we will return to often in this book. The term survives in our word 'virtue', which we tend to think of as a spiritual or moral quality. However, it contains the Latin word *vir* which means 'man' (as in 'virile'). Initially, 'virtue' meant something closer to 'masculinity' and was bound up with notions of physical strength. The martyrs display heroic physical endurance over the course of their persecution, as well as enhanced physical attributes such as luminosity and beauty (though not always). Their *virtus* is the source of their miracles before and after death. It has been proposed that, in an age that saw manhood as a more developed form of womanhood, saints of any gender were, by dint of their spiritual strength, 'manly' to a 'super-manly' degree.

Agnes: Death in Aquarius

DIED 304
FEAST DAY: 21 JANUARY

The cup shone in the candlelight, reflecting the rich hues of costly clothing. Distorted faces laughed and chewed in the band of gold around the base of the lid. Some had an angelic look, even in bent image, others could have been the vices that leered down from the columns in the church. At the banquet there were many young men and women, robed, ornamented and plucked according to the latest fashions, but the truly powerful were set apart by their red noses, exhausted eyes and full cheeks, the fruits of decades spent eating and drinking to excess. Candles illuminated the heavy damask tablecloth with its crop of gold plates, bowls and spectacularly ornate, half-useless vessels, while lapdogs scampered between the dishes, making away with a bread roll when indulgent hands were too slow to bat them away. All the reflections were parodied in the gold. All was reflected in the metal of the cup in mischievous caricature. But the cup itself – a gift – stood silent and still amid the commotion, unnoticed but for its general aura of luxury. The treasure was not for scrutiny but for joining with all the other riches on the table to tell the diners of their own magnificence. Peals of fevered laughter, all too ambitious for the jokes they followed, crashed around the work of sublime craftsmanship. But it was not just a cup. It was a story.

A frieze around the lid bore scenes in white, red, blue and green enamel. Together they told a tale of a girl called Agnes, accosted, while walking to school with her sister, by the son of the Prefect of Rome. The enamel showed the gold and glass image of the boy asking for her hand with a box of jewels and Agnes refusing him, declaring her chastity, her Christianity, and her conviction never to sacrifice to the Roman gods. At this, as rendered in the metal and glass, the young man's father sent her to a brothel and his son tried to rape her but dropped dead at her feet. Agnes resurrected him and ordered him to lead a good life as he knelt with his hands clasped in prayer. But, by now, the Roman priests had heard what was happening and tried to burn her. Agnes did not die from the red flames they put her in; these refused to touch the holy girl. She died when a soldier thrust a spear into her neck.

The feast went on late that night, raucous and oblivious. It was the eleventh day before the Kalends of February, the eve of the feast of St Agnes, and as the hour of midnight approached, the final scene of Agnes kneeling in the flames, the spear tip poised to puncture her skin, glowed a

Agnes: Death in Aquarius

little brighter. Her eyes were shut and the only movement on the gold surface was the dancing light of the candles and reflected gesticulation of the guests. But then a bell tolled somewhere beyond the hall and the flames about her legs began to flicker and her enamel eyes opened wide, drinking in the scene, the stained sleeves and bodices, the loosed hair and barely hidden groping. If any of the revellers noticed her watching from the pyre, they put it down to the wine.

❖

A thirteenth-century biography of St Hugh of Lincoln describes how, after feasting in hall, he would withdraw 'to his chamber . . . taking with him the more distinguished of the company'. There they would enjoy 'an even more magnificent and attractive spiritual banquet . . . inspired by his accounts of the sayings and deeds . . . of famous men'. The fourteenth-century poem *Gawain and the Green Knight* expresses a more secular version of the same notion. King Arthur will not start eating until he hears 'an uncouth tale of some adventurous thing, of some great marvel that he could believe, of ancient heroes, of arms, or of other adventures'. Both Hugh of Avalon and the fictional Arthur season feasting with a twist of worthy action. And indeed, the gentry of medieval Europe were hungry for stories of secular heroes like Charlemagne, Arthur and Alexander the Great, as well as saints and especially martyrs.

The first centuries after the Crucifixion saw an especially violent opening drama in the story of the human struggle for salvation. It centred on the persecution of Christians by hostile Roman emperors and yielded such super-saints as Stephen (the *proto-* or first martyr), stoned to death; Sebastian, shot all over with arrows; Felicity and Perpetua, one pregnant, one nursing her young son, executed in third-century Carthage, modern-day Tunisia; Apollonia, de-toothed and burned alive; Lawrence, cooked on a griddle; Bartholomew, skinned; Valentine, decapitated; and many more besides.

Historically speaking, the last and most extreme bout of anti-Christian action, Diocletian's persecution, began in 303 CE. It centred on the heartlands of the Empire, especially around the Mediterranean and North Africa, but extended even as far as Britain, as you will read in June. Christians who refused to sacrifice to Roman gods and deified emperors faced incarceration, torture and execution. Some believers accepted death rather than agreeing to comply.

It is here that the medieval cult of saints starts. In this early period, there was no official 'canonisation' process to recognise sanctity within the Church. Popular opinion was enough to transform the heroic Christian dead into martyrs and make shrines of their tombs. Over the subsequent decades, stories about them would be preserved in collections called martyrologies. Once Christianity had been made the Empire's official religion in 313 under Constantine the Great, their cults enjoyed more open patronage. By the Middle Ages, manuscripts known as *Passionales* preserved collections of lives and, in the later thirteenth century, Jacobus de Voragine produced his widely read *Golden Legend*. As the stories of martyrs took shape and the ranks of saints swelled, their setting remained broadly historical, but the increasingly elaborate accounts of their deaths and miracles took on a legendary hue.

St Agnes is one of the early martyrs, traditionally held to have been barely out of childhood when she died. She is one of many female virgin saints who saw great popularity throughout the Middle Ages. And yet, even in the early years of her cult, Christian pilgrimage and the veneration of saints were subject to suspicion, especially by Jewish and Muslim groups, who accused them of fostering idolatry and polytheism. Historian Ralph Finucane writes how, as early as the fourth century, 'the seeds of ambiguity, of paradox within the "official" Church, were already taking root'.

The Royal Gold Cup, a poleaxingly fine object, resides in the British Museum and bears scenes narrating the legend of St Agnes. It is a 'hanap', or decorative drinking vessel, made in or just before 1391, when it came into the possession of the French King Charles VI. It appears to have been among gifts from the very same Jean, Duc de Berry, in whose famous *Belles Heures* we found St Jerome's accidental transvestitism.

The Royal Gold Cup indicates just how thoroughly saints' stories suffused medieval culture, especially among the elite. But they were accessible to the non-elite as well. By the late Middle Ages, these tales were on tiles, they were painted onto walls, they could be found on tapestries and vestments, as well as on the outsides of civic and ecclesiastical buildings. But the ubiquity such images would one day have was not a guaranteed outcome.

In the seventh century, Serenus, the Bishop of Marseilles, set about destroying images of saints in the belief they provoked idolatry. But Pope Gregory the Great wrote to him, telling him that 'to adore a picture is one thing, but to learn through the story of a picture what is to be adored is another'. He reasoned that, in a picture, 'even the ignorant see what they ought to follow; in it the illiterate read'.

The letter remains a monument in the history of Western European culture, the artistic heritage and monumental landscape of which would be very different without orders like the one it contains. Whether their images were ever venerated or served only to bedazzle a noble company, objects like the Royal Gold Cup are miracles in the literal sense: they are objects of wonder, artefacts of unparalleled craftsmanship and witnesses to the dynamism of stories. And the pictures that adorn such objects exist thanks to an early policy decision by the Western Church to let holy tales be told in pictures. The decision was ever controversial, but, without it, surely, images of the legends and legendary figures described in this book would never have been made. And such artworks would never have grown in number in close symbiosis with burgeoning popular devotion until that popularity began bursting the seams of orthodox theology. And none of the drama and intrigue that followed, none of the folk beliefs, rituals and charms, none of the conflicts towards which this story runs, would ever have come to pass.

February

On the February calendar page, Pisces' fish remind medieval readers to look to their feet and to tumours, while little men painted in egg tempera and gold leaf warm their own chilly toes before a welcoming hearth.

Of the putative list of saints beside them, I have chosen Brigid, Werburgh and Ia; female virgin saints whose feasts stand at the threshold of spring. The feasts offered here sit either side of the Purification of the Virgin Mary on 2 February. The Purification marked Mary's first visit to the temple with her child at the end of her forty days' *post-partum* seclusion. Among the Christians of medieval England, the feast was known as Candlemas, the last hurrah of the Christmas cycle, and it saw whole villages coming together to have candles blessed and borne in procession around the church. Such rituals were, in the words of Eamon Duffy, 'eloquent evocations of the universal symbolism of light, life and renewal'.

But, then again, you would do well not to cause offence in the wake of Candlemas, for the blessed candles were powerful tools of vengeance, as well as protective objects. Go out into the snow with one of the candles lit, drip wax into the footprints of your enemy and wait by their cottage for their screams. According to the early fifteenth-century theological text *Dives and Pauper*, the act was believed to cause the victim's feet to rot off.

February challenges us, and not just by being dark and cold. The legends here reflect ideals we may find uncomfortable, even uncanny, like an icy draught on the back of the neck.

Brigid: Virgin, Again

Died 525
Feast Day: 1 February

The stories say that Brigid rejected the pleasures of the flesh; that she chose another path and did not stray from it even for a moment. By the time she had reached adolescence, the young men who lived near to her home in Kildare had made her many offers of marriage. But God repelled them, giving her the strength to burst her eye with her own finger in front of them. After that, the suitors turned their attentions to other girls. Later, when Brigid had died, better men would come to her as monks and congregate in the monasteries not far from her tomb. There, they would pen the first tales of her life and wonders.

It is said in these tales that, when she had been only a child, she had given away the butter she had spent all morning churning and the same amount had reappeared in her churn so that she would not disappoint her mother. Then, when she was older, they would say that Brigid had professed herself to God at the altar and the wood had come to life with a cracking, wet sound. Pale roots had twisted into the earth and never lost their sap. Then, when Brigid had run into the convent to escape a sudden shower of rain, she had draped her cloak over a sunbeam.

But, among these, the story of the foetus was surely strange even when it was first told. It related how one of Brigid's followers found out she was pregnant, but at first she did not tell. Maybe she prayed she would be allowed to carry on with her life as before, learn her lesson and suffer no consequences, that she would deliver, in the end, no child. Maybe she told herself it had all been a dream, for she must have been scared of giving birth in a community of Virgins; women who had given up home and motherhood to follow a holy life, who scorned fleshly appetites and worked wonders by their restraint. When the girl's child was born, she would have to leave. So, against her will, the girl's body softened and swelled. The inevitable day drew closer. She knew she would have to confess and Brigid's judgement would be God's judgement. What hope was there that she would be allowed to stay?

It is not said what that moment of confession was like when it came; whether the girl's hands shook or were steady. It is not said whether the words slid from her like a splinter as Brigid watched, then joined her in kneeling on the floor, cupping her belly in her hands and starting to pray aloud.

Brigid's touch showed the roundness under the girl's habit. But then the fabric was crumpling as the flesh drew back. Soon, the saint's hands were full of folded cloth, the

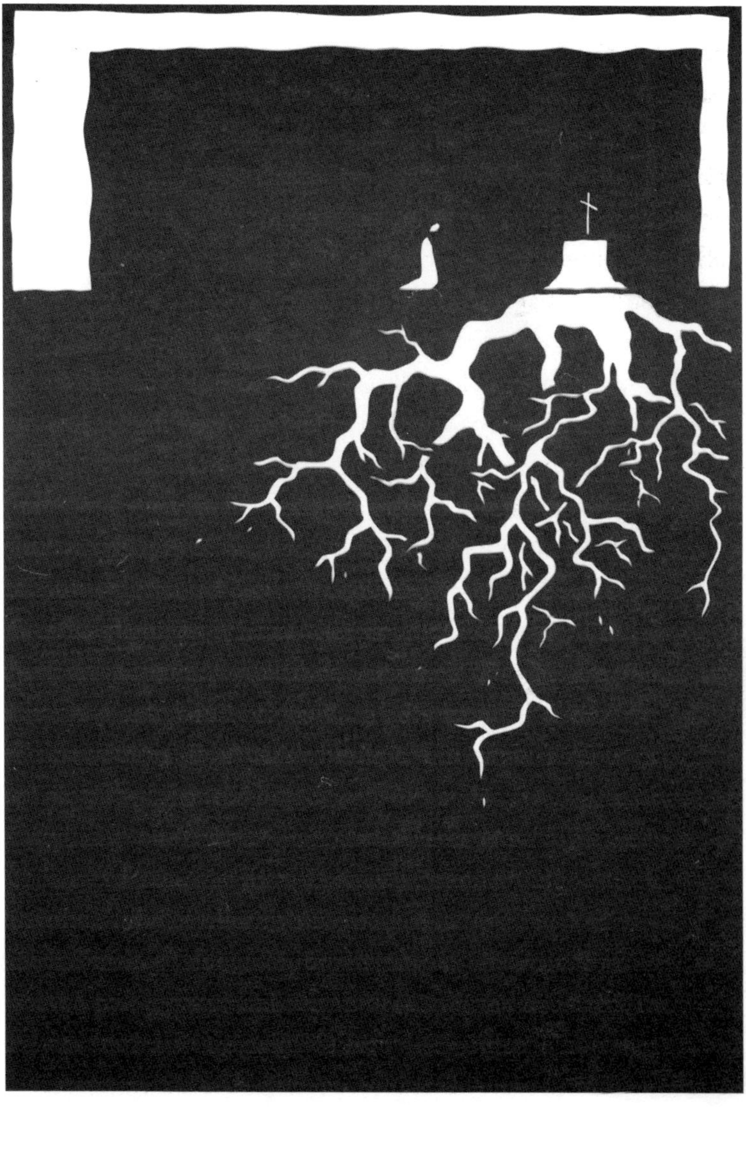

stomach beneath them flat as it had been months ago, when the girl had laid down with her lover to the hymn of bees and cattle.

It is said that the child inside Brigid's follower vanished without pain. Gone, as if it had never been. It is said the girl gave thanks.

❖

Brigid may be connected to a pre-Christian goddess or group of goddesses. In an early glossary of Irish words, attributed to Cormac Cuilennáin (a royal Bishop of Munster who died in 908), she is described as:

> A poetess, daughter of the Dagda [a Father god belonging to the Tuatha Dé Danann of Irish myth]. This is Brigid the female sage, or woman of wisdom, i.e. Brigid the goddess whom poets adored, because very great and very famous was her protecting care. It is therefore they call her goddess of poets by this name. Whose sisters were Brigid the female physician. Brigid the female smith; from whose names with all Irishmen a goddess was called Brigid. Brigid, then, bro-aigit, breo-shaigit 'a fiery arrow'.

Here, Cormac could be referring to an earlier, pre-Christian cult, from which the cult of the Christian Brigid grew. Her feast, still widely celebrated, falls on 1 February, around the date that the pre-conversion Irish celebrated the

Brigid: Virgin, Again

festival of *Imbolc*. Cormac Cuilennáin gives *Imbolc* the folk etymology *ói-melg*, meaning 'ewe-milk', because, he says, 'that is the time that sheep's milk comes'. As ewes living in an Irish climate deliver their lambs in the last weeks of winter cold, they would, one can assume, also produce milk around the start of February. Perhaps the goddess' cult was celebrated in conjunction with *Imbolc*, and so, therefore, was the feast of her milk-marvellous Christian counterpart. While Brigid was and remains the centre of a major Irish cult, she had a foot in the village of Beckery (erroneously translated as 'little Ireland' in a twelfth-century royal charter), near Glastonbury, which she and Patrick were said to have visited and left so-called contact relics (holy items touched by saints). There is likewise at least one medieval carving in the vicinity of Glastonbury Abbey thought to show Brigid milking a cow. It can be found on the late medieval tower of St Michael's Church on the neighbouring tor (for more on archangels and high ground, see late September).

Brigid's role in guarding the purity of her female charges is not quite unique and the miracle perhaps not as liberal in relation to female reproductive autonomy as it initially seems. Take the story of the Irish St Samthann's vengeance on a lusty monk intent on sleeping with one of her virgin followers. The monk, having crept out of his monastery, begins crossing the river to the convent, when an enormous eel – grey, muscular and spear-toothed – launches itself out of the water, biting down on his genitals and coiling itself around his waist. The monk somehow makes his way back home, but the eel will only unclamp its jaws once Samthann has personally administered her forgiveness. Here, we see a saint defending the virginity of one of her own and, as I will explain more fully, Brigid's 'abortion' miracle may reflect a similar intention.

Brigid is not the only medieval 'abortionist' saint, though all are Irish and held to have lived in the fifth and sixth centuries. St Ciarán hears of a young girl called Bruinnech who has been abducted from a convent by a king and violently impregnated. Seizing her back from her kidnapper, Ciarán presses his crucifix down upon her womb and 'forces' it to be emptied. Elsewhere, St Áed spots the pregnancy of a consecrated virgin while dining with her community, induces her to confess her secret sin and perform penance, then blesses her womb and causes the pregnancy to vanish. Likewise, St Cainnach is asked directly by a pregnant woman to bless her womb because the child within was conceived through secret fornication. The consequence of his blessing is the termination of the pregnancy, though the text remains silent on whether this is what the woman wanted; she does not ask for the pregnancy to end. Brigid's miraculous termination, the only one performed by a female saint, is also the only one in which the mother thanks God and is said to experience no pain.

Brigid: Virgin, Again

Still, perhaps the word 'abortion' is unhelpful in relation to this kind of miracle. Maybe it is too loaded with modern ideas. Maeve Callan has shown that, according to some early Irish penitentials (books of penance), the status of a consecrated Virgin was not 'lost' until a baby was actually born. And 'virginity' could even be won back after seven years' penance. In one account of his deeds, St Patrick crushes one of his penitent pregnant followers with his chariot, sending her soul into heaven. Callan has suggested that the punishment administered the physical penance (acts of fasting or self-mortification to atone for sin) needed for her to be absolved and enter heaven. There's another broadly historical story of a twelfth-century Gilbertine nun from Yorkshire who became pregnant during an affair with a lay brother. Her fellow sisters imprison her, chain her up and force her to castrate her lover, whose testicles they then hurl in her face. When she finally goes into labour it is night and she is alone. She receives a vision of two celestial women and a bishop. According to the narrator, the trio delivers her baby and disappears. In the morning, the castigatory nuns return to find that the imprisoned woman is neither pregnant nor showing any signs of ever having been so:

> They prodded her womb and behold, such slimness had succeeded the swelling that you would think her belly attached to her spine. They prodded her breasts

but drew no liquid from them. Not sparing her, however, they pressed harder, but they expressed nothing. They ran their fingers over each of her members, they explored everywhere, but they discovered no sign of a birth, no indication of a conception.

In the cases given above, the miraculous undoing of a pregnancy provokes no physical reaction. It simply returns the recipient to a pre-pregnancy state. When coupled with punishments administered by the community, it's clear that this is less about the removal of the foetus than it is about the miraculous restoration of purity. Likewise, when Brigid causes her follower's pregnancy to vanish, it might have been seen by many medieval readers as a conservation of virginity, not the loss or termination of a pregnancy in the manner of a miscarriage or abortion. The unborn child disappears, returning to its maker, never truly manifest. The life potential of the virgin womb remains unrealised.

And so Brigid is a reminder that medieval saints' legends are built on cultural and religious assumptions very different from our own. They are gateways to different ways of seeing the world and understanding the body. And, at the start of spring, it is the perception of the untapped vitality of the 'virgin' that we recognise in these tales.

Werburgh: The Goose Princess

DIED 700
FEAST DAY: 3 FEBRUARY

It was said that certain geese hatched spontaneously from barnacles, so this story might have begun in the sea, with a gosling, newly delivered from a pale clutch, dangling by her beak from the barnacle tree. As the weeks passed, her adult feathers grew. Then she and the others dropped one by one into the water. Those birds that did not sink soon recovered themselves from the fall and took flight. Our gosling, now a goose, was among them.

She had practised flapping while hanging from the tree, but after a few days' flying, her wings and back ached. Her goose mind filled with gladness when she at last saw land with its weaving rivers and streams and with the white and grey of birds just like her clouding above them. She and her siblings strove on till they had joined a mighty flock.

Together they ate and slept, flew and swam, paddled and sang for a whole summer, each bird guided by a spirit much bigger than its own. They were not a thousand geese, but one great goose with two thousand wings. The goose was part of that massive body and knew no other state of being.

On the morning they woke to find ice on the rivers too thick to swim through, they took off in great formations to the south, darkening the sky in a blizzard of plumage. There they entered a land which froze less hard in winter and where their food was easier to find in the cold. For the whole winter they travelled from place to place, eating until the food got scarce, then moving on. Months passed and the days shortened until they lengthened again. Before long, the flock began sensing the need to return to its summer haunts. Ahead of the long journey north, it would need to fill its many gullets.

The flock passed over a region that smelled of smoke, of humans, but also of plump green shoots. Making up its mind, it circled lower and landed in the ridged fields.

Blades of winter wheat pierced the black soil like a thatch of green hairs. The geese bent their long necks and nibbled them, squeaking and chattering. When the humans noticed and came crashing from their homes with anything they could find that made noise, the geese were only a little disturbed. Every now and then, those at the edge of the flock flew to the middle and the rest just carried on eating. They carried on, that is, until that particular human arrived.

The barnacle geese were lulled by her presence, and though they had not experienced maternal love, she was a

Werburgh: The Goose Princess

comfort to them. She kept her eyes downcast. And she did not make great crashes and clashes like other humans. She spoke softly, so that only the geese just beside her could hear. Understanding spread from them through the flock. Moving as one, as they always did, they began to follow her. It made them happy to do so. Each goose lowered its head trustingly, discovering as it walked behind her tall figure what it would have been like to follow a mother goose, protected by her sharp eyes and comforted by her presence.

She led the geese into a great sheep pen and shut the gate. They stood silent, her silhouette reflected in their black eyes. Then she asked them quietly to go and find food elsewhere. When she had finished, she opened the gate again and the geese at the front ran out, beating their wings until they were airborne. The rest of the flock followed, until every single goose had returned to the sky. Every goose, that is, except one.

Our goose had followed the others out the gate, running and beating her wings, and there was noise and commotion as there always was when the flock took off. So she did not see the man until he had grabbed her by the tail and pulled her under his coat. The darkness stunned her to stillness. She shut her eyes and felt no fear until suddenly it was light again and she could see only a square of sky and, so far off she could hardly hear them, her flock leaving her behind.

There was a wooden bench on the floor of the thief's house. Clamping her wings to her side with one strong hand, he laid her neck on it. Then he cut off her head with an axe.

Werburgh hugged the children of the village of Weedon Bec as their parents thanked and blessed her for ridding them of the flock of geese, which would have eaten all the wheat they had sowed the previous autumn and destroyed any hope of bread and ale at the end of the coming summer.

'We would have starved,' they said to her.

'How can we ever repay you?'

'The way the geese hung their heads . . . it was such a sight!'

She told them it was nothing, kissed the children's heads and went back into her chapel to pray. She felt very happy that the life she had chosen, one that would never give her children of her own, meant that she could show God's wonders in this way. Etheldreda, with her budding, blossoming staff, would be watching with pride from her throne in heaven. To commune with the birds had been beautiful and sacred. Werburgh remembered them following along behind her like the farm goslings followed the mother goose. In the privacy of the chapel, where she was not a princess but a child again, she laughed, reaching up to the thatch, then dropped to her knees before the altar.

Night fell and Werburgh went back to her chamber and slept, but the next morning she was woken by a deafening clamour. She ran outside and saw that many of the villagers had stepped outside their doors as well. The flock was back and seemed even bigger than before. It was filling the sky like a storm cloud, blocking out the light, and was inexpressibly hostile.

It was making such a noise that she could hardly hear her own voice as she cried, 'What is it? What has happened?'

Their answer came not as sound but as a sick feeling in her chest.

Betrayed.

'I have not betrayed you!' she called in response. And then the feeling came again.

Betrayed.
Betrayed.
We trusted you.
You have hurt us.

Werburgh brought her hands to her face and tried to think what could have happened. And then she felt someone touch her arm. Turning around, she saw one of her servants, a timid man with bags under his eyes and grease stains on his jerkin.

'I stole one of the geese,' he said.

'You did what?'

'I ate it last night with my family.'

Werburgh pitied him, knowing it must have been a rare treat indeed for his children. But to let the theft go would be to invite the flock back to the fields and consign the whole village to famine. She bent her head and prayed.

The goose he had eaten was not conscious of coming back to life until all her vertebrae had reconnected and her spinal cord fused to her brain. Then her round black eyes saw her skin covering the bare sinews of her muscles and feathers growing out of her skin. Her feet, once she had them again, were folded under her downy belly, warmed by the human's hands. When she heard the urgent calling of her own flock, she felt herself being placed on the ground. The goose ran, beating her wings, until she was in the air with her neck outstretched and the shapes of her own kind expanding in her vision.

On the ground below, the servant collapsed to the floor in a pool of his own vomit. Werburgh stood tall beside him, her face tilted up to the sky.

❖

Sometime in the thirteenth or fourteenth centuries, Werburgh's shrine in Chester Cathedral, then an abbey, received its own pilgrim souvenir. It showed a flock of geese in a pen, reminding her pilgrims of their patron's most famous miracle.

Werburgh, born around 650, was the daughter of an Anglo-Saxon king of Mercia. As an adult, she entered the Abbey of Ely, which had been founded in the East Anglian Fens by her great-aunt Etheldreda. In time, Werburgh rose to the rank of Abbess, following in her Aunt Etheldreda's footsteps, as well as those of her grandmother Seaxburh and her mother Ermenilda. The Old English names Æðelþryð, Wærburh, Sexburh and Eormenhild translate into modern English as 'Noble Strength', 'True City', 'Bright Sword' and 'Battle-Great': a formidable troop of women, if their names are anything to go by. The vast and muscular Gothicised cathedral that stands in Ely today barely does them justice. The most famous of them, St Etheldreda, was known by later devotees as 'Audrey'. An international cult centred on her shrine and is the original source of the term 'tawdry', which is a compression of 'St Audrey's' lace or 'tat': the cheap cloth tokens sold there.

We have touched on Mungo's many saintly contacts among the territories and allies of the Western Britons, including David, Serf and Columba. Brigid and Patrick, along with other Irish saints, wander in and out of one another's legends. The same is also true of the earliest English saints. According to the medieval legends, Chad of Lichfield educated Werburgh, and we're told that Etheldreda embroidered a stole for Northumbria's Cuthbert. Werburgh was a close acquaintance of Wilfrid of Ripon. He, in turn, was a friend of the historian of the English Church, the Venerable Bede.

By the later Middle Ages, shrines to Chad and Wilfrid could be visited in Lichfield and Ripon respectively, while the relics of Bede and Cuthbert both resided in Durham, and those of Werburgh lay in Chester and of Etheldreda in Ely. The shrines might have been scattered across England, but the legends – part marvelogue, part history – make much of the contact the saints had in life. In death, their shrines joined hill, fen and island together under a great veil of sanctity.

Werburgh died on 3 February 700 CE. She was buried at Hanbury in England's North Midlands, but devotees moved her coffin within the refortified walls of Chester after ninth-century Viking raids. The church in Chester was dedicated to her in the late tenth century, when the cults of early Anglo-Saxon saints were revitalised as part of larger reforms within the English Church. In 1180, her shrine, carried around Chester, was said to have saved it from fire.

In the fourteenth century, carpenters carved an illustration of her goose miracle into the oak of a misericord (a small shelf-like seat) for the choir of St Werburgh's Abbey, now Chester Cathedral. In Goscelin of Saint-Bertin's eleventh-century *Life of Werburgh*, she simply resurrects a dead bird. On the misericord, the stolen goose comes to life having already been eaten.

Brigid and Werburgh often appear on later medieval calendar pages made in Britain. Their commitment to monastic living, including chastity, earns them the power to work wonders, and they are members of larger communities shaping cultural identities within Ireland and Britain. Likewise, the animal world around them reflects their north-westerly domains; these are not Middle Eastern saints like Jerome and Mary of Egypt with their tame lions, or Menas with his camels, but they are cast in a happily derivative mould. These are saints who work wonders among robins, oxen and migratory geese – and you will meet more besides, what with the otters, whales and wolves to come. So writers of saints' legends, reinventing the authoritative tales of animals and saints that had arrived from afar, looked locally for their heroes' wild allies.

Alongside the ability to withstand physical pain, abstain from physical pleasure, defeat monsters and suffuse all they touched with life and vigour, saints' animal and avian friends represent an especially endearing device in the legends' repertoire of wonders.

Ia: The Impossible Boat

Died 6th century
Feast Day: 3 February

Ia watched the boats vanish into the dusk. She and Gwinear's missionaries should have travelled to Britain together, but one missed step and they had left her behind. She stamped her foot and the cliffs behind her shook.

There she stood, wrapped up for a sea voyage, everything she owned bundled in her shoulder bag, but with no boat, no friends, no option, it seemed, but to give up and go home. Now she would have to face those she had left behind and tell them what had happened. Now she would have to listen to them saying it was for the best, that her dream had been dangerous and it was, at last, time to behave.

The seawater rushed up to and away from her toes as Ia turned her face and palms to the sky, feeling them flecked with cold rain. For a long moment, she offered it all up. When she looked down again, she saw a leaf floating towards her on the water.

In another story, it might have carried on with all the other debris on the surf, just another leaf, but in this story

Quikening

her gaze struck it like a fist. The leaf bowled. Then it grew. Then it spread. And Ia stepped onto it.

She was not going home, nor was she turning back. She was going to cross the sea.

In another story, the miraculous vessel might have split, might have dropped her into the endless deeps like a stone. But in this story it held as surely as a boat of solid wooden board.

Had anyone been watching as night fell, the woman sailing on the leaf would have been indistinguishable from the black waves and the black sky, and indeed Ia herself could see nothing. But she could feel the wind finding gaps in her clothes and the water rolling and flexing like

Ia: The Impossible Boat

giant muscles under the membrane of the leaf. Invisible and unseeing, she floated on until morning, then she glimpsed land and the glimmer of dawn. When the water was shallow, she stepped into the breaking waves and on up the beach towards the sunrise. Behind her waited the leaf. Then it was small again. Then the current caught it. Then, as if it had never carried a saint, it spun away on the surf.

❖

The western Cornish village of St Ives, at the toe of southern Britain, owes its name to St Ia. The *v* in the placename's modern form is a later intrusion, stemming from confusion with a separate male saint called Ivo. His name is preserved in the village of St Ive (eastern Cornwall) and St Ives in Cambridgeshire. The uncorrupted form survives in thirteenth-century sources, which refer to Ia's titular village as Porthye or Porthia ('Port Ia'), or Sancta Ya ('Saint Ia'). What little we know about St Ia's legend resides in a *c.* 1300 *Life of Gwinear* in which Gwinear leads an Irish mission to Britain but leaves Ia behind. She follows them on a leaf.

The saints of Cornwall are many and varied, with connections to Ireland and Brittany, as well as further afield. In the *Life of Gwinear*, Ia is an Irish woman. However, it has been suggested that, despite the later medieval (and not very trustworthy) account of Ia's origins, earlier legends would have placed her a great deal further east. Her story is set in the sixth century, in the misty days between the end of the Roman occupation of Britain and the conversion of the Anglo-Saxons. This was an era in which the Romano-British had powerful kingdoms in western Britain, the commercial reach of which is demonstrated by archaeology. Tintagel, for instance, in north Cornwall, was the royal centre of the Brittonic kingdom of Dumnonia. It has yielded Byzantine pottery wine carriers called *amphorae*, indicating trade with the eastern Mediterranean. Meanwhile, isotopic analysis of human remains in contemporary cemeteries in Wales shows that people with North African heritage were living and dying in those regions as well.

Then, as now, trade and migration connections fostered the transmission of spiritual as well as mercantile materials. Amazingly, a site near Chester has offered up sixth- or seventh-century clay vessels bearing images of St Menas, an Egyptian martyr. This object type is usually found near the saint's Egyptian shrine and represents one of the earliest surviving forms of Christian pilgrim souvenir. Perhaps it came to Britain with a North African trader, who had also once been a pilgrim.

A saint called 'St Ia' features in the writings of the mid-sixth-century Greek scholar Procopius. He describes his own experience entering the gates of Constantinople and finding, on the left, 'a martyr's shrine of St Ia, fallen in ruins', which the Emperor Justinian had 'restored with all sumptuousness'.

Ia: The Impossible Boat

Justinian ruled from 527 to 565. At around the same time, therefore, that he was restoring the Byzantine shrine to St Ia, *amphorae* were being landed in Dumnonia and natives of Byzantium were settling in Wales. According to Persian martyrologies, the Middle Eastern St Ia was killed during a fourth-century persecution of the Christians under Shapur II, ruler of the Sasanian (or Second Persian) Empire. If Caitlin Green is correct in her suggestion that devotion to St Ia of St Ives arrived in western Britain along with people and wares from the eastern Mediterranean, then St Ia was no Irish missionary at all; she was a Persian martyr.

As to the voyage on the leaf, the origins of that tale are a mystery. Miraculous ways of travelling often appear in medieval saints' lives (as the next story will show) and maybe this trope filled a gap when her Persian legend was forgotten. The leaf-boat surfaces again in a late medieval Dutch translation of *The Voyage of St Brendan*. While at sea, he and his monks encounter a dwarf sitting on a leaf. The dwarf, who holds a cup and a stylus, repeatedly dips the stylus in the sea and lets the water drip from it into the cup. He explains that he is measuring the sea and will do so until the end of time. When Brendan exclaims that it is impossible to measure the sea, the dwarf replies:

> Just as it is impossible for me to finish measuring the sea before doomsday . . . so it is impossible for you to be able to see all the wonders of God's creation in the

sea and on the land, much of which is still unknown to you.

The sea-measuring dwarf recalls a story told by St Augustine of Hippo (died 430) and which became closely associated with him in late medieval European art. He relates how he met a boy on a beach striving to fill a hole in the sand with water. The boy tells Augustine that he has more hope in achieving his goal than Augustine, who strives to understand the divine mysteries.

We might imagine a story of Ia being read aloud in the eye of a Cornish winter, the sea shaking off a storm carried from the Bay of Biscay. In this western spur of land, travellers brought legends that residents made their own. Fantasies – or, for some, memories – of Persia might have filled the listeners' minds as their bodies warmed by the fire. And, if the storyteller knew their trade, Irish Ia and Persian Ia would each have brought something of the world's unimaginable size and uncountable wonders travelling in on the wind.

March

In medieval calendars, a figure tills beside the horned face of Aries. Now is the time for digging the soil in preparation for the spring and, under Aries, to assess afflictions of the head and face. While March's labour makes seasonal sense, digging could itself be dug for its sombre spiritual meanings. Christmas festivities had ended. March was a time for delving into the soul and preparing the ground for Easter; it would see the observation of Lent, a time of fasting and other forms of abstinence as Christ's earthly life reached its close. In late medieval England, Good Friday saw parishioners and priests 'creeping to the cross' barefoot and on their knees. March was a bare month, the month for cleansing the soul.

Medieval readers, contemplating their March calendar page, might have recalled Genesis, when God tells the fallen Adam, 'Cursed is the ground because of you; through painful toil you will eat food from it all the days of your life.'

A twelfth-century stained-glass window in Canterbury Cathedral shows Adam, naked to the waist, working with a spade, his bare foot pressing down on the top of the blade, pushing the metal into unforgiving stones. An adze or hoe for loosening the ground hangs in the lower branches of the tree beside him. The image expresses the burden of Original Sin that Adam passed to his descendants after the Fall.

In March, we come to David, Patrick, Cuthbert and William of Norwich. We will meet heresy, purgatory, penance and prejudice. And we will dig in turn into each legend, discovering how they told their readers what was and was not orthodox, as well as who should and should not belong.

David: Shifting Ground

DIED 589
FEAST DAY: 1 MARCH

A sea-monster carrying an Irish monk washed up on the beach below the cliffs at Mynyw. Blond-haired Barra, watching from the cliffs, saw to his joy that it was none other than Scoithín, whom he had once seen walking on the ocean. He climbed down to meet him and, when they had embraced, Scoithín explained.

'Aidan, my abbot, has sent me from Ireland to perform an important service for Bishop David.' But Scoithín would reveal no more.

On that Easter Sunday, Barra saw Scoithín conversing with David in the refectory. They knew each other well, for Scoithín had trained under David. When they had finished speaking, a deacon had come in with a basket of bread; Scoithín insisted on taking it from him and serving David himself. Abbot Aidan had been warned in a dream that the bread, Scoithín now explained, had been poisoned.

Now David divided the bread into three portions and got up from his seat. He gave the first portion to a dog lying outside the door and the second to a raven nesting in an ash tree. After watching the creatures die in agony, their skin splitting and the fur and feathers moulting, he blessed and ate the last portion of bread himself. Though all the monks watched him closely for several hours after that, he neither died nor suffered any ill effects at all.

Barra, whom some called Finbarr because of his light-coloured hair, was staying with David, having received an invitation on his way back from a two-year pilgrimage to Jerusalem. While Barra had been eager to resume the rhythms of monastic life with his brothers in Ireland, as well as his duties as abbot, he had accepted, delaying his homecoming by several months for the honour of time with one so holy as David.

Eventually the day dawned on which it had been decided that Barra would leave and make the final part of his journey across the sea to Ireland. He woke early and ran down to the shore, keen to see his beloved monastery again. But disappointment overwhelmed him. The wind had dropped so low that sailing was impossible.

Joining him on the sand, David offered Barra his horse. Barra almost laughed, thinking at first it was a joke. But then, remembering Scoithín walking on the water and riding a sea-monster to Mynyw, Barra mounted the horse and rode it off the beach. David's horse could walk on water and Barra was crossing the sea without the need of a boat.

David: Shifting Ground

Once Britain was out of sight, he saw land ahead and frowned.

'We can't be home yet,' he said to the horse, which shook its mane and snorted.

Barra could see a shaly beach now, with grey pebbles and fragments of black rock rising out of the water. Beyond was a forest, becoming a wooded hill and a jagged mountain. Then he glimpsed movement. Barra pulled the reins and the horse stopped, water lapping its hooves.

There was a flash of white cloth, bright among the darkness of the trees, then a hand grasping one of the narrower trunks. As Barra watched, a frail old man climbed down the hill and onto the beach. His feet were bare and his body clothed in a long robe. His white hair had been tonsured in the manner of an Irish monk. Barra called to him.

'Brother, who are you and what is this place?'

'Greetings, Barra, the white-haired one,' the man replied. 'I am Brendan and this is my home.'

Everyone had heard of Brendan. He had left the shores of Ireland in a hide-covered boat, visited many marvellous islands and discovered an earthly paradise. And as a young boy, Barra had met Brendan at Crossybrennan. He looked very different now, after all these years at sea. Then Brendan spoke again, telling Barra how he was borne to this place by one of God's creatures, though he had long had a reputation for preferring the ways of the Devil.

Barra didn't understand and said so to Brendan, causing the old voyager to point into the water. Barra looked. Then he looked again. Watching him from under the waves was a great green eye. It blinked and rolled to meet his own.

Under the eye, part of a wide grey-lipped mouth was just visible in a shaft of sunlight. Above the eye, scales turned to shale and broke the surface of the water. This was no island after all, Barra realised, but the stone-strewn, forested flesh of a whale.

'Iasconius!' Barra cried.

'The very same!' laughed Brendan, clapping his hands.

Barra had read about the diabolical beast, but he had not believed he was real.

'Once,' said Brendan, 'he nearly dragged my brothers to the bottom of the sea, but I stayed on the boat. I hadn't tamed him then.'

'What made you come back?'

'I wanted to stop his mischief. And I knew that none before me had knowingly set foot on his back. I prayed as demons tortured and tempted me, but in time the noise in my head fell silent and I was here alone, but for Iasconius, who has become my friend.'

Barra shook his head wonderingly, then told Brendan that it had been a great honour to meet him, but that he longed now to continue his journey home.

'Then I will leave you,' replied Brendan, 'with my blessing.'

David: Shifting Ground

Barra watched the island swim away, the old man waving goodbye all the while. Then Barra kicked David's horse and they went on with their journey, the horse's hoof prints leaving tracks in the water, then vanishing almost as soon as they had been made.

When Barra arrived back in Ireland, his community wondered at his story and received David's horse with honour. Barra and his monks even made a golden image of it when he died.

❖

After the martyrs and missionaries of the early cult of saints, we see the work to achieve redemption translated to the monastic cloister, where heroism is in the daily grind.

St David, like Brigid and Werburgh, belongs to the host of early medieval monastic saints. While the word 'monastic' comes from the Greek term for 'solitude', it was, by the Middle Ages, a communal endeavour, solitary only insomuch as it was set apart from secular society. The monastic communal model, which originated in Egypt, stipulated separation from the wider world and life according to a rule. In medieval Europe the rule of St Benedict, whose feast was celebrated on 22 March, became the prevailing system for much of the period covered by this book and, in broad terms, it encompassed a lifetime of diligent prayer and labour. Monks and nuns were expected to maintain their virginity alongside daily disciplines of reading, worship and manual work. It fell to the head of the community, the abbot or abbess, to enforce that rule; the monastic community was like a body, the condition of any part directly affecting the whole.

St David is a historical figure, a Briton who is now the patron saint of Wales. He is held to have lived in the sixth century and to have founded monasteries and churches from Brittany across Dumnonia and into modern-day Wales. The most famous of these was a religious community on the southernmost tip of Pembrokeshire, at a place then called Mynyw. The monastery and the town that grew up around it came to bear his name: St Davids.

Just as rules governed the monastic community, so the Church at large needed constant regulation. Throughout its long history, ideas and interpretations of Scripture gained popularity that challenged the orthodox doctrines. At the Synod of Brefi in Ceredigion, for instance, David is said to have spoken out against the Pelagian heresy, a belief system established by a Romano-Briton called Pelagius a century or so earlier. It held, among other ideas, that humans were not born with Original Sin, that is, belief in the innate fallen state and inclination to sin. According to the *Life of Saint David the Bishop* written in the late eleventh century by Rhygyfarch – a scholar and teacher educated at St Davids – the ground raised David up on a new hill as he condemned the heresy. So history and myth come to us entwined.

David: Shifting Ground

In the late eleventh century, when Rhygyfarch was active, Wales was suffering the effects of relentless Norman invasions. He composed a poem about it, known as *Rhygyfarch's Lament*, which portrays a kind of collective paralysis on the part of his people, leaving them incapable of rising up in defence of their territories and yet numb to the things that had always brought them joy, including stories and songs.

Rhygyfarch writes how Non, David's mother, conceived the saint after being raped by the King of Ceredigion. During the attack, stones broke from the ground at her head and feet. Likewise, when she delivered the future saint on the peninsula to the south of modern-day St Davids, she leaned on a standing stone that divided down its length in sympathy with her pain, her hands leaving their imprint on it. The ruins of a medieval chapel to St Non, built on the legendary site, may be found there to this day.

We might speculate that Rhygyfarch saw Non's violation by an earthly king – as well as her agony in delivery – as a symbol for the Norman invasion of his native land: who can say? But these various miracles of David are, in the end, about the power of monasticism to overcome the world's forces, both natural and political. Horses walk on water, hills swell under David's feet, and sea-monsters deliver monks onto the beach, all in the context of the religious community.

We will meet Brendan again, but it's worth noting here that the voyage at the heart of his legend sees him and his brethren visiting many of the same islands year after year for seven years, after which they at last discover the earthly paradise they have been seeking. Thus, their diligent, repetitive and searching communal labour prevails, as it might have done in the cloister.

Patrick: The Dreadful Door

Died c. 460–490
Feast Day: 17 March

Patrick, Bishop of Ireland, wept. Each time he closed his eyes, he had visions of the men and boys he had baptised only days ago. They had still been wearing their white robes, the oil with which he had anointed them still on their foreheads, and he had recognised their faces, remembered their personalities, some of them shy and smiling, others solemn. Now their throats were cut, their skin was grey and the blood which had stained their robes scarlet had already faded to brown.

Patrick had been told that Coroticus' men had dragged the women and girls away from the dead men and boys and Patrick knew from his own memory of slavery what the brutes would be doing to them now. He knew what it was like for those who were not built for work in fields and farms. He lay down in front of the altar and cried until he had no more tears. Sleep took him.

Far from the chilly chapel, Patrick found himself standing in a field. Breathing in the scent of warm earth, he looked around. He saw a man beside him and knew him to be Christ.

Christ passed Patrick a book wrapped in gold and set with gems, and so heavy that he knew it could not have been written or bound by human hands. He opened it and turned its leaves, learning secrets of Heaven, Earth and Hell.

Christ gave Patrick a staff. In his lifetime, it would be his instrument against the Devil and would come to be called the Staff of Jesus. Then Christ began to walk away and Patrick followed, the book in one hand and the staff in the other.

As they walked, the green and gold grasses of the meadow became brambles, nettles, dock and burdock. The butterflies and bees became wasps, crane-flies and gnats, and the birdsong turned to the croaks and cackles of ravens. Patrick followed Christ, lifting his habit away from the snagging thorns and pushing stems aside with his staff. Then the wilderness became a desert.

After a time, Patrick saw they were approaching a hole: huge, perfectly round and so black it seemed to eat the very light. The pair stood on the precipice, their toes touching the infinite darkness, and Christ explained that sinners fell into this hole after death. The less they had sinned, the shorter the time they would spend down there in the darkness and the sooner they would climb the road to Paradise. Patrick looked down. He smelled sulphur and heard screaming, along with the beating of drums. It reminded him of his days as a slave, marching shackled, the slave drivers setting the rhythm of their steps. He felt himself start to fall.

Patrick woke. He was freezing cold and could hear the bells ringing in the monastery beyond the chapel. Upon opening his eyes, he saw the great book and the shining staff lying next to him on the ground. Then he thought of the hole in the ground and the darkness and the dread. If Heaven was anything like as kind as that pit was perilous, then at least the men and boys he had baptised were safe. They were martyrs, bound for Paradise.

The image he saw whenever he closed his eyes was of the women, suffering like the sinful souls in the depths of that great hole Christ had shown him. The next day he wrote a letter to be read aloud in front of Coroticus, the British slave dealer whose soldiers had killed the newly baptised men and stolen away their wives and daughters. Patrick disowned the slavers as his countrymen. He condemned them for allying with Picts and Scots who had no Christian faith. He chastised them for killing those who had been gathered for God from the ends of the earth. He told them that Hell awaited them if they did not repent, do penance and set the women they had taken free. He urged Coroticus to imagine what a terrible thing Hell would be; though he knew in his heart that the slave driver would spend eternity in shackles, scourged with hooks and tormented by the beating of drums.

❖

Much of what we know about the historical Patrick comes from a text called the *Confessio* that he wrote himself in middling-quality Latin. (When we were given it to study as undergraduates, I took out a translation from the English Faculty Library. When I reached the line 'I can't express myself with the brief words I would like', I saw that someone had written in the margin, 'Oh but please try.') The text tells us that he was born in Britain shortly after the end of the Roman occupation in 410 CE. He was raised and educated in a Christian Romano-British household. At the age of sixteen, he was abducted and sold into slavery in Ireland, apparently with thousands of others. Patrick then endured six years as a slave in what is now County Mayo in the far west of Ireland, before escaping. Though his family welcomed him home, he had his own plans. Having grown even more devout in his years as a slave among non-Christians, he stayed in Britain long enough to be ordained as a deacon, after which he went back to Ireland to preach the Gospels. Patrick returned to Britain at least once when he was somewhat older to be tried for a past offence, though the *Confessio* does not explain the nature of the crime.

Close study of the *Confessio* has shown Patrick's use of rhetorical techniques, learned, presumably, during his Latin education in post-Roman Britain. Rhetoric, or the art of persuasion, is primarily concerned with speech-making and would have come in useful for someone bent on converting people to a new faith. And in this aim, he was very successful. While Patrick is not single-handedly responsible for the conversion of the Irish (as tradition claims), he probably played an important part in the process.

There is ample historical evidence for the far-reaching, tireless missionary work that gained momentum across Europe and North Africa from around the fifth century. Its agents, Patrick among them, were fuelled by the words spoken in the Gospels by the Resurrected Christ:

Go ye into all the world, and preach the gospel to every creature. He that believeth and is baptised shall be saved; but he that believeth not shall be damned. And these signs shall follow them that believe; In my name shall they cast out devils; they shall speak with new tongues; they shall take up serpents; and if they drink any deadly thing, it shall not hurt them; they shall lay hands on the sick, and they shall recover.

In the only other surviving work written by Patrick, a letter to the slaver Coroticus, the Bishop of Ireland describes the white robes and anointed foreheads of the people he has baptised, though they are already dead in the description. Purgatory would have been among the doctrines they would have learned from Patrick; a place the soul would go after death to be purified of its sins through suffering. Purgatory was different from Hell, because the soul, once purified, would ultimately be delivered to Heaven. Hell was forever.

The St Patrick of shamrocks and banished snakes known to today's culture is largely the product of legends written down hundreds of years after his death. One important biography was composed around 1200 by Jocelyn of Furness, whom we have already met in relation to St Mungo. Various rituals, charms and spin-off stories associated with Patrick are somewhat older, including the one known as Patrick's *lorica* ('breastplate'). The full text for this Old Irish prayer of protection survives in an eleventh-century manuscript of hymns. Most of its verses begin 'I bind to myself today' and are followed by a list of powers. These include divine and saintly powers such as 'the power of the Crucifixion', 'the faith of the confessors' and the 'purity of Holy Virgins', as well as natural forces such as 'the stability of the earth' and 'the hardness of rocks'. A short passage introduces the prayer, explaining that it was used by St Patrick for protection against an ambush, so that when he passed it with his followers, those lying in wait had transformed into a herd of deer.

The story of St Patrick's vision of the entrance to Purgatory appears first in an eleventh-century Latin text called *The Treatise on St Patrick's Purgatory*. The majority of the text concerns a knight called Sir Owein, who decides to enter the hole discovered by Patrick. It is therefore rather more in the tradition of a medieval romance (in the sense of a quest, rather than a love story) than a saint's legend. It was translated into Anglo-Norman French by the brilliant Marie de France (who also wrote a verse life of St Etheldreda) in around 1200, and a Middle English verse translation, known as *Sir Owein*, was also made. This provided the part of the story above concerned with Patrick's dream; the poem opens with the sleeping Patrick encountering Christ, who gives him a staff, a book and a view into the Abyss.

If you want a sense of how medieval readers might have imagined Purgatory, then there are worse places to start than *Sir Owein*. When the knight journeys into the hole, the text reads, 'At last, as he went along the cavern a tiny glimmer of light began to shine weakly . . . but there the light was shining only as it shines on earth in winter after sunset.' When the demons flew in and seized him, it is said that they 'dragged the knight for a long time across a waste land. The soil was black and the land dark and . . . a burning wind was blowing which could barely be heard but which seemed nonetheless to pierce his body with harshness.' At last they reached the first place of torture where the 'plain was full of human beings of both sexes and all ages who were lying naked on the ground on their bellies, stretched out by burning iron nails driven into the ground through their hands and feet'.

Avoiding or reducing time in Purgatory was a major fixation for medieval Christians. Penance on earth could help. Some years after my time with the *Confessio*, I was working on a penitential, a manuscript dealing with different kinds of penance, and found myself reading a line of Latin that roughly translated as: 'If you have knowingly drunk blood or semen: two weeks of bread and water.' It led me to a genre of medieval text concerned with the scope and variety of human sin. In the early eleventh century, for example, Burchard of Worms listed numerous specific and very elaborate sins and gave the penance required. Women's sins are especially imaginative. For instance, if a woman had lain face down on the ground, exposed her buttocks, had someone make bread on them and then baked the bread and fed it to her husband in the hope he would love her more, that would be two whole years of penance.

By the later Middle Ages, pilgrimages and special purgatorial discount vouchers known as 'indulgences' could reduce time in Purgatory. In the year 1300, Pope Boniface VIII issued an indulgence saying that, to honour the centennial, any pilgrim or outsider who came to Rome and visited the basilica of St Peter every day for fifteen days would be granted 'the fullest possible pardon of all their sins'. What an incentive that must have been for anyone living in terror of millennia of agony after death.

There is a cavern on an island in Lough Derg that has been known as St Patrick's Purgatory since the Middle Ages. The cave's association with visions may be explained by the theory that it was once a prehistoric 'sweat house' for inhaling herbal smokes. And, indeed, a curious anecdote in a fourteenth-century French chronicle hints that the medieval custodians of the shrine were not above creating hallucinogenic vapours for visiting pilgrims. Froissart reports how a knight called William Lisle once spent a night at the site and told Froissart of his experiences as they rode together from Kent to London. Lisle had accompanied a royal expedition to Ireland and visited St Patrick's Purgatory with a fellow knight. He said that they had been enclosed in the cavern from sunset till sunrise and that, as the gate had closed behind them, they had descended as far as three or four storeys, when they had begun to feel heavy and irresistibly drowsy. Sitting down on the stone steps, they had fallen asleep. Froissart, having asked what visions the men had received, reports Lisle's answer:

> They launched out in their sleep into strange dreams and great imaginings and saw, they felt, very many more things than they would have done in their own beds at home.
>
> 'But when we woke in the morning . . . we came out and could not remember a single thing we had seen. We considered it had all been a delusion.'

Nowadays St Patrick's Purgatory is closed to visitors and we must look to the medieval narratives for a sense of its mind-bending, vision-inducing powers. In the saints and spirituality of these stories we enter a realm of black, wasted and fire-swept soils, of naked bodies writhing on spits and dreams that can't quite be remembered; one can't help thinking that this is a realm in which the early twentieth-century psychoanalysts would have run amok. And, more broadly, legends which touch on the afterlife reveal how the cult of saints operated within a grander network of beliefs regarding the story of the universe from Creation to Last Judgement and the fate of every human soul.

Cuthbert: Otters in the Cold

DIED 687
FEAST DAY: 20 MARCH

The sea beyond Holy Island was cold all year round and the wind that scraped over it only a little kinder. Wade in and the breath caught at first and the skin burned, but persevere and slide each foot over the weed-slithering, anemone-pocked stone and the water rose over the groin – another intake of breath – and up to the nipples – and again – and then into the cold arms of the sea. Stand still and wait. Wait till it happens.

Peace.

Total separation.

Oneness with the deep pulse of creation.

The hermit's home.

Cuthbert's bare, buffeted shelter stood on Farne Island, even further out to sea than Holy Island's Lindisfarne. He lived amid a thousand seals and a hundred as many seabirds of all different kinds; a community unlike that of the monks on Lindisfarne. Here, the air was always full of the noise of birds, especially in spring, and the sea and the wind added their own voices. But in all other ways it was the quietest place on earth.

One night, after standing in the water as he did every night, Cuthbert turned and waded back to land. Out on the naked, elemental rock, the water ran in rivers down his pimpled legs, pooling at his feet and trickling back into the sea.

As he bore this second immersion, he thought about what the messengers from Holy Island had come to tell him that day. They'd invited him to accept the office of Bishop of distant Hexham. Cuthbert pondered it now.

It would mean moving a long way inland. It would mean episcopal duties and heavy, uncomfortable clothes. It would mean constant talking, constant appeasement, constant confrontation with the knotty human world. Cuthbert felt weary. Then he noticed a sliver of reflected moonlight snaking onto the stone beside him. An otter had crept out of the sea, its oiled fur slick and glossy. Then another whiskery head broke the water and a second otter joined the first. The pair raised their blunt noses and shook themselves dry. When their pelts were fluffy as dandelion clocks, they sprang forward to wind themselves around the hermit's legs, weaving in and out, whisking away the wetness and breathing on his skin in warm puffs.

Watching the miracle, Cuthbert knew that he never wanted to leave these islands, this life out on Farne was blessed beyond reckoning. But perhaps he should rejoin the world a little. Perhaps it was his duty. Cuthbert lifted his eyes from the otters and glanced over at Holy Island. Some lights still glimmered in the chapel windows. Eata was Bishop of Lindisfarne now. Could there be a compromise? Would he be willing to trade his post for the bishopric at Hexham, so that Cuthbert could stay on as Bishop of Lindisfarne, within sight of his hermitage?

The otters squeaked as they finished their work. The messengers had said they would come back in the morning for his answer. In his heart, Cuthbert sensed that leaving this place, even only to live again on Holy Island, would kill him. He just hoped that he would have time to come back and that his friends, some nesting on the cliffs, some sleeping on the beaches, two now sliding into the sea, would remember him when he did.

❖

God's approval of Cuthbert's cold-water dips in the North Sea is shown by the ministration of a pair of otters. This is not an isolated motif. In medieval accounts of St Brendan's journey to the Otherworld, he and his monks encounter Paul the Hermit. The old man, completely covered in white hair, receives fish and fuel from an otter. An early twelfth-century Anglo-Norman version of the encounter reads:

> For all of thirty years I had a servant who cared for me constantly, an otter which regularly, three days each

week, brought me fish and fed me with it . . . round its neck hung a satchel packed full of dry seaweed, with which I could cook my fish . . . after thirty years the otter did not return; this was not out of reluctance or because it despised me, but because God . . . created for me here the spring which supplies everything I require.

In the Brendan narrative, the otter is the stepping stone to a further sixty years living on water alone. It teaches Paul the Hermit to put his faith in God's provision.

The story of Cuthbert and the otters survives in the work of St Bede, who lived from childhood in the Northumbrian monastery of Monkwearmouth Jarrow and died in 735. His *Life of Cuthbert* and *History of the English Church* tell us that Cuthbert was born in the 630s in Dunbar in the far north of the Anglo-Saxon kingdom of Northumbria (nowadays Dunbar lies within East Lothian in Scotland). At this time, not all Anglo-Saxon kings had yet been converted, but King Edwin of Northumbria had been Christian for several years thanks to the Irish mission. Irish monastic communities had founded monasteries in Northumbria and brought with them a love of the hermitic or ascetic lifestyle.

Cuthbert, despite being English, was raised in the Irish tradition. He initially joined a community at Melrose, Northumbria, which had been founded by the Irish missionary St Aidan (died 651). There, Cuthbert rose to the rank of prior. In 664, he travelled to Lindisfarne's Holy Island and entered its monastery, also founded by St Aidan. There he enforced recent reforms from Rome, but, in 676, retired to one of the nearby Farne Islands. When he was made Bishop of Hexham just under a decade later, he almost immediately exchanged the role with the contemporary Bishop of Lindisfarne, but returned within a year to his hermitage, where he died.

Cold-water immersions like those practised by Cuthbert recur in Bede's own work. He describes how, when he was living in Melrose, Bede heard the story of an ordinary man called Dryhthelm who died and experienced a vision of Hell, Purgatory and Heaven. Coming back to life, the man entered the monastery and became a great ascetic (one who eschews all physical pleasure). As often as he could, he would plunge into the River Tweed and sing the Psalms. He would do this even in winter; even when he had to crack the ice with his bare hands. Whenever he had finished his immersion, he would climb out and wait for his clothes to dry against his skin. Upon being challenged by the other monks as to how he could bear such cold, he would reply, 'I have seen colder.' And when asked how he could endure such hardship, he would answer, 'I have seen harder.'

And it's not just Bede who tells such tales. In Jocelyn of Furness' *c.* 1200 *Life of Mungo*, the narrator describes Mungo (otherwise Kentigern) observing a similar ritual. The saint rises from his bed – which is 'a rock hallowed out like a grave' – and slips off his penitential hair shirt, before stepping into the river:

> And there . . . no corruption of his eager flesh, either awake or even sleeping, defiled or stained the lily of his white genitals . . . this just man sprouted before the Lord like an un-withering lily . . . he was no more pricked by the sight or touch of the most beautiful girl than of the hardest flint.

As for Cuthbert, the efficacy of his ascetic lifestyle was held to have been proven when, eleven years after his death, he was exhumed and his body discovered to be incorrupt. The monks translated it to a wooden coffin for display above the ground. This coffin went with them when, in 875, the community gave up resisting Viking attacks and left Lindisfarne for good. They relocated to Chester-le-Street. Then, in 995, they carried Cuthbert's coffin up to Durham, where it has lived ever since. The church built there by the community became the centre of a monastic settlement and then a town. Durham, as a great cathedral city, owes its existence to Cuthbert's remains and Cuthbert's coffin represents the oldest extant fabric of a saintly shrine from Britain.

Cuthbert's incorruptibility was a symptom of his *virtus*, which could provoke other physical symptoms. For instance, the corpse of St Hugh of Lincoln (who in life was said to have been beloved of a whooper swan) disgorged mouthfuls of sweet-smelling oil, while the hair and nails of St Edmund (the wolf tamer you will read about in November) kept growing in the grave.

This tenacious *virtus* focused on the saint's body, but it extended beyond it too, into the landscapes and materials it had touched in life, creating a solar system of contact relics. Prudentius describes how 'the land of Spain', following the martyrdom of Emeterius and Chelidonius, 'drank in the warm stream when it was wetted by the slaughter of the twain, and now its people throng to visit the ground that was coloured with their holy blood, making petitions with voice and heart and gifts'. *Virtus* radiated from saints' bodies like the sun's heat, soaking into their very clothes, their possessions, their places of martyrdom, their sites of burial. It could transfer to the dust that settled on their shrines. It was a spiritual sunbeam in which demonic motes could not survive.

When, in 1104, St Cuthbert's coffin was opened, the community found a postcard-sized Gospel of John, as well as a garnet-inlaid cross and an ivory comb and imported fabrics. These were removed to be venerated as relics. The comb may have been used to tend Cuthbert's corpse and survives, along with the cross and the Gospel Book, which, with its red leather binding and embossed foliate decoration, constitutes the earliest extant and intact European book. The British Library acquired it for £9 million in 2012, making it one of the institution's most significant and costly acquisitions of the past twenty years.

In 1401, Cuthbert's bones and original coffin were housed in a great shrine which boasted a jewel known as the 'Great Emerald'. Even at this date, it was valued at £3,336. By the high Middle Ages his shrine stood at the heart of a thriving metropolis, with grateful pilgrims offering gifts as strange and exotic as griffin claws and eggs, unicorn horns and elephant tusks.

The shrine is lost, but by the nineteenth century the saint's body was preserved in a larger tomb along with the pieces of his early medieval coffin, which have now been conserved, reassembled and put back on display in Durham Cathedral. They bear incised images of the four evangelist symbols (a calf for Luke, a lion for Mark, an eagle for John and a man for Matthew), alongside one of the earliest representations of the Virgin and Child to survive from outside Rome. The inscription gives the names of Christ, the four Evangelists and the Virgin in a combination of encrypted runes and Greek and Latin characters. Such mixing of alphabets would be hard to explain in isolation, but other related discoveries, including the Lindisfarne Gospels, the Anglo-Saxon whale-bone Franks Casket and inscribed stones from Lindisfarne, show the coffin's debt to a fertile confluence of cultures.

Cuthbert: Otters in the Cold

The cult of Cuthbert is a lesson in how pilgrimage centres evolved in relationship to the many political upheavals of the ages. Without the Vikings, there might be no Durham. Chester, too, would be a very different place without the revenues to Werburgh's shrine, brought within its walls because of Norse incursions. The stories that sustained Cuthbert's cult are early, barely a century younger than the man himself. When we read them, we are reading the legends that compelled the Lindisfarne monks to carry his relics with them as they fled south, that were in the minds of the twelfth-century ecclesiastics who opened his coffin and found a manuscript and ornaments inside, that shaped the commission to the goldsmiths to house the ancient timbers in a reliquary set with precious gems. Saints' legends were, in short, vital to the institutions that claimed them, as well as to the pilgrims who came to venerate the subjects' relics. It follows that the physical survivals of the medieval cult of saints, including, in some cases, whole cities, depend on legends.

William of Norwich: The Body in the Woods

DIED 1144
FEAST DAY: 26 MARCH

The night after Passover, a nun had come running into Norwich claiming she had seen a ladder of light shining from the sky into Thorpe Wood. Following it, she discovered the dead body of a boy hanging from an oak tree, wearing only his coat and boots, his head shaved. Two holes pierced his left foot, a ring of wounds encircled his forehead and bruises surrounded his neck and mouth, which was closed around a spiked teasel. There were another two holes in his left palm. The skin around them looked like raw pork that had been doused with boiling water.

'There were ravens trying to peck at his eyes,' the nun had said, 'but they couldn't get close enough. Some power kept them away.'

The boy's body was buried where it was found, but a priest called Godwin went there to see if it belonged to his nephew, William, who had gone missing. He reported how the earth seemed to fling itself out of the hole as he dug, so that he began to hope the boy was still alive. But when he had reached his body, there was no doubt the boy was dead.

Still, the corpse had not been quite like any he had seen in all his years as a priest. It had smelled like honeysuckle flowers.

On hearing the news of her son's murder, William's inconsolable mother explained that, the Monday before, she had opened the door to a man she did not know. He told her that he was cook to the Archdeacon of Norwich and needed an assistant, but she had turned him away, distrustful. When he had come back the next day with a bag of coins, twelve-year-old William had joined her at the door, saying:

'Let me go with him. In the house of the Archdeacon of Norwich, I'll be a proper servant and earn twice as much as I do working in the skinner's shop.'

William had persuaded her to change her mind. That Tuesday, the man took him away and she was left with the money bag.

A rumour began, stirring up an old resentment; a resentment that some justified with Christian Scripture, which said that their Messiah had been tortured by Jews. There were plenty of Jews in Norwich, invited by the Norman lords to carry out moneylending. Anger rose against the community, which lived in its own quarter of the town. When the city sheriff invited the accused ones to stay in Norwich Castle until the furore had died down, they gladly accepted.

The Jewish children asked to explore the castle and their parents let them, eager to discuss evil rumours that had led the Christians of Norwich to accuse them of murdering a child. They had heard the whispered words as they had hurried through the streets, carrying their overnight bags, wondering when it would be safe to go home.

'Killed on Good Friday!'

'Wounds to his hands and feet.'

'Thorns piercing his poor forehead and a stab wound in his side.'

'Wasn't his mother paid blood money, like Judas?'

'William worked at the skinner's shop. The Jews go there for their furs.'

There was more, much more, but, in truth, for anyone to think they were capable of such a deed was all they needed to know. They had known this kind of hatred before. This was a trap much bigger than Norwich: much bigger, even, than England.

The singing of a blackbird rang out in the evening air. Inside the castle, the hostages lapsed into silence. What more could be said? There was nothing to be done. The real killer had masked his crime well enough, timing and staging William's murder to cast suspicion on the Jews. He had been lazy enough about it, knowing that the Christians of his city would jump at an excuse to let the dormant bud of an old hatred bloom.

The oldest of the Jewish men found himself listening to the blackbird and for a moment the threatening aura of the city beyond the castle walls left his mind. The song drew his gaze out of the window to where a cherry tree blossomed. It shone in the twilight like a many-branched menorah and, almost without conscious thought, he began to speak the ancient blessing for the first flowers of spring.

His voice delved through the night, silencing the blackbird, but offering a new music in its place. Then the other men joined him. And all present prayed aloud or in their minds, because the tree was beautiful indeed and all they could do was trust that God would, somehow, provide.

❖

The mythic Jews of medieval Christian literature are inversions of religious ideals that, as Debra Higgs Strickland puts it, 'tell us next to nothing about medieval Jews, but . . . reveal a great deal about medieval Christians'.

The young William of Norwich was murdered in his home town in 1144 and certain aspects reported about the state of his body encouraged the city's majority Christian population to pin the crime on the Jews. A vehemently antisemitic cult sprang up around the grave of the dead boy, who was hailed as a martyr, and the story, along with its vilification of the Jews, was crystallised by Thomas of Monmouth, a monk in Norwich Cathedral Priory in the years just after William's death. Thomas' *Life and Miracles of St William of Norwich* began a tradition of blood libel against Jews.

William's body was buried in the monks' cemetery at Norwich Cathedral. Six years later, on 7 March 1150, Thomas of Monmouth claims to have received a message in a dream from Bishop Herbert, long-dead founder of his community, that the body should be 'translated' into the interior of the church. Thomas writes that he ignored the instruction three times, finally inducing the Bishop to appear holding the young William's hand, threatening Thomas with his crozier and pinching him so hard on the arm that his thumb marked the skin. Thomas went to his superior, Prior Elias, and the translation took place on the Wednesday before Easter 'with utmost reverence', though Thomas admits hiding two of William's dislodged teeth in 'a secret place'.

The translation boosted William's status as a martyr and that was a boon for Norwich Cathedral. It hadn't had the privilege of a saint's cult until now and, as Miri Rubin has observed, might have been looking a little inadequate compared to the cathedral in neighbouring Bury St Edmunds, with its vibrant cult to Edmund the Martyr.

Thomas' *Life* presented and popularised the idea that Jews chose, hunted down, tortured and murdered a Christian child every year around Passover. William's was the

William of Norwich: The Body in the Woods

first such legend but not the last; the body of a young boy found in a river in 1168 led to the attempted creation of a cult of St Harold of Gloucester, killed, it was claimed, by Jews. In 1181 similar accusations were made in Bury St Edmunds. Later, the disappearance of a Lincoln boy called Hugh, and the subsequent discovery of his body at the bottom of a well, led to the hanging of Copin, a Jewish resident of Lincoln, and the execution of a further eighteen Jews of that city. A shrine was created to the child saint 'Little St Hugh of Lincoln' in the cathedral, already the site of a shrine to St Hugh of Lincoln, a former bishop of the same name. Thirteenth-century historian Matthew Paris writes of Jews coming from all over England to re-enact on Hugh the torture and death of Christ. And he lists all the injuries consistent with a pseudo-crucifixion, finally adding that 'they took the body down from the cross, and for some reason disembowelled it'. As with William of Norwich, the medieval account leaves questions unanswered, but assumes its reader will need little persuasion of Jewish guilt.

Francophone Jewish groups began arriving in England after the Norman Conquest and settled in various major cities, Norwich among them. Among the catalysts for their migration were persecution in the Rhineland and northern France and the invitation to act as moneylenders to the Norman ruling classes (a profession forbidden to Christians). For all that these communities were protected by the Norman elite, antisemitism flourished, rooted in Christian biblical representations of Jews torturing and killing Christ, as well as anger around taxes to fund the Crusades. There were anti-Jewish riots at Richard I's coronation in 1189 and in the following year a mob set upon the Jews of York. According to William of Newburgh (died *c.* 1198), an Augustinian canon from Yorkshire and author of a *History of English Affairs*, the victims, led by a man called Joceus, sought protection in Clifford's Tower at York Castle. They were beset by a mob so violent and terrifying that the Jewish families resorted to mass suicide as their only means of escape.

Blood libel drew the cult of saints into a wider antisemitic narrative. Giles de Bridport, Bishop of Salisbury between 1256 and 1262, made it his mission to convert Jews in his diocese (the area under his authority) and sought to enforce numerous restrictions on their lives. He even commissioned a manuscript known as the Abingdon Apocalypse with an illustration of a tall bishop (presumably Giles himself) barring from heaven a Jewish man identifiable by his hat and already well-worn antisemitic physiognomy.

Giles stood close to the climax of a cultural, economic and religious campaign of Jewish persecution that culminated in 1290, when King Edward I of England ordered the expulsion of all Jews from England. He decreed that it must be done by the first of November – All Saints' Day – of that year. All debts were cancelled. Jewish families fled.

William of Norwich: The Body in the Woods

And artefacts like the thirteenth-century bronze Bodleian Bowl, found in a disused Norfolk moat and bearing French heraldic motifs and a Hebrew inscription pertaining to a pilgrimage to Israel, give us glimpses of the stories of expelled Jews and the fate of their treasured possessions. The edict would remain in place until the seventeenth century.

It was not hard to transform 'murder' to 'martyrdom' in the case of William of Norwich. Within a few years of his death, his feast day appears in monastic calendars from as far away as Bavaria. Thomas of Monmouth describes his numerous miracles; how, for instance, the young nephew of Prior Elias recovered from a mortal illness when his parents made a candle the same length and width as his body. Dedicating the candle to St William, the boy's father bore it to the tomb and left it there. Sure enough, it was claimed that, by the time he got home, his son was no longer at death's door, but up and fit and well.

The William of Norwich story demonstrates how saints' legends helped express and communicate medieval England's antisemitism. Popular stories were powerful tools then as they are today. We underestimate them at our peril.

Part Two

Outsending

❖

MENEDEMUS But what strange Dress is this? It is all over set off with Shells scollop'd, full of Images of Lead and Tin, and Chains of Straw-Work, and the Cuffs are adorned with Snakes Eggs [rosary beads] instead of Bracelets.

OGYGIUS I have been to pay a Visit to St. *James* at *Compostella*, and after that to the famous Virgin on the other Side the Water in *England*.

MENEDEMUS What! out of Curiosity, I suppose?

OGYGIUS Nay, upon the Score of Religion.

Desiderius Erasmus,
A Pilgrimage for Religion's Sake (1526)

April

April is a fine month in medieval calendars, calling readers to pick flowers, prune trees and enjoy the spring. Thanks to the moon in Taurus, this is the month of the neck and throat, as well as bad breath.

The privations of Lent are probably over and done with and the Easter sepulchre may even now be standing gloriously in the church. This would be a spectacle indeed after the stripped altars of the preceding weeks. In late fifteenth-century Bristol, the gilded sepulchre in the church of St Mary Redcliffe showed the risen Christ, a hell-scene with thirteen devils, angels with detachable wings, soldiers sleeping at the tomb and the descending forms of God the Father and the Holy Ghost.

In the stories to come, we will meet holy warriors, a Thames fisherman and the spirit of an ancient pagan, and we will discover how legend could serve the dominant powers of the age.

George: The Princess and the Dragon

Died 303
Feast Day: 23 April

To Una, whose young life had known nothing but the silk slippers and sweet fancies of the palace, the dragon seemed far away. She heard the stories with exaggerated horror, gasping as her ladies-in-waiting told her how, each night, the beast had been wrapping itself around the city walls and breathing fatal fumes from slits in its snout. The poorer families whose homes rested against those walls knew nothing but the tightening of their lungs, then the scrabbling of their own and their relatives' hands on blankets and pillows, and, finally, the terrified resignation to death.

Una, who prided herself not only on her appearance but on her political learning, thought favourably of her father's idea to start sending lambs and calves to distract the dragon. Una's father was the King of Silene and had converted his council chamber, where once he had plotted conquests of far-off kingdoms, into a library of dragon destruction. He had shipped scrolls and translators from throughout

Africa and Asia to stock his shelves and provide, in time, an answer.

Dragons are hungry, said letters inscribed with reeds from the Nile and brushes of black rabbit fur. *Give dragons food*.

For a while, it worked. The dragon would carry the sheep and cows tethered outside the gates to an underwater cave, and stopped killing the people altogether. It was deemed a great victory on the part of the King and his council of barons. And it bought them time to think of a way to annihilate the beast. Trembling artists sat on the ramparts after dark and came back with blurred impressions of something with malicious, intelligent eyes, serpentine, long as five full-size crocodiles nose to tail. They said the creature lived in the lake on the other side of the plain, darted like a lizard and breathed a noxious miasma that curled black over the earth, darker even than the night. None of the generals was willing to risk his troops against such an enemy. They had no doubt that the Underworld was wreaking some punishment upon them.

When Silene's homegrown supply of livestock began to dwindle, which took longer than it might because the people had soon given up eating it themselves, Una's father called in favours from his allies beyond Libya on either side of the Mediterranean Sea. At first, they helped willingly, sending caravans of their own animals to keep the dragon at bay. But after a few months, his messengers came home with nothing. The favours had run out and so had all the meat.

Una's father often let her sit in on council meetings, saying that it would stand her in good stead for queenship of some foreign land if she understood the subtleties of political debate. When it came to the dragon, she enjoyed the puzzle, as well as the barons' admiring expressions when her well-timed contributions showed her grasp of the situation's delicacy. When the city was down to its last few sheep and calves, the discussion was fierce. Without meat tethered outside the gate, whole households would die every night. Without their labour, the city's economy would crumble. If there were no animal flesh and the dragon needed flesh to be appeased, then that left only people. Of the population of Silene, those old enough to work were essential for the running of the city and those too old might anger the beast for being tough and sinewy, but there was a surfeit of children, especially among the poor families, and anyway, young meat in any creature was preferable to old. It was therefore agreed among the King and his council of barons that lots would be cast each day, choosing first a district of Silene, then a street, then a household, from which a child would be selected. It was a temporary but necessary measure, just until they had found out how to destroy the dragon completely.

Una went to bed feeling very grave that night, knowing it had been a hard decision for her father to make, but one that proved his strength as king. She drifted off imagining the first family giving up its child for the sake of the city. Their nobility of spirit made tears seep from between her eyelashes and soak the silk cushion under her head. In the nights that followed, she heard distant crying and she felt more pity than ever for those poor, dutiful parents.

Then, within a few days, something happened that neither Una nor her father had foreseen. They had never imagined that when the lots were cast, the district chosen would be the royal district and the street chosen would be that on which the palace stood and the household chosen would, that day, be theirs. And what her father had forgotten was that his very own Una was, in the eyes of the law, still a child. When the dice fell, it did not matter that she was on the cusp of womanhood and that she would soon be old enough to marry. It did not matter that she was a princess and that her father was the King. All that mattered was that it was she who had been chosen to be given to the dragon that night.

The barons, whose own children were all grown-up, sent messengers into the streets, informing the people who the evening's child would be, as they did every morning. The King tried to overturn the decision, but the crowds would have none of it, even when he resorted to begging.

'My Una, not my dear Una. Please, I beg you!'

'Hypocrite!'

'We have all given up our children!'

'But I am to see her married. I am to see her bear my grandchildren.'

'You think yourself an exception, just because you are King? We had hoped for the same for our children, but you sent them to die.'

In the lake, the dragon heard it all. Fish kissed at the scales round her jagged mouth as she digested the words. She didn't suppose princesses tasted better in any real sense, but the pleasure of listening to her father grovel and whine before the people was a novel delicacy. As evening approached, the dragon kept her eyes just above the water. She wondered what the girl would look like. She hoped she was plump.

Darkness fell and so did a tantalising hush. The gates of the city were shut. She waited. At any moment, a white-clad shape would be led from the great wooden doors and left at her mercy. Oh, she would make her last as long as she could. She would savour this one.

But no princess appeared that night. Not after one night, not even after two. On the third, the dragon swam to the shore, wrapped herself around the city walls and exhaled. She heard again the last, desperate gasps of the dying and thought of the King safe at the heart of the city and the furore the morning would bring.

The day after that the dragon could feel the crowd's vibrations even from within her underwater lair. When her head broke the surface of the lake, an angry hum rose from inside the walls. Today, she thought, he will relent. But the evening came and no princess at the lakeside. That night, she breathed them dead again. The next day, riots. The King gave in only after a full week had passed.

Una had bitten her nails to the quick and been sick so many times that there was nothing left to bring up. Her father led her on foot to the gates of the city. She had never been so far from the palace. She saw drawn, thin faces looking out of windows and from the shadows of stinking alleyways.

Soon they were at the gates. The guards were opening them, her father had let go of her hand and she was walking out of the city. As she turned around to cry out, the gates slammed shut. The last thing she saw was her father's rigid, grief-stricken face.

She looked over her shoulder at the lake. Then she turned and started walking towards it, her treacherous feet acting, it seemed, without her permission. Her silk slippers were turning brown. The sky was turning purple.

When she reached the edge of the lake, she saw the stake to which her predecessors had been tethered. She saw blood-stains around the base of the stake. It was incomprehensible to her that she was going to die. And the loneliness, the terror, the longing for a parent to shake her awake and smooth the nightmare from her brow . . . Was that how all the others had felt?

Una saw movement on the surface of the water. A

Outsending

V-shaped current was rushing towards her. Then, just as a form split the lake in front of her, she heard thundering hooves. And then, just as a terrifying, reptilian face with razor teeth and jet-black eyes broke from the water, a horse leapt over her, bearing down, colliding with the dragon.

Having already leapt from the water, the dragon did not see the horse and its rider till it was much too late, nor did she see the lance until it had penetrated her neck. Her jaws snapped closed onto nothing, the lance snagged across her gullet like a splinter of bone. Her body thudded onto sharp rocks, twisting round so that her pale, tender parts felt the cold night air.

There was a long silence, then her attacker said, 'Put your belt over her head.'

She felt the girl's shaking hands tying a belt around her neck. Through bleared vision she saw her face, her set mouth, her round, shocked eyes, not quite silhouetted against the last light. Then the princess took the loose end and pulled it tight. The leather constricted against the lance, the dragon's breath caught in her throat and pangs of agony stabbed down her spine.

'Now lead her to the city,' said her attacker.

The dragon had no choice but to roll over and follow the princess as she picked up the end of the belt and walked towards the gate.

Out of the corner of her eye, Una could see the rider beside her, tall and clad in glittering armour. When they passed through the gates, people crept from their houses, until hundreds were lining the street. She fixed her own gaze ahead, unable to look at them as she led the dragon to the middle of the city.

❖

The archetypal dragon-slaying incident in the Christian canon lies in the Book of Revelation (12: 7–9), known in the Middle Ages as the Apocalypse, in which St Michael the Archangel defeats the dragon, a symbol of Lucifer, once and for all:

And there was war in heaven: Michael and his angels fought against the dragon; and the dragon fought and his angels. And they prevailed not; neither was their place found anymore in heaven. And that great dragon was cast out, that old serpent, called the Devil, and Satan, which deceiveth the whole world: he was cast out into the earth.

Saintly dragon-killings rehearse Michael's ultimate defeat of Satan, to which we will return in late September. They are not the end of the Devil. They always leave space for a sequel. George's is just one of a host of dragon-killing saints, but his story has proved especially tenacious.

According to legend, George was a Roman soldier from Cappadocia (modern-day Anatolia, Turkey) who was subjected to torture and execution for refusing to renounce his faith. Even as early as the fifth and sixth centuries, St George was venerated in Armenia, Constantinople, Jericho, Arabia and Syria, with cults focusing on his prolonged and elaborate martyrdom. In the earliest source, which dates to the fifth century and is known as the Vienna Palimpsest, George experiences a multiplicity of tortures, including being immersed in hot lead, made to wear boots full of sharp nails, drink molten iron, have his skin torn apart with hooks and have nails hammered into his skull. He dies three times and three times the Archangel Michael brings him back to life and all the while George works miracles for the faithful. When he is finally beheaded, water and milk gush from his severed neck.

In the thirteenth century, writer Jacobus de Voragine included St George in his popular collection of saints' lives known as *The Golden Legend*. This version, which still ends with the saint's martyrdom, also popularised the now famous story of the dragon, along with George's banner: a red cross on a white ground. Both the dragon-slaying and the flag would become powerful political symbols. In late medieval art, the dragon is frequently represented lying on its back, exposing a gaping vent, a kind of anus or vulva, and the trend is explored in the work of Samantha Riches. George's aggressive, phallic lance and the passivity of the vanquished, penetrable dragon make this a fertile topic for the fields of psychoanalytic and feminist theory.

George is a soldier and a martyr. He therefore came to represent the idea of the *miles Christi*, or soldier of Christ. When Christendom embarked on Crusades in the Holy Land from the late eleventh through to the thirteenth centuries, warrior saints became especially useful emblems of divine approval of war. But the banner of St George continued to inspire the idea of Holy War long after the Crusades had ended, giving him a political function. He is patron saint of Portugal, Ethiopia, Georgia and Lithuania, along with many other countries and cities.

In Christ Church, Oxford, under the shelf-mark Christ Church 92, is a manuscript made in 1326 for a young

Edward III. He was not quite King of England yet, but its contents were designed to prepare him for that office. The manuscript was probably commissioned by his mother, Isabella of France, who would bring about the deposition and death of his father Edward II within a year and put a teenage Edward III on the throne, so that she could rule as regent. The text is a treatise on kingship by a cleric called Walter Milemete and the many heavily gilded images reveal much about the psychological condition of the contemporary ruling elite. One illustration shows St George, wearing his red cross on his tunic, personally handing the arms of England to the future Edward III. Along with his father's throne, Edward would inherit conflict with the Scots, ongoing since the days of his grandfather Edward I, and a furious flock of barons poised to resume civil war. An image of St George showing his personal support for the young Edward III at least promised that his fights had divine sanction.

Once he had become king, Edward III showed no signs of insecurity on that front. In 1330, when he was just seventeen, he exiled his mother and executed her lover and partner-in-politics, Roger Mortimer. Edward then assumed his full authority as king and spent his long reign making war and shaping ideals of English chivalry. He founded the Order of the Garter in imitation of Arthur's Knights of the Round Table and built a chapel for its peers at Windsor, which was dedicated to St George. Prior to the fourteenth century, it was more common to see Edward the Confessor or Edmund the Martyr represented as England's patron saints. But from this time on the part is increasingly given to George. As George protected the Order and the Order protected England, the saint led the charge.

Mellitus: Sacred Salmon

Died 624
Feast Day: 24 April

While Columba and his followers roamed the northern territories of Britain, spreading the Word of God, visitors from beyond the eastern sea had docked their ships in the very south. Like many of his neighbours, the fisherman had worked on the wide Thames all his life and, having been raised to worship Woden, Frigg and Thor, he didn't like the visitors' ways. He didn't like the way they emptied the old temples for new altars to new gods, but he had no more power to stop the changes than he had to turn the tides that ruled the river. The new priests had built a church upstream on one of the ancient shrines; they called it St Paul's. They were building another on Thorney Island; there would be a strange name for that one too.

The fisherman sat in his boat, preparing for a night at his nets, while a crowd of converts gathered on the foreshore, waiting for one they called Father Mellitus. The fisherman had heard of Mellitus, who lived beside the new church downriver. Mellitus was neither an Angle nor a

Briton, but a swarthy man with a strong accent, who had come up from hot lands beyond the sea to bring his faith to London. The fisherman cast the crowd a suspicious glance, then carried on readying his nets.

When a man on the bank started calling out for passage across the river, the fisherman kept his eyes downcast. Let one of the other fishermen answer him. What business could anyone have on Thorney Island who was not wealthy enough to have their own boat? As he lowered his nets into the water and settled to wait for a catch, he stole a glance at the stranger. The night was not warm; the wind over the Thames was full of sea chills, and the fisherman himself was wearing a thick woollen coat, but the man on the bank was in nothing but a light shift. His arms and ankles were bare and the skin of his feet was visible through his shoes. The fisherman did not like the look of him.

The man went on calling and his voice echoed through the bands of mists from the eastern marshes. Suddenly the fisherman realised he was alone on the river.

'You! Yes, please take me across. You will be richly rewarded!'

The fisherman frowned, then raised his net out of the water. It had only one small roach in its weave. So he rowed to the bank.

The pair crossed the river and docked at Thorney Island. As soon as the boat had crunched on the gravel shoreline, the man leapt out and made for the great doors of the new building. The fisherman followed him, running to catch up. He did not want his passenger to go into the church, as they called it. They would both get in trouble. It was on royal land. The traveller had already opened the great doors and stepped inside. When the fisherman crossed the threshold, he forgot what he had been about to say.

The man was standing in front of the high altar, glowing like the moon and sun together. The beams that radiated from him ignited the candles fixed about the church. Winged beings appeared who were sprinkling the walls with water from golden vessels. As the beings rushed over his head to anoint the outside of the church, the man began reciting prayers. The whole building was dripping with water and resonant with the sound of the man's voice. When all the prayers had been said, the man walked past the fisherman to an area of sand beyond the door and began to inscribe strange characters in it with his finger. When he had finished, the beings vanished and darkness fell.

'Are you still there?'

The fisherman stuttered. The man replied.

'I am hungry. Do you have any food?'

'I have been so blinded by all this that I have not gone back out on the river. I have nothing but one small fish.'

'Return to your boat and cast your nets out again.'

Shaking, the fisherman left the church and slid down the bank to his boat. As he pushed off from the shore, his vision was still blurred and full of brightly coloured spots and his

Mellitus: Sacred Salmon

heart was pounding. When he was out on the muddy water, he put his net over the side and felt it fill with fish as if they had been waiting to be caught. He hauled them into the boat and saw by the growing light from the east that he had landed a whole shoal of salmon. There were more salmon now sparkling at his feet than he had caught in his whole life on the river. Then the man said:

'Bishop Mellitus will be waking up soon and preparing to come and dedicate this church to Saint Peter, companion of Saint Paul and keeper of the keys of Heaven. I am Saint Peter and I have dedicated it on his behalf. Go to meet him and take one salmon with you. Tell him it is from me and tell him what I have done. Tell him also that he will know the truth of your story by the moisture on the walls, the remains of the candles, and the Greek alphabet that I have twice inscribed in the sand beyond the door.'

Setting out into the dawn, which though bright and new seemed stale and dark compared to the light he had seen in the church, the fisherman did as he was told.

Mellitus, hearing the news from the fisherman and seeing the signs, believed his every word. Though kings of the old faith would soon drive him from his home and be buried again in their longboats, flooded with gold and sunk in the sand, according to the old customs, the English Church would not fall. The Bishops of London would return to St Paul's and when King Edward came to the throne, he would restore St Peter's Abbey to glory.

As for the fisherman, he embraced the new altars in the old shrines with more zeal than any of the converts on the riverbank. And, in every year that followed, he and his descendants gave one tenth of their catch gratefully to St Peter's Abbey at Westminster. And that tithe was enjoyed by the monks, as well as the kings, queens and courtiers who made it their personal temple.

❖

In 597 CE, Pope Gregory the Great sent a group of missionaries from Rome to Kent. They succeeded in converting King Æthelberht of Kent, whose wife, Bertha, was a Christian Frankish princess, and their leader, Augustine, became the first Archbishop of Canterbury.

Bede tells us that, in 601, a certain missionary called Mellitus joined the Christian community in Canterbury and became the first Bishop of London, which was ruled by Sæberht of Essex, Æthelberht of Kent's brother. (Incidentally, Bede writes that both Æthelberht and Sæberht were descended from the Saxon, Hengist, who, according to British myth, had come to Britain in the fifth century and, with the help of his daughter, Ronwen, had duped Vortigern the British usurper into giving them lands in Kent.)

According to Bede, Mellitus remained Bishop of London until both royal Christian brothers died and the territory fell to Eadbald, said to be a fornicator and devotee of the

Mellitus: Sacred Salmon

Germanic gods, Woden and Thor among others. Mellitus was therefore forced to flee to Gaul, only returning in 617–19, when Eadbald had converted. At this point, Mellitus becomes the third ever Archbishop of Canterbury. He is laid to rest there after his death.

The main miracle ascribed to Mellitus in Bede's *Ecclesiastical History of the English People* concerns a fire in Canterbury. Through prayer, the aged saint caused the wind to change direction and the fire to go out. However, in twelfth-century sources, we find him playing an important role in the foundation myth of St Peter's Abbey, Westminster.

The name of Thorney Island derives from the Old English word *Þorn* (pronounced and meaning 'thorn'), and *īeg* (pronounced *ay*, meaning 'island'). Together the two words translate, rather obviously, as 'thorny island'. But the rivulets that once surround Thorney (let's leave out the 'Island') have since disappeared with increased management and control of the waterway. 'Westminster' has replaced the name 'Thorney' and means 'a minster or church to the west'.

The churches of St Paul and St Peter rose from a cityscape already full of non-Christian temples and shrines to Roman, Celtic and Germanic gods. What should become of these is addressed in a letter to Mellitus from Pope Gregory the Great:

> Tell Augustine that he should by no means destroy the temples of the gods but rather the idols within those temples. Let him, after he has purified them with holy water, place altars and relics of the saints in them. For, if those temples are well built, they should be converted from the worship of demons to the service of the true God. Further, since it has been their custom to slaughter oxen in sacrifice . . . They will sacrifice and eat the animals not anymore as an offering to the Devil, but for the glory of God to whom, as the giver of all things, they will give thanks for having been satiated.

We see here how Gregory the Great urged the missionaries to refashion old customs for the new Christian faith. Converts should be invited to celebrate the 'day of the dedication of their churches [or] the feast of the martyrs whose relics are preserved in them . . . with religious feasting'. This will serve as an incentive, Gregory explains, for, 'if they [the pagans] are not deprived of all exterior joys, they will more easily taste the interior ones'. Gregory's instruction to appropriate and adapt the religious buildings and practices of would-be converts is evidence of a process known as 'religious syncretism'. The letter also suggests that, to make missionary work easier, the Church authorities allowed for a degree of 'wiggle room' in terms of Christian practice as well.

Mellitus: Sacred Salmon

My retelling of the salmon legend comes from the same *History of Saint Edward the King*, by the monk of St Albans, Matthew Paris (died 1259), that I used for the tale of Edward the Confessor in January. It relates how Edward, living some centuries after Mellitus, rebuilt the dilapidated abbey and justifies his efforts with the story of Mellitus, St Peter and the salmon. However, this is not just about St Edward. Matthew Paris' *History* was written during the reign of King Henry III, who was himself refurbishing St Peter's Abbey, Westminster, as well as the cult of St Edward the Confessor, whom the King claimed as a personal patron. Henry even gave the saint's name to his son, the future Edward I.

The tale of the salmon met numerous needs for Henry III. For one thing, it elevated the abbey's dedication to St Peter by claiming the saint had performed it in person. For another, it traced the abbey's origins back to the dawn of the English Church in the days of St Augustine and St Mellitus, which lent the whole institution the authority of age. And, as well as these, it connected him to Edward the Confessor, who had also refurbished the abbey. In short, it links Saints Peter, Mellitus and Edward the Confessor with Henry III in an unbroken chain of architectural patronage.

Despite Henry III's best efforts, Edward the Confessor's shrine was never that popular. At least it produced a number of pilgrim souvenirs. The most elaborate, in its complete form, takes the shape of a circular border, almost like a crescent moon, enclosing the image of a king giving a ring to a beggar. A scroll between them identifies the king as 'Edwardus'. According to another legendary episode, the beggar proves to be none other than St John the Evangelist, disciple of Christ. The ring was Edward the Confessor's primary contact relic.

If, nowadays, you were to visit Westminster Abbey and go into Henry III's 'Little Chapel', you would find yourself looking down on medieval floor tiles showing, alongside Edward and John, a small but accurate image of a salmon. These rectangular fish-bearing tiles look very similar to the illustration of the salmon being presented to Mellitus on a rectangular board in the Westminster copy of Matthew Paris' *History of Saint Edward the King*. It is no great surprise. They come from the same visual world.

In addition to its many advantages to England's royal and ecclesiastical corporate image, the salmon legend offered the community at Westminster Abbey an excuse to dine on salmon on 29 June, the feast day of Peter, the abbey's dedicatory saint. And if your own hypothetical trip to Westminster Abbey were on that date and if you were let into the private rooms of the Dean and Chapter, you might still find diners sitting down to a meal of salmon with the Worshipful Company of Fishmongers. So lore endures in the abbey's rituals, even if the Thames' stock of leaping ocean fish may now only be found in a legend.

Mellitus: Sacred Salmon

But the historical Mellitus brings different insights. His letter from Gregory the Great, for instance, suggests that, while medieval Christianity was in many ways profoundly different from the religions it replaced, it might still have preserved some of the locations of their spiritual sites and subsumed some of their feasts. But here it would be easy to exaggerate. We inherit the tendency of much later centuries to accuse medieval Christianity of 'paganism', to call every Catholic festival *saturnalia* or *bacchanalia* in disguise. This bias endures, and though we may judge it an enhancement of medieval Christianity today, there was a time when it was the gravest slur.

Erkenwald: A Secret under St Paul's

DIED 693
FEAST DAY: 30 APRIL

In ancient days, Britain was called Albion. It was said to have been named by Albina, a Syrian princess, who came to its shores with her sisters. They ruled and lived off the land, but, lacking any men with whom to engender heirs and, being sympathetic to creatures who rarely receive affection, they slept with a posse of demons. Their children were the giants of Albion, who ruled the islands until a fleet of Trojan ships led by Brutus docked, killed them off and claimed Albion for themselves. Brutus installed himself as the new king, renaming the islands 'Britain' after himself and building a New Troy either side of the Thames. Many kings and queens came after him, ruling and dying while Moses parted the Red Sea and Elijah made prophecies in the desert. Some of those rulers were good, some were bad. Some were unfairly deposed: some treasured. One revered king was Belinus, whose younger brother, Brennius, tried to unseat him many times. Belinus passed good laws. The officials in his court were just and under his government the people of Britain felt safe. They felt even safer when the brothers' mother, Conwenna, bared her breasts on the battlefield and convinced Brennius to give up his fight.

But these were still days of darkness, for Belinus and his people worshipped old gods, brought to the islands by their Trojan forebears, and Christ had not yet been born. For Belinus and his people, there was no salvation. When they died, they all went to hell, no matter how virtuous they had been. But when eventually Christ was born and sacrificed himself, so that he could let the good souls free, almost all of them escaped.

Six centuries later, the descendants of Brutus had gathered in the west of Britain, while settlers from Saxony and Denmark established kingdoms in the east. London fell under their rule and they called themselves the 'English'. Augustine and his missionaries had brought the Christian religion to them from Italy and seeded it in the soil of Kent. In the meantime, Irish monks had been sowing Christian teachings in the North.

When Erkenwald rose to the rank of Bishop of London, the city formerly called the New Troy, he decreed that the greatest of the city's pagan temples should be uprooted and the church of St Paul's extended. The job was long and he did not stay to oversee it. Indeed, he was in Essex visiting an abbey when the old foundations were being excavated and the workers' shovels and picks hit the hard stone that would show them the greatest wonder their eyes would ever see.

They brushed away the earth and revealed a slab of veined grey marble. The workers dug around and cleaned it, the better to see what they had found. It was a sarcophagus inscribed all over with gold letters. They called on learned priests, who copied the letters down and took them away to their cells, but declared their meaning elusive. Guild masters and practitioners in all kinds of trades also puzzled over the inscriptions. But no one could devise an intelligible translation. As news of the mystery spread, people began flocking to the place where the sarcophagus lay.

One morning, at the heart of the confused crowds, the Mayor of London spoke up.

'It must be a coffin of some great person or other. We should open it and see what else we can learn.'

So the workers prised off the lid and all the people gathered round.

He was no bigger than most men, but to those who saw him for the first time that morning, he was larger than life. He was dressed in a woollen robe, shot with silk and hemmed with pearls and gold. A golden belt encircled his waist and ermine lined his collar. His great head bore a crown worked with spiralling designs in silver and red enamel and a sceptre lay across his chest. All those close enough to see him well felt the hair rising on their arms, for not only were his clothes as bright and clean as if they had been presented by the tailor that morning, but his skin was plump, smooth and soft, and blood flushed his lips. All this in a sarcophagus that must have been underground for many hundreds of years.

'A great person indeed,' whispered a pale monk, who loved reading the chronicles in the monastery library. 'His name must surely reside in the history books. If only we could find out what it was.'

But the history books yielded nothing. Excitement at the mystery was rising to such a pitch that the rivers and roads bore Erkenwald word of what had been found in his church. He lost no time in riding home from Essex. Then he locked himself away in his palace and prayed all that day and night to learn the identity of the richly attired, centuries-dead man.

When Erkenwald left the palace the next morning, he resisted hurrying to the worksite to see the wonder. Instead, he said Mass in St Paul's surrounded by his clergy and a host of high-born men and women in luxurious robes. Then he processed with the whole company to the place where the dead man lay and there was extravagant ceremony in the arranging of the lords and priests and civic officials. As was fitting for such a morning, Erkenwald made speeches about the fruitless attempts to decipher the inscription and the futile searches in the history books to find the identity of the man. It fell to God alone to reveal it.

Outsending

Erkenwald knelt at the head of the tomb and reached his hands down to the dead man's face. Then, gently, he slid back the eyelids and spoke.

'Lie down no longer, corpse, for Jesus orders you to rise. Tell us who you are, when you lived and which world your soul inhabits now. Are you damned or saved?'

At first, nothing happened. Then a breeze seemed to stir the corpse and the mouth made a sound.

It was not quite a human sound. It was a ghost sound, mournful as wind in sails. Everybody there shivered and the spring sunlight lost its warmth.

'I cannot disobey,' said the body, 'even if obeying robs me of my eyes. Your authority comes from one to whom Heaven and Earth submit and I am much less than these.'

To the onlookers, all London was still. Nothing moved from the bed of the river to the highest pinnacle of the church. And the people themselves were like statues. To them, only the lips of that long-buried corpse were in motion.

'I lived here in the New Troy, four hundred and eighty-two years after Brutus and one thousand and fifty-four years before the birth of Christ. I lived in the days of King Belinus and his brother Brennius, and I was a judge.'

'Then why do you wear a crown?' asked Erkenwald, who now knelt beside the tomb.

'For over forty years, my jurisdiction covered the whole of the New Troy. In that time I suffered much at the hands of the wicked citizenry, but never once did I bend from justice. My judgements were never made for love of money or fear of punishment. This was a precious thing to the better people of the city and when I died, they mourned. To honour me, they dressed me in a long gown. It symbolised my virtue. My belt symbolised skilled governance and my ermine collar stood for loyalty. The crown, to them, symbolised my kingship over the highest judges of the New Troy; those who had been before and all those that would ever be. And the sceptre marked my devotion to rewarding the righteous.'

To this Erkenwald replied, 'How is it, then, that all your garments are intact?'

'It must be God's doing, for He loves Justice above all virtues.'

'Then, tell us, is your soul with God?'

And now the man's mouth stretched wide and, whereas his voice had been soft and ghostly before, now it wailed.

'When he descended in light and broke down the doors of Hell, I watched my loved ones flee. I watched them flee to a place of feasting, kindness, sunlight and soft shadows. But I could not follow. My chains held firm. He left me there. *He left me.* And what, after all, was my goodness worth when, even now, I speak to you from dark, cold captivity? Even now, among the dead and damned, I starve, I thirst and I pine for friends I hardly remember.'

And now there was movement in the watching crowd,

for tears were running down the people's cheeks. Erkenwald was no less moved. He bowed his head and wept.

'Don't go,' he said to the corpse. 'Stay just long enough for me to get holy water and baptise you in the name of the Father, Son and Holy Spirit.'

And as he said the holy words, one of his tears fell onto the full, flushed face of the judge.

'I will not stay,' he said.

Erkenwald looked back and the judge spoke again. His voice was brighter than before:

'I will not stay, because that tear will do. With the holy water of your eyes, dear Bishop, you have baptised me. And even now a shaft of light falls from Heaven to where I lie. And even now I am flying upwards. Even now, I am walking to the table. And even now I see them all. My friends. My place has been made ready.'

Erkenwald made to take the judge's hands in his, but no sooner had he reached forward than the eyes and skin turned grey, and all the flesh fell away. And the whole body and all its ancient finery disintegrated, till all that remained was dust.

❖

This story comes from a late fourteenth-century Middle English poem called *St Erkenwald*, inspired, it is thought, by an earlier legend about Pope Gregory the Great saving the soul of the dead Roman Emperor Trajan. *St Erkenwald* is set just under a hundred years after the conversion of the English. The dead judge, however, lived centuries before the birth of Christ. He lived, he himself explains, during the reign of the legendary British King Belinus. Many of its first readers would have recognised the name: he appears in Geoffrey of Monmouth's *History of the Kings of Britain* (c. 1136) which inspired numerous adaptations in vernacular languages, known collectively as the *Brut* chronicles. The story of Belinus features his troublesome younger brother Brennius and their mother, Conwenna. But Geoffrey also emphasises Belinus' strength as King of the Britons. He builds the Roman roads and promulgates good laws. *St Erkenwald* shows the imaginative pervasiveness of Britain's deep myths. And it is no coincidence, as others have noted, that the ghost is a judge; the poem is all about what is 'right'.

Back in March, on the southernmost tip of South Wales, we heard St David speaking out against the Pelagian heresy. This belief-system, which flourished in Britain in the fifth and sixth centuries, challenged the orthodox idea that humans were born stained by Adam's sin and required baptism to be set free. And while Pelagius was no longer a threat to mainstream Christianity in the late fourteenth century, when *St Erkenwald* was written, there were new heresies gaining ground. Lollardy, for instance, had been flourishing for some decades in England. It challenged the veneration of saints and their images. It also, like the

Pelagian heresy, denied the necessity of baptism for salvation. With the Bishop's weeping and speaking of the names of the Trinity, *St Erkenwald* boldly presents ritual words and holy water as how the judge's deserving soul at last finds Paradise. It endorses the sacraments as the means to salvation.

According to Bede, the real Erkenwald became Bishop of London in 675. By 1245, Erkenwald and Mellitus' shrines stood side by side next to the high altar of St Paul's Cathedral. The shrine of the former was, according to a medieval inventory, 'wood inside and covered with silver plates with images and stones'. And, together, these magnificently entombed characters were an important part of London's spiritual mythology.

I have already talked about the medieval Christian idea of history as a narrative focused not on how events from the past led to the present, but how events from the past relate to Judgement Day, the future event which will see the culmination of the war between Heaven and Hell and the division of all human souls into the blessed and the damned. Seen in this light, the story of the judge in *St Erkenwald* does not concern the judge alone, but the instrumentality of sacraments like baptism in freeing souls from the clutches of the Devil and delivering them to Christ.

May

May is a season for carousing, for loving the new sun and calling in the summer. Now the moon is governed by Gemini, implicating the arms and shoulder blades.

Turn to May in a medieval calendar and you find its illustrated population courting, hawking and enjoying leisurely pursuits. Gemini looks down on the scene, its twin siblings perhaps too old to be in such a close, naked embrace. May is a profligate month that verges on indecency, casting off winter cloaks with reckless abandon.

With Brendan and Mary, we will encounter a talking skull with dark ideas and a miraculous cherry harvest that bids us to seize the day. The question of where true riches lie comes to the fore in May; when there is such abundance outside and so many pleasures to be plucked and savoured, how do you know if fleshly delight has strayed into sin? And, if it has, might you just choose to stay there?

Brendan: The Skull

Died 575
Feast Day: 16 May

The monks left the boat and scuttled in a pod across the beach. They were making for the curiously shaped white boulder that had washed up on the beach during the previous night's storm. While the shipwrights made their finishing touches, Brendan followed them, his feet pressing into the wet sand. When he rounded the side of the boulder, he stood still in amazement. The brothers fell back in terror.

Anemones plugged what appeared to be nostrils. Seaweed lashed the hollows of empty eye sockets. Great teeth, what was left of them, leaned this way and that, with colonies of mussels in between like heaps of prayer books bound in purple leather.

Brendan had read about giants and now he was staring into the skeleton eyes of just such a being.

'What were you like in life?' he thought aloud, not imagining the skull would answer.

Wind off the sea, cries of gannets, the whimpering of

Brendan: The Skull

his companions; then a creak from the jaw hinge and the great bone mouth began to speak.

'A rogue,' it said in a voice of breakers on shingle.

The brothers scattered, but Brendan would not be moved.

'Where are you now?'

'The Pit.'

'Hell?'

'Hell.'

'And what sent you there?'

Now the shadows in the eye sockets rolled.

'I was a hundred feet tall. I used to wade into the sea and wait for ships, then I would plunder them. I sent many souls into the depths for the sake of treasure. I had a good and safe living. Even during storms the sea never rose higher than my chest. But then one storm came that was worse than any before. It took the waters over my head and my feet slid from under me. I tumbled in the black water till I drowned. Then my real suffering began.'

Brendan held out his hands.

'If I prayed for you to come back from the dead, would you accept baptism and live a Christian life?'

A grinding, churning laugh.

'Well, what if I said yes? And what if I fell once again into sin? And, having sinned again, die again, feel my body break, my memory fade and my blood vessels burst again. And, after that, don't you think I'd be damned worse for being damned twice?'

'Perhaps.'

'Then, no. I would not live again if you owned the world and if it were solid gold and if you gave it to me with two thousand years to delight in it. I fear death too much for that.'

Brendan's hands dropped. It was no good. Behind him, he could hear the cases and coffers being loaded onto the ship. He turned and gestured to the trembling men who would be accompanying him on a quest for Paradise.

As they pushed off into the water, leaving navigation to God, Brendan gazed back at the skull. He had hoped to save the soul that had once lived within it, but it had gone back to a place to which he could not – and hoped he would never – travel for himself.

❖

The tales of Brendan's voyaging are full of hope and a sense of adventure. According to one Irish annal, he was born in 486. Various others date his death to 575. In his early medieval *Life*, his mother's name is given as Broinngheal, or 'bright breast', which refers to a vision she receives before his birth of gold filling up her bosom and making it shine like snow. Brendan undertakes a long and itinerant religious education within Ireland and then embarks on an even more wandering mission over the sea to find an earthly paradise.

In *The Voyage of St Brendan*, an Irish Latin text dated to the ninth century, Brendan's quest takes seven years. He and a group of monks visit many strange islands, some of them annually. Finally, the company passes through a dark mist and discovers the longed-for paradise. It is not exactly Heaven, but it has heavenly qualities, including perpetual fruitfulness. With each retelling of his voyage legend in Catalan, Occitan, Anglo-Norman, Middle English and more, the islands visited by Brendan and the brothers transform. Of the earthly paradise, the Middle English *South English Legendary* tells us, 'It was thickly planted with trees, and the trees bore heavily, the apples were all fully ripe, just as if it were autumn.'

The abundance of Brendan's earthly paradise is just one of many marvels in the many versions of Brendan's voyage. Of Brendan's discoveries, we have already met the whale posing as an island, as well as Paul the Hermit with his attendant otter and its pouch of inflammable seaweed. But there are many we haven't met. Take the island on which, every Easter, fallen angels take the shape of white birds and sing the Psalms. Other wonders include the story of the monks travelling for days encircled by a great sea-monster with its mouth clamped on its own tail, like the Midgard Serpent of Norse myth. Then there's the island of black cliffs to which one of the brothers is irresistibly drawn, jumping from the boat into the clutches of a multitude of demons, never to be seen again. Another is an island with a church full of crystal altars, the candles of which are lit every day by a burning arrow that comes in through one window, flies around the church, and disappears out of another. Just as the dwarf on the leaf told us back in February, there's no limit to the world's wonders; the story could always be retold.

Such was the reach of the Brendan legend that his paradise was judged to be real. On the *c.* 1300 Hereford Mappa Mundi (or World Map), 'St Brendan's Isle' lies south of the Pillars of Hercules, off the coast of Africa in the Great Ocean, somewhere in the region of the Canary Islands. It also appears on the earliest surviving globe, the so-called *Erdapfel* globe finished in 1492, which literally means

Brendan: The Skull

'earth apple' (not, as in modern German, 'potato'; potatoes had not yet come to Europe).

Medievalist Glyn Burgess likens St Brendan to Ulysses or Sinbad, seeing in the saint's legend, and its many translated forms, 'fragments of Indo-European folklore, echoes of Sumerian epics'. The story of the giant skull on the beach comes from a Dutch iteration of the *Voyage* preserved in two manuscripts from *c.* 1400. It is an exploration of who and what can be saved. Is the giant's choice to remain damned an inevitable consequence of his gigantic nature? Or do some of his kind roam Paradise? We shall have to wait and see.

Mary: Cherry Time

DIED 48
FEAST OF THE VISITATION: 31 MAY

The thatchers staged their play on a wagon they had roofed themselves. They had also, less expertly, painted the backdrop to look like a road through a dark and snowy landscape to a city lit by one large star. On the floor of the wagon stood a manger and cast of animals all made from straw. The pageant wagon and its props were at least as intricate as the ones built by the shipwrights further down the street, showing Noah's ark and all kinds of strange creatures walking two by two. And every wagon in the town that day displayed to technical perfection the skills of whichever trade had decorated it, for today was the feast of Corpus Christi and, under the hide-and-seek sun of early summer, it was the guilds' annual opportunity to show off their craft to the townsfolk, as well as to each other.

One of the apprentice thatchers, with hairy forearms and a sunburned nose, had borrowed a blue dress and stuffed a small bale under his costume to make himself look

Mary: Cherry Time

pregnant. Mary, for that was whom the apprentice played, sat on a straw donkey with seed heads for its mane and tail. Behind him, a burly, sweaty Joseph scratched his chest, bundled up against imagined cold with woollen socks, mittens and a thick hood and collar.

Now Mary raised a hairy hand to above the snowy backdrop, where a tree towered over the scene. Its trunk was artificial, made of painted timber, but its long branches had been cut that morning from the real cherry tree that grew in the master thatcher's garden. Leaves and ripening cherries, damp and glistening from an earlier shower of rain, clustered on the boughs. Standing in the street below, the wives, mothers, daughters and young sons of the thatchers clapped their hands as more townspeople congregated around them.

'Look at this tree, husband mine,' the apprentice Mary piped. 'It is bearing fruit despite the winter season. If you could climb it and gather our fill, we'd have a feast of cherries!'

But Joseph spoke in disgruntled tones that may or may not have been affected.

'To harvest these would be wild work. The tree is too tall! Why doesn't the one who got you pregnant in the first place pick the cherries for you?'

The watchers laughed. Above everyone's heads, the tree began to shake, shedding water droplets on Mary and Joseph's heads. Then, with a creak, one of the longer cherry boughs began descending over the canopy. When it dangled within reach of the couple, Mary squealed with delight, and the cherries trembled as her impersonator said:

'See how it bows down to us! God be praised! Now we may pick our fill!'

'I spoke unkindly,' Joseph said. 'I see from this miracle that she is favoured by God and so is the child inside her.'

Then, sliding his collar round so that his hood hung down his chest, he started picking the cherries with large, calloused hands. And then he stopped picking, turned to face the crowd, dived his hand into the hood and flung the fruits into the crowd. Apprentice Mary laughed as Joseph,

Mary: Cherry Time

grinning now, leaned out of the wagon, and put a cherry into the hand of a child. The boy, whose skin was pitted with scars from the pox, nibbled the flesh from the stone, then pulled a face at its sourness. Still, he held his hands out for more.

When it had all happened for the first time, outside Bethlehem, the tree had borne not cherries but dates, yellow and round as egg yolks. And the weather had not been that of a western island in the Great Ocean, but of a much larger land bordering the eastern edge of the Mediterranean Sea. And the tree had not bowed down for a bundle of straw, stuffed into a dress. It had bowed to a deity, curled up in his mother's womb.

❖

Medieval Christians venerated Mary, the mother of Christ, with a passion. By the later Middle Ages, she had many feast days marking moments from her life as told in gospels both apocryphal and Scriptural. One of her feasts fell on 31 May and celebrated the biblical story of the Visitation, when the pregnant Mary meets her cousin Elizabeth, who herself is carrying John the Baptist. The child leaps in Elizabeth's womb, acknowledging the Messiah. I have not told that story here, but instead I have told the story of the miraculous fruiting cherry tree said to have bowed down to Mary on the wintry road to Bethlehem. Perhaps you'd think I should have put this chapter in December, around Christmas. I haven't, for reasons that I hope will become clear.

In the British Museum's department of Britain, Europe and Prehistory, a storage chest of drawers holds over seven hundred medieval pilgrim souvenirs and secular badges. Many of these invoke Mary, some in the shape of a crowned capital M, others as she is often depicted in medieval paintings, seated and holding the Christ Child, and some as the Virgin of the Apocalypse, with a starburst behind her as if she is lying on a sea cucumber.

There were so many shrines to Mary in medieval Britain, Ireland and beyond, that it's often hard to know where the badges come from or what exactly they meant to their wearers. And yet, when I was working at the Museum, digitising the badge collection and redrafting the catalogue entries, I found a couple of shrine-less Marian badges that piqued my curiosity. One was in the Museum of London and was the shape of the typical crowned capital M, except the crown was decorated with minuscule acorns. I did some reading and found that Mary had a tendency to appear to people from trees in the Middle Ages and there was probably more than one hollow oak containing a Marian shrine. Perhaps the Marian acorn had been made for one of these.

There is another mystery badge that has intrigued me for years. It's not obviously Marian, though I now believe it had at least a tangential link with her cult. It shows a hood with its face-hole stuffed full of cherries, to judge by their long stems. A ribbon designed to hang from the point of the hood fastens the neck of the collar. If you turn the badge so that the hood is at the bottom and the collar is at the top, it looks like a makeshift sack, an item of clothing roughly converted to hold fruit. From the decorative 'dagging' on the hood's ribbon, it is datable to the later fourteenth or fifteenth centuries.

It is not the only surviving 'hood-of-fruit' image. I came across a similar example in the margins of the Luttrell Psalter (c. 1340). They ramble with bizarre hybrid beasts, episodes from saints' lives, and scenes from agricultural and noble life. Underneath the text of folio 196v, there is a lively illustration of a boy high in the branches of a wild cherry tree. His pointy-toed shoes lie abandoned on the ground. His left hand and red-socked feet rest on woody knots. He wears a collar and hood, which he has yanked round to hang against his chest, so that he can fill the hood with cherries. His right hand reaches to pick more, his cheeks bulge with fruit and his lips touch another cherry dangling near his face. Apparently he has scaled the tree to eat and gather as much of its fruit as he can before the owner, already running along the ground towards him, waving a stick with rage, forces him to flee. In this illustration, the hood enables the boy to take advantage of an unexpected harvest that must be enjoyed immediately or lost forever. Could the hood in the badge have a similar meaning?

There was a legend about a cherry tree that had a brief season of popularity in fifteenth-century England. One of its sources is the late medieval N-Town Plays (the 'N' being an 'insert-name-here' instruction in the manuscript). In the scene for the Nativity, Mary and Joseph encounter a tall cherry tree while on their way to Bethlehem. It bursts into fruit, despite the wintry season. Joseph refuses to pick the cherries on account of the height of the tree and the difficulty of the task, so one of its boughs descends, and Mary and a sheepish Joseph gather their fill.

The story derives from the apocryphal gospel of Pseudo-Matthew, in which the tree is not a cherry tree, but a date palm. However, in an English context the cherries would have made better sense, drawing on existing associations and even allowing actors to use the branches of real cherry trees, if the performance coincided with the cherry season.

The cherry, as we presumably all know, is small and scrumptious. It grows wild in north-western Europe, littering woodland floors with red, orange and yellow fruits during early summer. The fruiting season is brief but abundant and medieval cherry fairs took advantage of it. This led to the cherry season and the fairs as metaphors for life's fleeting pleasures. In the 1470 morality play *Mankind*, the character of Mercy says:

> So help me God, it is but a cherry time!
> Spend it well.

Mary: Cherry Time

And in a fifteenth-century poem, *How the Wise Man Taught His Son*, the narrator warns:

> Therefore beware the world's wealth,
> It passes like a cherry fair.

Perhaps a late medieval badge showing a hood full of cherries reminded wearers to gather their earthly joys, however fleeting. This sentiment is echoed in a line of medieval graffiti in the parish church of Little Dunmow in Essex: *Dum sumus in mundo vivamus corde jocundo*, or 'While we are in this world, we should live with a happy heart'. But the connection to the Virgin nuances the meaning. The cherry-tree story is shown on a late medieval embroidered *Opus Anglicanum* (or 'English-work') panel now in the Victoria and Albert Museum. It also appears in a disguised form in the Middle English romance *Sir Cleges*. Finally, recent conservation work on the Battel Hall Retable, an early fifteenth-century panel painting showing seven saints, has revealed that the figure of Mary was first drawn holding a lily, but then the painter ignored the instruction and gave her a branch of wild cherry. The story of the date palm or cherry tree taught that the child in Mary's virgin womb was like fruit on a tree out of season: that the Christmas cherry was like the embryo of Christ. The red juice, surely, offered the added connotation of the blood shed at his Crucifixion.

Town guilds performed mystery plays during the feast of Corpus Christi ('the Body of Christ'), the date of which was dictated by the movable feast of Easter. It generally landed in late May or sometime in June. The feast derived from the moment in the New Testament when Christ, sitting down to a final dinner with his disciples, breaks bread and drinks wine and shares it with them, saying 'This is my body' and 'This is my blood'. He then asks them to repeat the ritual in his memory. Christians call that repetition 'Communion' and many denominations still re-enact it as part of their formal worship. However, medieval Catholicism, like Catholicism today, also taught that, when the priest blessed the bread and wine on the altar in imitation of Christ at the Last Supper, a miracle called 'transubstantiation' occurred. Mainstream medieval Christians believed they witnessed the bread and wine transform into the true Body and Blood of Christ, the *Corpus Christi*, every time they went to Mass.

Just as what tastes sweet for one person cloys for another, so some detected rot in the merry beliefs of the feast of Corpus Christi. Even before the fifteenth century, reformers had started challenging key tenets of medieval Christianity, like the doctrine of transubstantiation. In 1395, the Lollards (adherents to the views of the English theologian John Wycliffe) produced its Twelve Conclusions. The fourth concerned 'the sacrament of bread' and declared, 'The service of Corpus Christi . . . is untrue and painted full of false miracles'. As for the veneration of saints and their images, that is treated in the eighth: 'Prayers, and offerings made

Mary: Cherry Time

to blind roods and deaf images of tree and stone be near kin to idolatry.' And so, with the fifteenth-century story of Mary's miraculous cherry harvest, we see how populations far from the biblical heartlands made its legends their own, adapting them to their own natural landscape and shaping them according to their own idioms and customs. For many of the faithful, it must have felt as though even saints with the most distant origins were no more than a village away, if not standing in their very churches.

June

Presided over by a moon in Cancer, June is the month of the chest and oesophagus. And it is the month for reaping hay, for holding the long handle of the scythe with both hands and sweeping its curved blade in front with measured precision. If the blade is sharp, the grass falls in clipped, sweet-smelling heaps. If the blade dulls, the reaper must stop, bring out a whetstone and slide it down the length of the metal. 'Making hay' remains synonymous with the sunny summer days necessary for a successful hay harvest. But the sharp, undiscerning blade gave reaping its darker side too.

In the fourteenth-century Middle English poem *Gawain and the Green Knight*, we sense the threatening connotations of the great scythe blade – long as the reaper's own arm – when the hero hears the Green Knight sharpening his axe in the cavern of the green chapel, 'as one upon a gryndelston hade grounden a sythe'. And, of course, in Western European art since at least the late Middle Ages, personifications of Death have held a scythe. Death works steadily, felling souls like blades of grass, the antitype of the glad haymaker.

Outsending

Still, there was one place in medieval Europe where June's scythe blades were harmless to all but vegetation. In his early medieval *Life* by Adomnán, Columba agrees to bless a slaughter-knife for one of his brethren while preoccupied with copying out a text. Without looking up from his parchment, Columba points his quill at the knife and makes the sign of the cross. The brother goes out and tries to use the knife to kill a bullock, but it will not pierce its skin. Upon discovering that the knife will not now cut any flesh at all, the monks melt it down and coat the monastery's sharp tools in the sacred metal, rendering them harmless to all living things.

In June we meet Boniface, missionary to the Frisians and destroyer of sacred oaks, while Columba transforms metal and directs the wind and Alban gives up his life to save his friend. As the medieval legends ring with optimism, the faithful line up to receive the sacraments and the churches are being filled to the very rafters with art.

Boniface: The Fallen Oak

DIED 754
FEAST DAY: 5 JUNE

At the great age of seventy-nine years, it seemed that Boniface, the tireless evangelist, would never die. Exposure had fissured and gnarled his skin. His hands were knotted, the hem of his black Benedictine habit so stained with travel that, when he stood to preach, he seemed to be growing out of the peaty soil.

When his killer's axe fell, Boniface held up a heavy book to defend himself. A dry, bloodless cut split its pages. When the axe fell again, it found its mark. Boniface toppled at once, his forehead gushing blood, and thudded on the ground like a fallen bough.

As the moon rose, Boniface's killer left him amid the bodies of his companions and helped push the dead missionaries' travel chests through the marsh and onto waiting boats. Then he in turn waited with the chests as his own gang went back for baskets of food and wine. When the camp was empty of valuables and the boats were low in the water, they picked up their oars and rowed away.

Outsending

When Boniface's killer had been a boy, he had watched the black-clad priest chop down Thor's Oak. There had been fury from the villagers at first. But then there had been wonder. Many people had said it was a miracle how, struck only once with the axe, the ridged bark barely dented, the great tree had split into four as it fell. The boy's neighbours had stopped shouting and sunk to their knees, shuffling on all fours to the priest, begging forgiveness, swearing that they would never again betray the true faith. But his mother and father had not been among them. They had taken their son's hand and led him home. That night, when they thought he was asleep, he had heard his mother crying and his father speaking over her tears.

'It was just a tree.'

'It was not and you know it to be true. We made offerings there when our babies died.'

'And our living son is strong as Thor himself.'

'And what will Thor do, now our village has betrayed him? He will have his sacrifices one way or another. What if he chooses me?'

The boy's mother had been ill since his birth. But she had made sacrifices at Thor's Oak every week, stealing to the place in secret, with doves and dormice hidden under her cloak. Still, he did not take his mother's worries seriously. He was interested to see what the missionaries were doing and went to the place of the felling to watch them trimming away the smaller, leafy branches, then setting aside larger limbs. He saw the men making beams, cutting away the bark and flattening the sides of each section by standing astride the timber and bringing arched blades swinging between their legs so that the chips of green wood flew up like sparks from a fire. The boy hung around, helping carry away the fragrant waste to the tannery or bringing food and drink to the workers. Then he watched them shape joints and lay out the parts of a building.

He didn't mourn the tree as his parents did. Change brought intrigue and action. The stump was sawn down to the roots, and a structure, which the priests called an oratory and used for their rituals, was constructed over it. Hazel from the nearby coppices filled the empty spaces between the timbers and supported a wet mixture of dung, mud and straw that dried to make walls. When the workers had thatched the roof all the way up to the ridge, they fitted a small fixture for a bell that rang many times a day.

After finishing the oratory, priests arrived with great wooden chests. These contained a gold cup, called a chalice, and a small plate and a box of fragile bones, but mostly the chests were filled with unfamiliar objects that resembled leather-covered blocks of wood. These strange artefacts opened to reveal hundreds of leaves of thinly stretched animal hide, covered in markings in gold and black and sewn together along one edge. The objects were the first books the boy had seen, and they fascinated him.

'Most belong to Boniface,' a missionary had told him as

the boy gazed at the golden words, 'but he'll leave one or two with whoever remains here as your priest. Books are very powerful.'

Later that month, his mother grew weaker and the boy urged his father to pray for her in the new oratory. He refused.

'She would never go into that place. To go there for her would be wrong.'

'Maybe, then, we could just pray over her with this?'

The boy put his hand into his coat and brought out a small book bound in red leather and decorated with a raised pattern of vines. He had taken it from the oratory secretly that day.

'Don't show this to your mother,' was all his father said, casting a look at where she lay in the corner of the room.

But that night, when his father was sleeping too, the boy took the book from his pocket and laid it in her hand. Then he prayed as he had seen the priests praying. He tried to stay awake, to witness the effect of the book's power, but after a while he too fell asleep.

In the morning, the boy had woken up to find his mother's hand stiff, cold and grey, her nails digging into the red leather binding. He took it back to the priests, crying and telling them that their books were not powerful at all, because they had not saved his mother. The towering, black-clad Boniface had leaned down towards the boy, laughing.

'Of course it didn't work, child. Your mother was a godless heathen.'

Then Boniface had pulled the red book from the boy's hand and returned it to the chest.

Once Boniface and the missionaries were dead, the thieves didn't hurry their boat downstream. No one was coming to stop them. They drank the wine stolen from the camp and discussed how to divide up the riches in the fastened chests. As the drink dulled their vision, other images sharpened; garnet-inlaid crosses, reliquaries, and the goblets used by Christians in their ceremonies – all gold, all waiting for them – and they were stirred to jealous violence. They moored the boats, stumbled onto the bank and brought out their axes and swords for the second time that night.

There was no loyalty among these thieves. They were mercenaries. Only one of them suspected that the chests' contents were not as rich as the others believed, but he still wanted to get at them. Boniface's killer fought as hard as any of the other men.

Soon, half the thieves were injured or dying, and those sobered by the violence agreed to share the booty equally. Each share would be bigger now that the others were dead. They went over to the boats, found the keys they had torn from the missionaries' belts and unlocked the first chest. Then they opened the chest beside it and then the one beside that. Seeing by the moonlight that only books lay

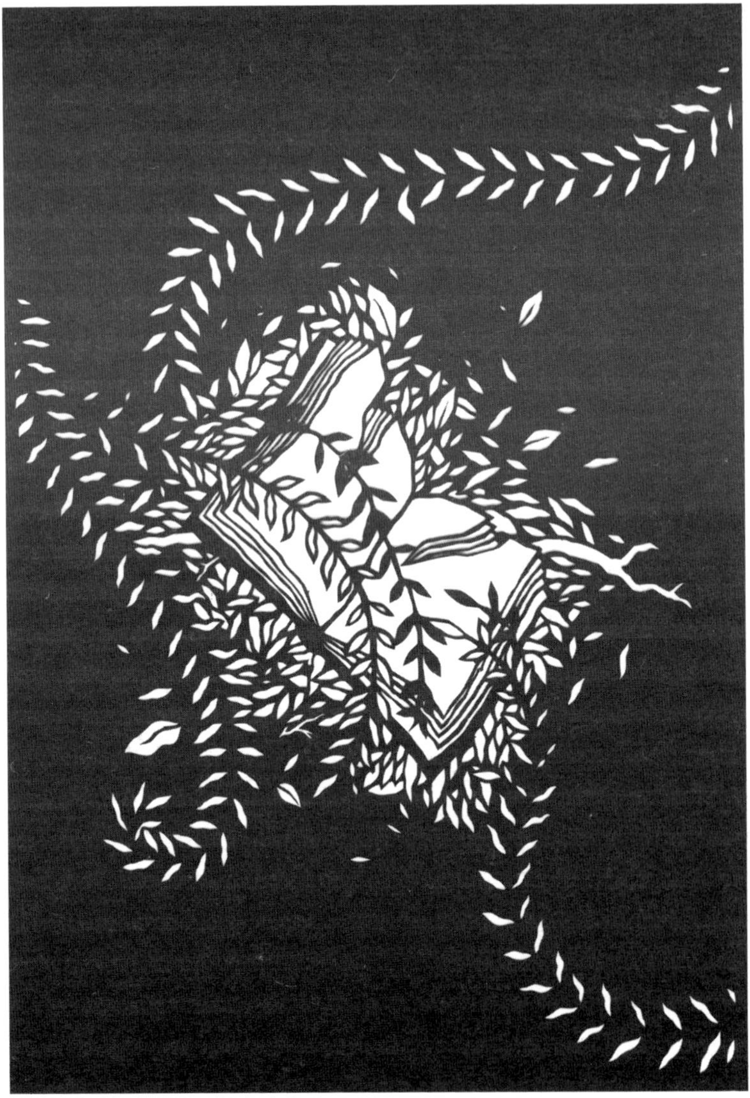

inside, they began to throw the chests' contents into the waters of the marsh, Boniface's killer working hardest of all.

There were some, in that land, who rejoiced at the old missionary's death. His killer was among them. But then Christian warriors, assembled in vengeance for the murder of Boniface and his priests, gathered and stormed the households that still worshipped the old gods. They put men to death and seized their wives and children. And faithful and fearful alike hailed Boniface as a miracle-worker, the saint who had saved the barbarians from darkness, whose manuscripts were found wondrously undamaged in the marsh. Only one of the books bore signs of the violence, and that was the one lying on the old man's corpse. And no one ever missed the red-bound volume buried in the Frisian bog, its white pages coppering in the peat.

❖

The English priest Boniface, christened Wynfrith, received his new name from the Pope in 718 to prepare him for his mission into the territories of modern-day Germany and the Low Countries. There, most of the population still worshipped the Norse and Germanic gods, though Irish missionaries had made some headway in converting the people to Christianity. Once Boniface arrived, he worked with the relentless tread of the reaper, weeding out Irish clerics who, by his own estimation, fell short of the standards set by Rome. He also cut down the sacred trees of the old religion and, so the story goes, used their timber in the construction of churches.

The tale of the loss of Thor's Oak survives in an eighth-century *Life of Saint Boniface* by one Willibald, who served beside Boniface as a missionary. He had been born in England into an almost completely alliterative family, with his brother Winibald, his sister Walburga, his mother Wuna of Wessex and his father, Richard. Both Willibald's siblings also became important religious figures on the Continent, helping Boniface to found and run a monastery in the territories marked for conversion. The tract concerning the felling of the oak by Boniface tells us how the 'pagans' of Hessian, while having nominally accepted Christianity, continued, 'some . . . secretly, some openly, to sacrifice to trees and springs'. Boniface chose sacred trees for destruction, including an oak 'of extraordinary size' called *robor Iobis*: 'Jove's Oak' or, interpreting the romanisation, 'Thor's Oak'. It must have been a magnificent thing, like the ancient and precious Capon Tree outside Jedburgh in Northumbria.

Willibald tells us of the miraculous demise of Thor's Oak. Boniface struck but one blow with the axe, but then a force from heaven compounded his effort and caused the tree to fall and divide into four parts. The text then goes on to tell us that the missionaries used the timber to build an oratory. I have it on good authority that there is unlikely to have been much wood in an ancient oak suitable for structural use, but perhaps that is the least of the reasons for scepticism.

Boniface: The Fallen Oak

There is a certain poetic justice to Boniface's death: felled in turn by one of those he had set out to convert. According to later traditions, his only defence was one of his trusty manuscripts. And while this detail is not historical, it is true that Boniface had a particular fondness for books. In one of his surviving letters, he asks an English nun, Eadburg, to make and send him a copy of the Epistles of St Paul written in letters of gold. This request by Boniface, along with Bede's descriptions of St Augustine arriving in Kent with silver crosses and other costly paraphernalia, suggests how the display of wealth by Christian missionaries aided the conversion of non-Christian populations. That being said, Boniface's books were not equated with treasure by his killers, who threw them into a bog. Though they are said to have been rescued unharmed, other early medieval books have been known to turn up in bogs. The Faddan More Psalter dates from c. 800 and was found in a peat bog in County Tipperary in 2006.

I have invented the character behind Boniface's killer and the story of the mother's death, but it is intended to acknowledge those nameless historical figures who, according to Willibald, continued to make sacrifices at the sacred trees and springs despite the Christian mission. What must the loss of those rituals have meant? And how did the oratories built around them relate to the transformation of shrines to the Germanic gods into Christian churches that we met in England with Mellitus? Little survives in north-western Europe of the pre-Christian monumental landscape, but, perhaps, traces of colossal oak roots tan the soil under more than one Frisian church.

Once Boniface was long dead and the conversion period a thing of the past, legends strengthened the links between the saint's remains and the contact relics associated with them. Tradition has it that the book Boniface used to defend himself from his killer is none other than an eighth-century volume known as the Ragyndrudis Codex, now in Fulda, Germany. This is also the location of Boniface's remains and shrine. The manuscript, which contains religious texts written by British and Continental scribes, bears deep incisions from sharp metal blades.

I cannot comment on the authenticity or otherwise of the Ragyndrudis Codex, but it does show the way in which cult objects shaped legend, as well as the other way around. Items associated with the saint might allow the custodians of their remains to give pilgrims more than just a shrine to visit at their destination. In Canterbury Cathedral, for instance, as we will see in December, there were several different stations, including the place where Thomas Becket had been killed by King Henry II's knights (marked by the sword-point which had broken on the stone floor) and the reliquary bust in the chapel, at the easternmost end of the church, which housed the severed disc of his skull. And so history shaped legend and legend gave meaning to material things, and all were sustained by the crowds of eager pilgrims.

Columba: The Wind Whisperer

Died 597
Feast Day: 9 June

Cormac and his brothers in Christ were sailing away from Ireland for the third time, off to find a desert in the sea. As evening fell after two weeks travelling north, they crossed an invisible threshold in the Great Ocean. They did not know it, but they had now gone further than anyone had ever sailed before. A pale night arrived and brought with it a wind from the south that lifted the brothers' tonsured hair and pushed them further north.

The midnight sun was low over the sea and dark creatures began to show themselves as shadows in the water. The men were frightened. Then a spiny tail arced over the boat and scared them so much that they tried to turn back, but the wind from the south only strengthened, forcing them on. More apparitions followed, more sea-monsters and more terror, then a threat more awful than any before appeared on the horizon and came rushing towards the boat.

At the very same time in Britain, an Irish holy man named Columba hurried into a church, beckoning to his monks to follow. He closed the new-hewn doors, gathered the men close and said:

'Our brother Cormac has travelled into a cursed region of the sea and a great multitude of monsters is about to attack his ship. He and his brothers will die if we do not help. We must pray for the wind to blow them south.'

Columba's monks bowed their heads and obeyed their leader's command, wondering how he could see what was happening so far away and in a place of which none of them had heard.

Far off, Cormac and his desperate brethren, though they were fighting for their lives, felt the air change about them. Their sail fell slack and their boat stopped speeding north. They rowed to turn their vessel around and as they did so, the sail filled with a new wind. Now their hair, habits and sail billowed towards Ireland and their boat sped away from the peril that had been encircling them. The men praised God as they left the monsters behind and entered homely seas.

When they at last arrived home, Columba and Cormac met on Hinba Isle, to the west of Britain. Cormac had travelled there with three others, including Brendan the Voyager. Speaking of the miracle of the shifting winds, Brendan and the others asked Cormac, 'What was there that made Columba help you? What peril attacked your boat?'

Cormac shuddered, then replied. 'We saw a swarm of monsters coming over the sea like a black mist. They hit

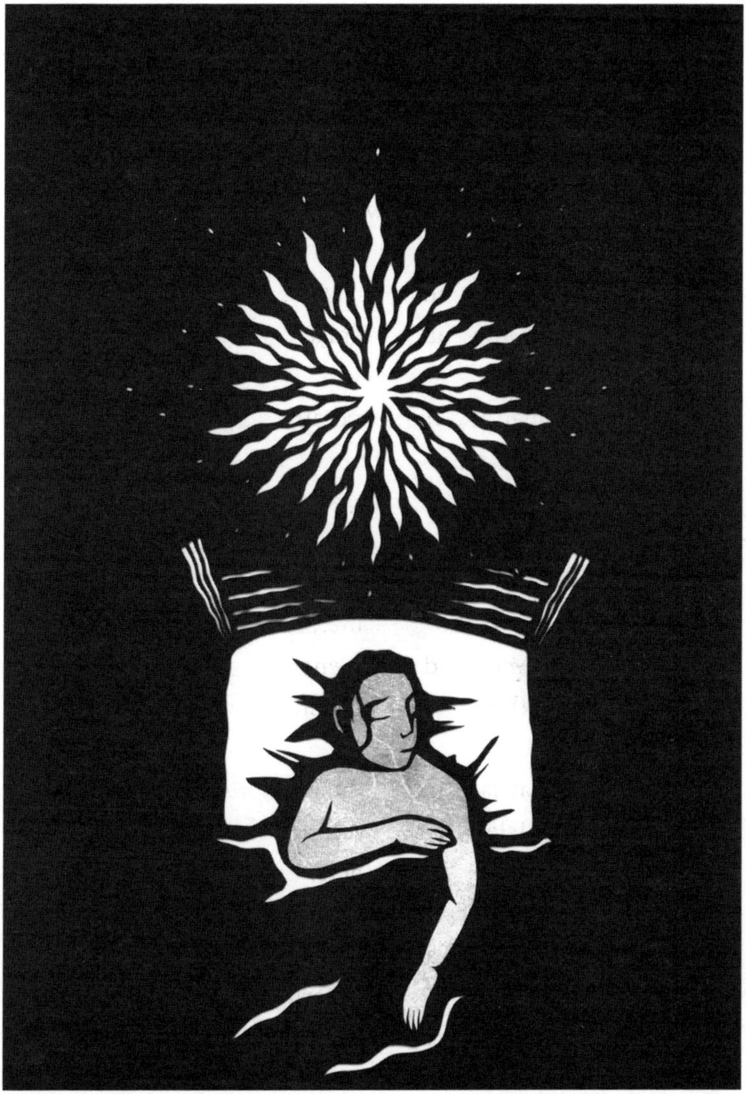

our boat on every side, the creatures climbing the oar handles, stinging everything they could reach. We thought they would pierce the leather hull and sink our boat.'

'How big were the creatures?'

'Small, like frogs,' Cormac said, 'But so numerous and so full of malice.'

Later that day, Columba celebrated the Mass. It had been rumoured that, when he was a boy, a ball of light had hovered over him while he slept, illuminating the whole monastery. Now, as he blessed the bread and wine, a sphere of flame burned again over his head, rising and rising until he stood under a column of light. Then they knew for certain the source of Columba's power and why his prayers were heard by the mighty, world-encompassing winds.

❖

It is said that the Irish missionary St Columba died on the western British island of Iona, in the church he had founded there. The date was 9 June 597, just over a century after St Patrick's death and some hundred and fifty years before that of St Boniface. And like Patrick and Boniface, Columba was a missionary, though his territory centred on what is now Scotland and its islands.

What we know of Columba is largely preserved in the *Life of Saint Columba* by Adomnán (died 704), the ninth Bishop of Iona. As with many of the official Lives covered by the preceding chapters, the tale combines what we

Columba: The Wind Whisperer

would think of as both history and legend. Columba is the saint's Latin name; in Irish he is called Colum Cille. Both mean 'Dove'. And he is not pure legend. Columba did live and work to spread Christianity among the Pictish tribes, as well as the early communities of Scots belonging to the Irish kingdom of the Dal Riáta, but among these historical details are numerous miracles that served to prove his special sanctity.

The story of the malicious swarm is one of many of Columba's monster-blasting marvels. Others include a sea-monster in the River Ness (flowing out of Loch Ness), which is pulled back as if by invisible ropes when it attempts to seize Columba's follower, Lugne; and the wild boar that charges Columba in the forests of Skye, but stops in its tracks and dies at a word from the saint. Monsters, in these contexts, are manifestations of chaos and the forces of the Devil. They are symbols of evil that the saint's *virtus* is able to defeat.

Columba's power imbued his relics. They include his *Cathach*, or 'Battler', a sixth-century manuscript of Psalms written in black ink and decorated with enlarged, ornamental initials. Tradition has it that the book was penned by Columba himself, though now its letters are more widely hailed as early examples of the style of script and decoration found in famous 'Insular'-style manuscripts like the Book of Kells and the Book of Durrow. The 'Battler' is so called because it would have been worn round the neck in a book-shrine called a *cumdach* and borne to the battlefield as a protective talisman. However, unlike the Ragyndrudis Codex used in defence by Boniface, the *Cathach* bears no scars from weapons of war, only from many centuries of neglect.

The *Cathach*'s eleventh-century *cumdach* survives as well. Set with great rock crystals, its embossed and gilded metal frontispiece shows Christ enthroned, flanked by an image of the Crucifixion on one side and, on the other, Columba in bishop's garb and holding the bishop's staff known as a crozier. In keeping with convention, the seated Christ carries a book, representative of the New Testament, and raises His right hand in blessing. Both Columba and Christ's books and benedictions express protection. What was holy power if not a precious resource for keeping humans safe from danger in life and damnation in death? The catalogues of miracles of which many saints' legends comprise testify to that power. Here, they profess, is a saint who will fight forcefully beside you.

Alban: The Unfortunate Executioner

Died 304
Feast Day: 22 June

The days of Agnes, George and Margaret made many martyrs. And most of them had been raised in the warm lands where the emperors could grow the best vines. But one martyr had grown to manhood on the westernmost edge of the Empire's domains. Now the Briton had angered the General of Verulamium and was about to be handed over to a soldier for execution. And that soldier would never kill again.

His earnings went back to Rome, where his mother, father and younger sisters lived. They were proud of their strong son and brother, having no notion that it was thanks to his strength that he was often given the job of executioner. He was stationed in Verulamium in eastern Britain. He had received orders to report to the town general, fetch a prisoner and put him to death. The prisoner, a young man, wore a blue cloak and a brave smile. He had been charged with sheltering a priest, then disguising himself as the priest by putting on his blue cloak. Thanks to this trick, the young man had been arrested and the priest had escaped the town. The sentence was death.

The soldier and two guards took the prisoner, already bruised and bloody from a beating by the general, and steered him to the bridge over the river, which would take them to the killing fields they used for executions. When they reached the bridge, they found it blocked by an inquisitive crowd. The soldier's hand went to his scabbard, ready to order the people out of the way, but he heard the prisoner praying. To one side of the bridge, the water started to churn, then it rose up in two shimmering waves, exposing a path. The soldier, who would not let witchcraft distract him from his task, gripped the prisoner's arm and pulled him down the riverbank.

Ascending the opposite side, the guards and the prisoner proceeded to the base of a hill. As they climbed, the crowd followed.

'I'm thirsty,' said the young man.

At his words, a gush of water bubbled up in the grass. The soldier, feeling troubled by this second display of sorcery, let the prisoner kneel for a drink. He had been planning to perform the execution once they got to the top of the hill, but here would do, given that the man had willingly dropped to his knees.

Standing behind his prisoner, the soldier slid his sword out of its sheath. He had whetted the blade that morning and knew it would make a clean cut. He raised it and

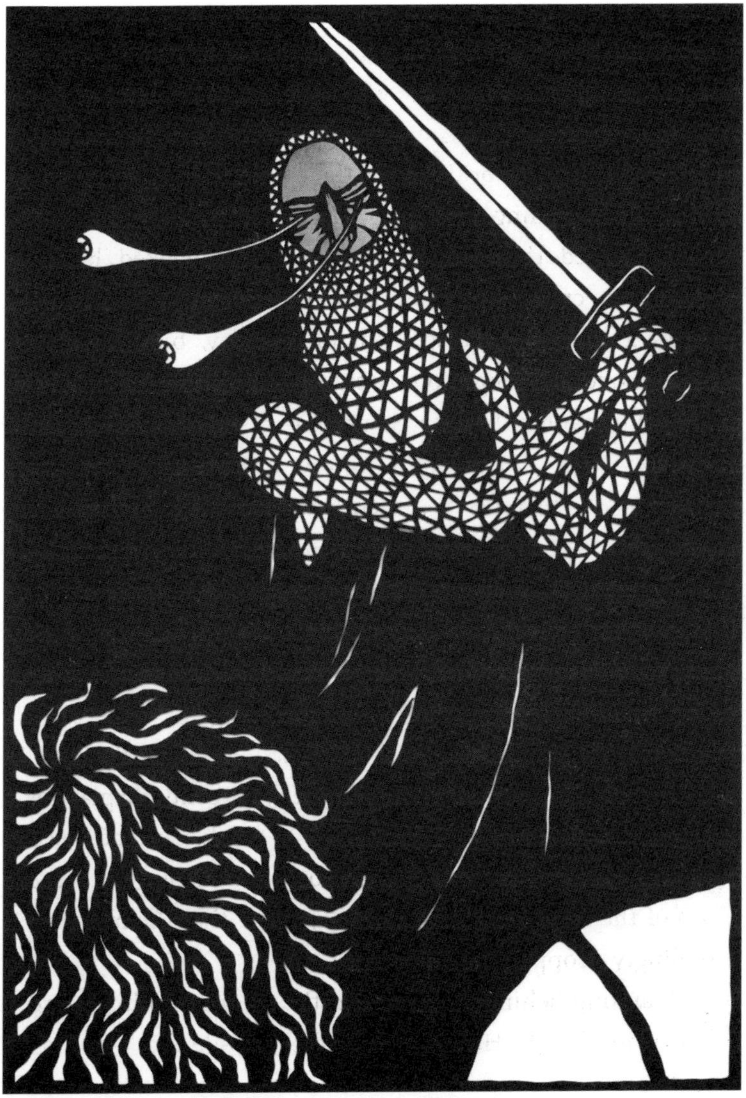

focused on the sliver of skin between the man's thick hair and the blue cloak that had fooled the guards and liberated the priest. Then he began to bring it down. The spring gurgled, jostling speedwells and buttercups, and reminding him of the flowers in the fields behind his childhood home with a pang so strong that he suddenly longed to drop the sword and abandon everything. But already the blade was falling hard and fast and his aim was so good now that there was no going back. And at the same time light bounced from the water in the man's cupped hands and blinded the soldier. Time slowed. Remorse struck like daggers into his eyes. Now, at last, he wished with all his might he could swap places with the man who was giving his life for his friend.

The sword sliced easily through flesh, bone and sinew, causing the head to spin upwards, so that its hair became tangled in a tree beside the new fountain. The blue-cloaked body fell to its knees, blood arcing from the wound, spattering the petals.

But the executioner saw none of it. At the very moment his sword had passed through the young man's neck, a great pressure behind his eyes had caused them to fly out of his head. He dropped the weapon and held up his hands, catching the two wet spheres and feeling them attached to the place where his eyes had been by long, bloody sinews.

A month later, the Roman army sent the soldier back to Italy. His family cared for him. In summer, they would lead

Alban: The Unfortunate Executioner

him out to the fields behind the house and he would sit in the grass, running his hands over the flowers.

He never told them any details of his time in the army, but he talked in his sleep and they learned a little from that. There was just one word they didn't understand. It was a foreign word and their sleeping soldier repeated it like a prayer.

Alban.

Alban.

Alban.

❖

St Alban's death dates to the same wave of Roman persecution that killed Saints Agnes and George, making him Britain's contribution to the early Christian martyrs. The earliest account of his legend is the sixth-century *Ruin of Britain*, by Gildas, in which the author celebrates Alban as a beacon of sanctity in a depraved, dying land. Thanks to the sinfulness of its kings, it is falling to Saxon powers. In Gildas' version of events, Alban parts the waters of the Thames on the way to his execution.

The story is told again, at greater length, in Bede's eighth-century *Ecclesiastical History of the English People*. Here we learn how Alban, still a pagan, shelters a priest and converts to Christianity after watching him practise his faith. He then helps the priest escape persecution by the Roman governor of Verulamium (the future St Albans) by wearing his cloak and assuming his identity. Alban is captured, tortured and executed. While being led to his execution, he parts the waters of the River Ver. When Alban is finally beheaded, Bede emphasises that he then receives 'the crown of life, which God has promised to them that love him'.

Every martyr's story, however marked it may be by feats of supreme endurance, ends in execution. And this, especially according to older ideals of heroism, can look rather a lot like defeat. In his *Crowns of Martyrdom*, Prudentius, a fourth-century poet from northern Spain, tackles just this paradox with reference to the martyrs Emeterius and Chelidonius: 'Written in Heaven are the names of two martyrs; Christ has entered them there in letters of gold, while on earth He has recorded them in characters of blood.' The dual calligraphy, a kind of holograph showing words first red, then gold, sums up the idea of earthly defeat *versus* spiritual victory. Though the martyrs' blood was spilled, though their bodies lie in the earth, their souls are glorified in heaven.

A thirteenth-century 'Book of St Albans', made at St Alban's Abbey by its resident historian Matthew Paris, tells Alban's story and follows it with that of Amphibalus, the name given to the escapee priest and which means 'cloak' in Latin (reflecting a certain amount of confusion, it seems). Alban's execution is depicted with the saint's body kneeling, while his head dangles from a tree and his executioner holds his own eyeballs in his hand. The same moment is shown on the medieval pilgrim souvenir for St Alban's shrine in his eponymous abbey and functions as a kind of holy logo. The manuscript also tells how Amphibalus, thanks to his escape, converts many pagans. Eventually, those converts are put to death, and so is Amphibalus, the massacre of the converts shown in Matthew Paris' dynamic style with Christians' severed hands and feet littering the ground as Roman soldiers charge the survivors, driving spears into their backs and through their foreheads. Matthew has made much of the blood spattering the ground. And yet, in the top right-hand corner of the scene, Christ is already swooping in with crowns in His outstretched hands.

According to Bede, when a bishop called Germanus travelled from the Continent in 429, he found the earth at the place of Alban's martyrdom still red with his blood. Germanus is credited with setting up a shrine to St Alban in what would become St Alban's Abbey. When a grave purported to be that of Amphibalus was discovered in 1170, the bones were brought to the abbey. The friends were reunited and the cult fortified.

Today, St Albans Cathedral is the only one in Britain to house two medieval shrine pedestals. Their great height reflects the perceived importance of the saints whose remains they bore and, like many other such shrine bases, they contain niches into which pilgrims could slide and have healing *virtus* rain down upon them.

But what might the shrines on top of the perforated stone pedestals have looked like? There are plenty of manuscript illustrations, including one of the St Albans shrine in Matthew Paris' illustrated retelling of the saint's life and miracles. Pictures like this suggest that the shrines were not unlike some Continental European survivals. For instance, the relic shrine of St Godehard in Hildesheim, Germany, is one of the oldest complete examples to have reached us from the Middle Ages. It dates to around 1140, is the size of a suitcase and is shaped like a house or hall, its oak substructure covered with gilded silver plate, chased and moulded with roof tiles and arcades of columns. The gold and silver columns shimmer with incised ovals that recall the fossils and veins of polished marble. Relief figures of the Apostles, Mary and John the Baptist, and Godehard, with two other Hildesheim ecclesiastics, populate the niches and bear endearingly alarmed expressions. Ornate openwork panels crown the ends of the gables and run along the ridge, along with a line of odd-sized lollipops of rock crystal, like spoils from Midas' sweet shop. It's a dazzling thing; an insight into the lustrous heart of the medieval cult of saints, the product of donations left by pilgrims, rich and poor. And as the Middle Ages progressed, the strength of that devotion grew, spreading across Christendom. In time,

Alban: The Unfortunate Executioner

the appetite for saintly protection would encompass not only pilgrimage to single cult centres like that of St Alban, but veneration of images in churches far away from their subjects' earthly remains. Now, it would be easier than ever for people to pay homage to their host of holy protectors.

Part Three

Mightsomeness

❖

Christ's passion here derided is with
>   sundry masques and plays,
Fair Ursula, with her maidens all, doth
>   pass amid the ways:
And valiant George, with spear thou
>   killest the dreadful dragon here;
The Devil's house is drawn about, wherein
>   there doth appear
A wondrous sort of damned sprites, with
>   foul and fearful look;
Great Christopher doth wade and pass
>   with Christ amid the brook:
Sebastian, full of feathered shafts, the dint
>   of dart doth feel;
There walketh Catherine with her sword in
>   hand, and cruel wheel:
The chalice and the singing cake, with
>   Barbara is led,
And sundry other pageants played in
>   worship of this bread.

>   Thomas Naogerg, *The Popish Kingdom*,
> translated by Barnabe Googe (London, 1570)

July

Now, over the summer's apotheosis, looms the heliacal ascent of Sirius the Dog, *Canis Major*, bringing the scorching *Dies caniculares*, the 'Puppy' or 'Dog Days', on the world. Illustrated beside the calendar text, the Zodiac symbol Leo burns in the sky, governing the heart, liver, sides and spleen.

The conventional labour for July is the harvesting of wheat. Medieval calendar pages troop with sickle-wielding figures — male and female — in wide-brimmed hats, their legs bare, with companions drinking from leather flasks or making sheaves. Against the ranks of corn, poppies and cornflowers shine red and blue.

From 1252, mid-July saw the annual celebration of Relick Sunday, when churches brought out the bones and possessions of the holy dead. We might imagine the interiors of parish churches with their small, enamelled reliquaries in the shape of houses or body parts arranged on the altar and illuminated by candles, all visible to the laity through the carved and painted wooden screen that divided the main body of the church, or nave, from the chancel. Above the screen hangs a large carving of Christ crucified, looking dolefully down at faithful parishioners venerating their resident saints. As images would have been venerated too, even without relics, in the later medieval period, we might add to this scene wooden panel paintings showing one or more saints, surrounded by further images painted in bright reds, yellows and greens on the undulating plaster walls. All these relics and images would have been cues for stories narrated from the pulpit or in the minds of the faithful, transporting them into familiar fields and distant deserts. The bumper crop of legends I offer for July does similar work, speaking of art made without human hands, as well as dragons, giants, devils and centuries of dreamless sleep.

Veronica: The True Image

Died 1st century
Feast Day: 12 July

It was evening and the ground was releasing the day's heat in waves. Veronica wiped her forehead, sat down and pulled out the small lead token that hung on a ribbon round her neck. The vernicle was tarnished and crudely made, bought by her mother at a London market stall. Now the bearded face it depicted stared directly into Veronica's eyes and she traced the downturned mouth, the large nose and the affronted eyebrows with her thumb.

Veronica stretched out her legs and pulled her skirts up to cool her feet. Her favourite telling of the tale had come from the book her father had given her on her namesake's feast, a new translation of *The Golden Legend*.

She heard a small voice calling for her. Her sixth child, Margaret, had escaped the house and was climbing up next to her. The girl reached up to the pendant in her mother's hand and Veronica let her take it. Then, even though it was too hot for closeness, she wrapped her arms around

Margaret and, as the girl scrutinised the little leaden face, Veronica looked in turn at the childish profile said to be her own in miniature. A few moments of stillness passed before she asked her daughter:

'Shall I tell you the story?'

'Yes.'

They rocked in the sun and Margaret rested her head on her mother's shoulder, as Veronica began to speak.

'A long time ago, when Jesus was alive, there was an old lady called Veronica. She lived in Jerusalem and would listen to Jesus as much as she could. She was scared of dying and he said things that gave her hope. Veronica was an artist, so she used to try drawing Jesus in the sand while she listened. Sometimes she would sneak off early, go home and try making the picture again on a piece of board. But no matter how many times she tried to paint Jesus' picture, it would never look quite like him. Sometimes his eyes were too small or sometimes his nose was too big.'

'What happened?'

'One day, when old Veronica was listening to Jesus, she managed to wait till he had finished talking without running home to her paints. But as soon as he had blessed them and stepped down from the rock he had been standing on to be seen by the whole crowd, she got up and started gathering her bits to leave. Then something amazing occurred. Jesus himself came over and touched her on the shoulder.

Veronica: The True Image

He asked her why she was always running off. When she explained, he took a napkin from her bag. Then he put his face in it.'

'Why?'

'When he gave it back to her, she saw that her napkin now bore a picture of Jesus' face. Veronica went home and used it to make lots more pictures of him. And after Jesus died, Veronica's cloth cured an emperor and became a mighty relic. We call it the Vernicle, along with all the other versions of it, like this one.'

Veronica held up the pendant.

Margaret sat up and looked at the token. Veronica looked at it too.

It was no fine work of art, but those eyes locked on hers with a force like touch. And she cherished the thought that here, waiting for dinner in the heat of a July evening, she could see the face of God.

❖

When I was a child, someone showed me a postcard of the Shroud of Turin. They told me it bore an image of Christ's face burned on to a sheet of linen at the very moment of Resurrection. I was so thrilled and unnerved I couldn't be in the room with it. Records of the Shroud of Turin go back to the fourteenth century, but there are even older candidates for the Veil of Veronica. All have to do with popular devotion to the Holy Face.

Twenty or so years after meeting the postcard, I was at my temporary desk in the British Museum scanning a Holy Face or 'vernicle' pendant badge. It is a lead alloy copy of Christ's face as seen on the Veil of Veronica. His beard divides into three tapering points, not unlike the roots of a tooth, and his head is a distorted rectangle. But later medieval Christians knew that gaze and silhouette. They may well have known its implications too. According to the medieval tradition, Veronica meant 'True Image'.

Veronica is all legend, but her story endures in the Catholic account of Christ's death. Traditionally, she is held to have met Christ as he carried the cross to the site of his execution. There she is said to have used her veil to wipe his face, transferring its image to the cloth. However, in William Caxton's 1483 English adaptation of *The Golden Legend*, she is an elderly devotee who keeps attempting to paint Christ's portrait after listening to him teach. Eventually he transfers the image of his face to her handkerchief so that she has an exact reference. In artworks showing the veil, the face of Christ has no neck, as though he has pushed his head through a hole in a white wall. So distinctive was the design that it translated easily into other media and was copied into books, cast in lead, painted onto wood and carved into stone.

Regardless of the quality of the copy, the vernicle's frontal stare holds the power of Christ's own gaze. Images like this are known by the Greek word *acheiropoieta* – an icon made without hands. This term applies not only to the original miraculous images, but also to copies made of them, however lowly, like the pendant badge. Similar images, not quite *acheiropoieta*, but immensely authoritative nonetheless, included those painted by Christ's followers, such as the portrait of the Virgin and Child attributed to Luke the Evangelist and the Holy Face of Lucca, in Italy, which was a crucifix purported to have been carved by Nicodemus, who helped St Joseph of Arimathea entomb the body of Christ.

Like the progeny of a fallen grain of wheat, a single cult image could generate many copies. Pilgrim badges from Cologne's Shrine of the Three Kings contain mirrors, in which the faithful could capture the reflection of the holy place they had come to see. Most other pilgrim badges depict a cult statue, such as that of Our Lady of Rocamadour or Our Lady of Eton, and allowed pilgrims to take a simulacrum home. Nail holes in some survivals suggest they were pinned up in the domestic space, perhaps above a bed or on lintels over windows, doors and fireplaces, which, in later centuries, became the site of scratched or scorched marks to ward off witches.

Veronica expresses something of the frenzy of images yielded by the cult of saints, especially in the later Middle Ages. On one busy day in 1392, forty thousand pilgrims passed through the gates of Munich, Germany, and were counted by dropping peas into a jar. The city only had a population of ten thousand, so it must have made for a tight squeeze in narrow medieval streets, confined by city walls. A century after that, Aachen boasted an influx of 142,000 pilgrims over the course of just one day to see, among other relics, the tunic of the Virgin Mary. Canterbury must have hosted similar numbers to the shrine of Thomas Becket. And all those pilgrims, like tourists today, wanted something to take home. The massive popular demand created by pilgrimage to saints' shrines revolutionised European cultures of mass reproduction.

A man called Johannes Gutenberg developed technology for the city of Aachen, repetitively die-stamping thin metal discs with sacred imagery to satisfy pilgrims' desire for souvenirs. He went on to use that technology to develop movable type and, from there, the printing press. It is therefore in no small part thanks to the popularity of the medieval cult of saints that you are holding a printed book.

Uncumber: The Golden Shoe

UNKNOWN
FEAST DAY: 20 JULY

Once upon a time, in the days of jousts and tournaments, when kings were eight feet tall and lived in castles, a minstrel entered a church. He was so hungry that if he had possessed any oats to leave, as was customary, before the image of St Uncumber, he would have eaten them. But, as it was, the only offering he had for the statue of the woman on the cross was the music he could make with his fiddle. He brought it to his chin and, standing at the feet of the saint, he began to play. In long strains and trembling scales, he played the tune of his poverty. He played the tune of his hunger. In his hands, his fiddle sang of terror at sleeping on the streets and of bitter disappointment with himself.

As the notes soared, hopped and trembled in the empty church, he grew calm. In this, if in nothing else, he was a master.

He looked up at the statue, and Uncumber, golden and stretched out on the cross, looked down at him in return.

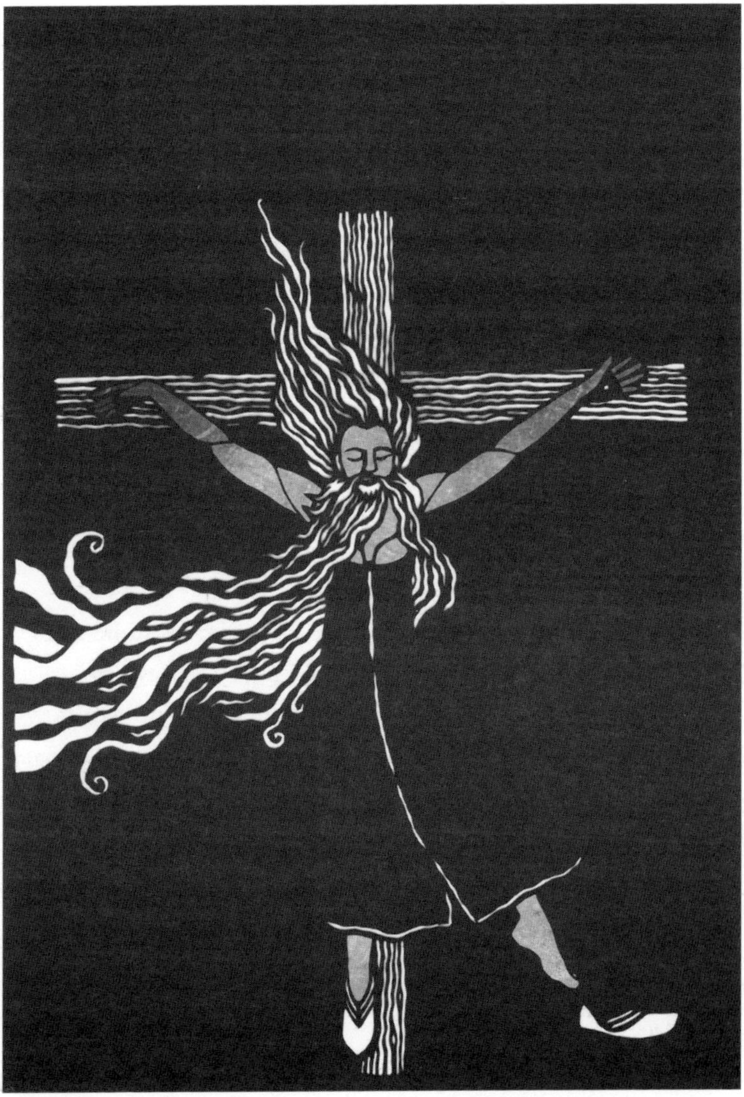

Was it his imagination, or had her eyes shone with more than reflected light?

'What do you care for me?' he said. 'My suffering is nothing compared to yours.'

And now he played a new melody. It was wistful, full of longing and defiance; the minstrel was playing the saint her own story.

It had come to pass in time out of mind, when Uncumber, the King of Portugal's daughter, was a girl. She had been raised in a chamber comfortably furnished with soft couches, fine hangings and a choice selection of books. Teachers had visited her there and taught her to sing, dance and do all the things a princess should do. Though her world was small and well protected, she had discovered a faith not shared by her father and cleaved to it like ivy to a tree. When the King himself came to see her, he stroked her long black hair and told her how proud he was to have her.

'Soon, you will marry a prince and then all will see how lucky I am.'

'Thank you, Father,' his daughter replied, 'but I don't want to marry. I want to live in prayer.'

He said, 'Of course you do,' but he did not believe her.

Sometime later, he visited her with news that an emperor from a wealthy neighbouring kingdom had asked to marry her.

'You will be an empress and your children will be heirs to many lands.'

Uncumber: The Golden Shoe

But his daughter only said, 'I don't want to be an empress and I don't want children. I want to live in prayer.'

Sitting back on a velvet couch, the King asked her what kind of child acted so cruelly to their own, devoted parent?

She was saddened by these words, but she didn't change her mind. Her will remained strong and her thoughts very clear.

Each day the King gave her verses from the Bible to change her mind. '*Honour thy father and thy mother,*' he read to her, '*that your days may be long upon the land which the Lord thy God giveth thee.*' Then he asked her:

'Do you not see that God is giving you land to rule? Accepting His gift will lengthen your very life.'

But she only replied, 'I will never marry.'

The King's temper broke, and the princess found herself in a dungeon with mould spreading on the damp stones and no light at all. She still refused to give in and told herself, 'If I become unattractive to my suitors, they won't want to marry me and I will no longer be encumbered by them or my father's wishes.'

And she fell asleep using her hands as a pillow, praying to be transformed to repulse all those sycophants who might want to marry her.

When she woke up the next morning, she lifted her head from her hands and realised that her face was strangely heavy. She reached to touch her cheeks, but something was growing from them, flowing onto the floor and spreading across it. Delight bloomed in her heart; her prayer had been answered.

The King came down to see her that day, ready to offer new arguments and inducements to make her change her mind, but when he held the lamp over her, he jumped back in horror.

'What has *happened* to you?'

'God has set me free,' she said, stroking her great new defence.

He dropped his lamp and fled. Later on, the guards led her out of the dungeon to the place where they executed criminals. Soldiers nailed her hands and feet to a timber cross and raised her up on a plinth. And Uncumber was crucified at her father's orders. But God had his revenge on her father. Even as she was dying, a fire began in the palace and burned it to the ground.

Uncumber would have felt alone in her suffering if it hadn't been for the sight of her new full beard twisting and coiling in the wind. Her prayer had been answered; soon she would be in Paradise and all the pain would be gone.

The minstrel held the last note, golden and true, until he had come to the tip of the bow. Then he lifted it from the string so gently that the sound continued to hum in the church. But, all at once, a clatter cut it short. Something had fallen, flashing to the stone floor. The minstrel looked to see what it was.

Uncumber: The Golden Shoe

The statue of the crucified and bearded Uncumber had kicked off one of its golden shoes.

'Thank you,' he whispered, feeling the weight of the solid metal.

No one believed his story at first and the town forced him back to the church to prove it. Then the second golden shoe clattered at his feet and all saw he had been blessed by the saint. And the minstrel never again faced starvation and he made music ever after.

❖

It has been argued that the story of Uncumber arose from a misinterpretation of images of the Holy Face of Lucca. A popular Italian pilgrimage destination active from the start of the twelfth century to the present day, the cult crucifix shows Christ with open eyes, a crown and long, flowing robes. Scholars have argued that pictures of it travelled across Europe and, being misread as an image of a crucified woman, gave rise to the cult of the crucified bearded princess.

Found in European Christian literature and art from around 1400, St Uncumber is often depicted in a tightly laced dress and wearing a crown as she hangs on the cross, with her diagnostic facial hair. She was variously known as Wilgefortis, Débarras, Ontcommer, Kümmernis, Librada and Solicitus, though most of her names have similar overtones of liberation. For instance, in French, *débarrasser* means 'to get rid of', while in German, 'sich kümmern', means 'to care'. Only the name Wilgefortis breaks the mould. It may derive from *virgo fortis* (with the *v* pronounced like a *w*), meaning 'strong virgin'.

In an article published in the *Journal of Feminist Studies in Religion*, Lewis Wallace notes Uncumber's distinctive patronage of women eager to lose rather than gain husbands (which is the offering of saints like Agnes). He also writes of a practice that developed in both the Austrian Tyrol and the Low Countries of putting dresses on crucifixes to turn them into Kümmernis or Uncumber. Medieval accounts style her as a crucified bride of the crucified Christ. They emphasise the miraculous fulfilment of her desire to become 'ugly' and so more beautiful to God.

According to *A Dialogue Concerning Heresies*, a sixteenth-century pro-Catholic satire by Thomas More, it was customary for women to offer oats to Uncumber's image in churches, in the hope she would *unencumber* them of abusive or unwanted husbands. The character of the Messenger muses as to what offering oats might achieve, 'Whereof I cannot perceive the reason [unless] it be because she [Uncumber] should provide a horse for an evil husband to ride to the Devil upon'.

Uncumber is a prime example of how folk belief and ritual shaped the medieval cult of saints. Another example may be found in the French cult of St Guinefort, a greyhound killed by its master for eating the man's infant son, when it had, in truth, only saved the child from a snake. The master only realises his mistake when he hears his son's cries and finds him whole and sound under his overturned crib, the dead, dog-bitten body of a viper beside him. In shame, the master threw the dog's corpse down a well, which, when the story got out, became the focus of a popular pilgrimage. Even when the shrine originated, it was viewed with scorn by some. Guinefort's cult was, for instance, condemned by the Dominican preacher Stephen of Bourbon in his text *De Supersticione*, in which he writes:

> Offensive to God are those [superstitions] which honour demons or other creatures as if they were divine: it is what idolatry does, and it is what the wretched women who cast lots do, who seek salvation by worshipping elder trees or making offerings to them; scorning churches and holy relics, they take their children to these elder trees, or to anthills, or to other things in order that a cure may be effected.
>
> This recently happened in the diocese of Lyons where, when I preached against the reading of oracles, and was hearing confession, numerous women confessed that they had taken their children to Saint Guinefort.

Nevertheless, the shrine to St Guinefort, located outside Lyons, endured well into the twentieth century. Saints like

Uncumber and Guinefort show the unruliness of medieval sanctity. Their cults, coming into being after 1200, when canonisation began being managed by the papacy, meant there was no doubt that they contravened the regulations of the Church. Yet to take action against them would require reassessing the very foundations of the Christian faith and risking accusations of heresy. It would take a very tenacious movement indeed – and strong political motives – to square its shoulders against the intellectual battles and genuine political dangers such action might provoke.

Margaret: A Strange Gestation

Died 304
Feast Day: 20 July

Curled with her knees up to her chin, Margaret floated like a yolk in an egg. Pillows of warm flesh bumped against her back and arms. She could hear soothing sounds, deep and soft as distant thunder.

'I can't wait to meet you,' said a voice, 'I can't wait to hold you in my arms.'

Margaret smiled, feeling safe. All the pain had gone. She began opening her mouth to say, 'I am ready. I'll come to you now,' and then she wondered: *What pain?*

She moved her fingers. Then she stretched out her arms. There was no pain there. Then she ran her hands over the skin of her calves and felt bumps and gashes under her fingers. They were injuries, some of them terrible. Moving to her arms and shoulders, she found more cuts. She pushed her fingers into them and touched hard bone.

Why am I so wounded?

Now a view of a prison cell appeared like a shadow in her mind's eye and with it a feeling of melancholy. The image had the quality of a memory, and yet it seemed to be slipping away from her, as if she had fallen out of it and was sliding down a dark tunnel. And another question took shape sluggishly in her sleepy mind: *Where am I?*

She half resisted it. She was so very comfortable, so tired, so desperate to sleep. But, still, a sad voice within her said: *Remember.*

Her memory reached out and found a scrubby hillside. She was watching over a flock of sheep with a group of other girls, but the sight of a chariot coming up the track was making them turn their heads. The expensively dressed man in it was followed by soldiers. He had seen Margaret and ordered the soldiers to take her from the group and bring her with them. The track led to the important man's house, whose name was Olybrius. He had wanted to make her his concubine, but she had made him angry.

She had told him she was a Christian and refused his advances.

In a torrent of images she remembered it all. He had taken her to the centre of the city and tortured her in front of all the people. She had been whipped with hooks that had ripped her skin all the way down to the bone, and Olybrius, covering his eyes with his robes, had feigned disgust at her blood. After she had refused to renounce her beliefs, she was thrown into prison.

Alone, she had cradled her broken body and struggled to understand the hate in the man's eyes.

Margaret: A Strange Gestation

'Where does the hate come from?' Margaret had prayed aloud. 'Please, help me understand where such hate comes from.'

A creature suddenly appeared.

The dragon couldn't be seen all at once. It thrashed and curled in the prison cell like an angry snake, then it vaporised and formed again. She had stood, shaking from her injuries and from terror, and then the dragon took her in its jaws and swallowed her whole.

Now Margaret pressed her hands and feet to the walls of her warm, fluid-filled bed and understood: *I am inside the dragon.*

'I can't wait to meet you,' said the voice again, 'I can't wait to hold you in my arms.'

Margaret made the sign of the cross and opened her mouth to say, 'No.' And even as the sound left her, the fluid became unbreathable and rushed down her throat. She began to choke, kicking out with her arms and legs. She opened her eyes and saw a thin strip of light ahead of her. She reached towards it. She pushed her hands through it and tore it apart, forcing the opening to widen. When it was big enough, she pushed her foot through the gap. Then, feet first, she tore open the belly of the dragon and burst from it.

Margaret hit the hard stone floor and rolled onto her back, her injuries screaming, her clothes bunching under her arms and between her legs. Then she jumped up, ready

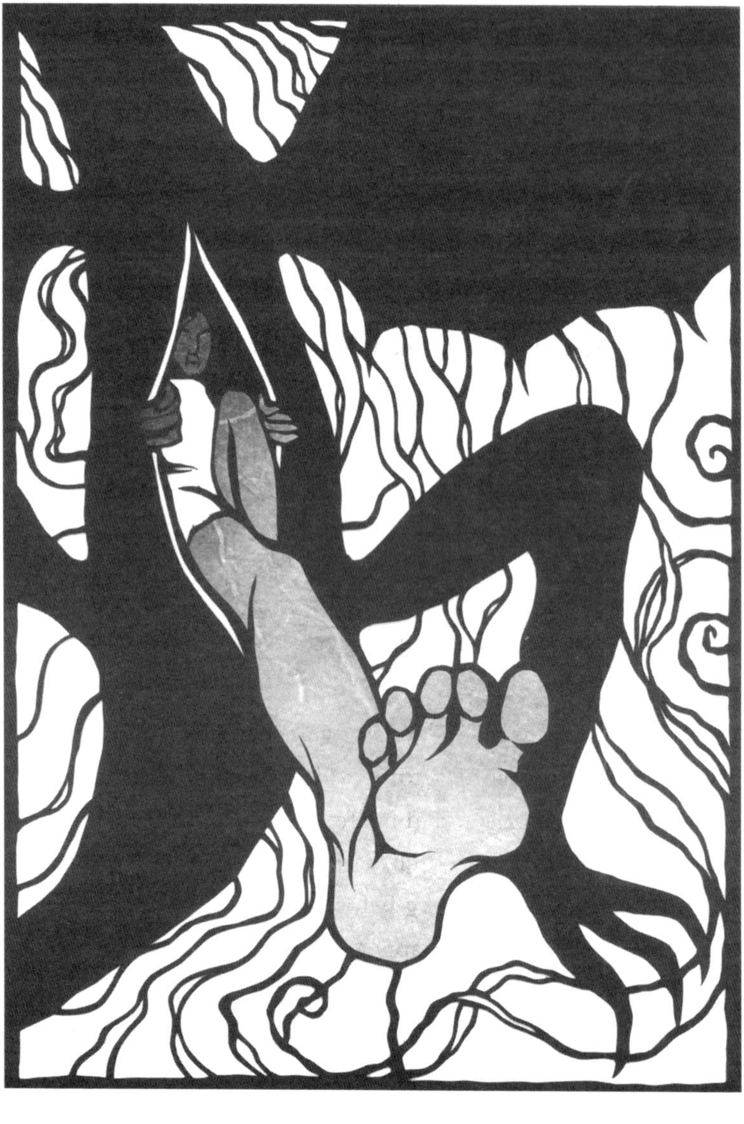

to defend herself against the creature that was the Devil himself.

But no creature stood there. Instead, there was just a man.

'You've done very well,' he said. 'But now, take my hand.'

The man, on the face of it, seemed kind, but he was not. He was Veltis, whom, long ago, King Solomon had trapped in a brass jar, but whom the people of Babylon had set free when they had broken it open in search of treasure. Margaret sensed his duplicity and roared with a force that seemed to come rushing up through the soles of her feet. Shutting her mind to her injuries, she flew up at the man, tugging her own veil from her hair and wrapping it around his head. Using the full weight of her determination, she dragged him to the ground. Then she put her right foot on his back and said, 'Don't you move, demon. I have won!'

Bent round with his wrists against his ankles, the man whimpered and whined to be unloosed. But at her words, the floor of the prison had melted beneath him and already he was slipping into such a deep chasm that the stone would seal above him long before he hit the ground. When he and the hole had disappeared, Margaret was left with just the echo of his words:

'I was bound as hard as a woman in the agony of birth! Now I will never be able to harm such a woman again.'

Margaret knelt, her knees burning in the liquid that had spilled from the dragon's belly. She understood that, even if she lived, she would never have children, but instead she would pray for those who did. She also knew that, unless she renounced her faith, Olybrius would order her death.

But Margaret was not scared.

❖

St Margaret of Antioch is a super-saint and one of the early martyrs said to have been killed, along with the likes of George and Agnes, during the aggressive persecution of Christians in the Roman Empire at the start of the fourth century CE. In the Middle English *Stanzaic Life of Margaret*, the saint uses her wimple (a kind of head covering) to bring down the demonic presence in her cell. When she defeats him, he cries out, 'You bind me with steel so that I may do no ill to woman with child!'

'Binding' and 'unbinding' are words associated in medieval English texts with childbirth. Their use in legends of Margaret reflects how, at the moment of her execution, she prays for women in labour and the health of their children. And one of her miracles in *The Golden Legend* is to raise a mother and child from the dead. Over the course of the Middle Ages, she became a patron saint of childbirth and many ritual practices sprang up around her cult. For one thing, Margaret's own name may have influenced the

Margaret: A Strange Gestation

medicines given to women in and after labour or encouraged its own association with those treatments. *Margarita* means 'daisy', the powdered form of which is recommended in the *Trotula* (a medieval compendium of texts concerning female health) to repair tears to the perineum after childbirth. *Margarita* also means 'pearl', the healing properties of which and their bond to St Margaret are expressed by the poet John Lydgate (died *c.* 1451).

> This stone's power is as to invigorate the heart,
> To be a great comfort to the spirit:
> Just as her heart was majestic –
> I mean, in power [vertu] throughout her life;
> For she vanquished with all her mortal striving
> The Devil, the world, so her story tells,
> And made a sacrifice of her flesh.

Thus, powdered pearls were given to wealthy women during childbirth.

But Margaret's legend had more direct links to childbirth too. It is thought that fifteenth-century French prayer rolls bearing her story were placed on the labouring women's bodies. Indeed, an English birth girdle of sheepskin parchment bearing prayers to Saints Quiricus and Julitta, also believed to be special patrons of women in labour, survives from around 1500 (it is now in the Wellcome Collection under the shelf-mark MS. 632). In 2021, scientific analysis performed on the parchment yielded proteins found in cervico-vaginal fluid, along with traces of honey, milk, egg and broad beans (all believed to have been beneficial in pregnancy and childbirth).

Women grateful for safe passage through childbirth would offer the umbilical cord as a votive offering at shrines to St Margaret. Thanks to the particulars of her legend, Margaret bore a special association with childbirth, but she was not the only saint to do so. Traditions varied from place to place. In late medieval Kelham, Nottinghamshire, a relic of St Stephen's finger was sent to 'lying-in women', and in Burton-on-Trent women in labour walked about and leaned on St Modwenna's staff.

All these practices were performed in the hope of ensuring safe delivery and, at the very least, enough life for the child outside the womb to allow for baptism. In the early fifteenth century, the Augustinian canon John Mirk called on the faithful to light candles in honour of Margaret on her feast day, so that 'Each woman that calls to her in time of travailing with child . . . may be sound delivered, and the child come to Christendom'. At least a little time in Christendom would allow the child to be cleansed of Original Sin and receive Salvation. One can only imagine the anxious desire this must have caused.

The veneration of saints and the religious magic performed to invoke their protection is therefore bound up with contemporary theology regarding the sacraments. It is impossible to consider one without the other; popular expressions of Christian devotion led, inexorably, to matters of high theological import, however harmless they seemed.

Christopher: The Wandering Giant

Died 251
Feast Day: 25 July

Scoundrel was a soldier, but never just one of the troops. He was set apart by his vast size. He was the main attraction, the one they brought forward to fight the enemy's best hero. And Scoundrel never lost.

After too many years doing the same thing for the same petty warlords, Scoundrel decided to find and serve the greatest prince in the land. His search took him to Canaan, where he entered the service of its prince.

Scoundrel followed the man wherever he went, killing as instructed, never feeling sorry, and coming to know all his employer's ways. One thing the prince did intrigued Scoundrel especially. Several times a day, he would say, 'By the Devil.'

Scoundrel wondered who this 'devil' was and what he had over the prince. Eventually, he asked him. The answer would lose the Prince his servant.

The prince said the Devil he spoke of was a mighty lord whom he did not want to offend. On hearing this, Scoundrel realised he was serving the wrong man. He wanted to be with the greatest prince and no other. He packed his few belongings and left.

Scoundrel didn't know where to go to find the Devil. Many knew him, but no one knew where he could be found. Scoundrel decided to cross the desert and try his luck in the cities beyond the border. But crossing such terrain is dangerous even for a giant. He walked over the dunes for weeks before, at last, spotting a glimmer of light on the horizon. Scoundrel made for it. Then he saw it was coming for him as well.

The light was not shining from a city. It was radiating from a man at the front and centre of a huge army, bigger than any Scoundrel had ever seen, stretching as far as the horizon, ranks upon ranks upon ranks of the most alarming soldiers. He could see one with the legs of a goat and another with wings like a bat. Another had the skin of a toad, another the body of a slow-worm. When Scoundrel was close enough to their shining leader to speak, he asked the man's name.

'I am the Devil,' he replied.

Scoundrel knelt down and the Devil made him his knight.

He worked for the Devil for a long time: killing, maiming, massacring, doing whatever he was asked to do. He got to know the Devil's ways. He was intrigued that the Devil would always take a long detour whenever he saw a certain symbol: a cross. Sometimes it stood at the side of the road or was scratched above a door. Sometimes it was a pendant on the neck of an enemy. Wherever it happened to be, the Devil avoided it. Before too long, Scoundrel asked him why. This time, the answer he received would lose the Devil a servant.

'It is the sign of a prince whose name I do not like to speak.'

'What is his name?' Scoundrel asked.

The Devil ground his teeth.

Then he breathed the word as if to say it above a whisper might kill him.

'Christ,' he said.

Scoundrel packed his few belongings and left in search of Christ.

If the Devil had been hard to find, Christ was harder still. Scoundrel searched high and low, crossing wastelands and cities, staying in villages and farms and, as with the Devil, though many had heard of the prince called Christ, none could tell Scoundrel where he was or how to enter his service. At least, not until he met the hermit.

That morning, Scoundrel had woken up after spending the night next to a wide river. He had been planning to wade across it that day and continue on his travels. But then he saw a man in rags with a beard down to his knees standing and watching him. Scoundrel asked him the same question he had asked every other person he had met on his fruitless quest.

'I want to serve Christ. Do you know where he is?'

The man looked at Scoundrel and then at the river.

'I don't know where he is, but I do know how you can serve him.'

The man, a hermit, explained that there was a village nearby that traded with a town on the other side of the river. But, as there was no bridge, the people would often wade across the river and all too often they'd drown. If Scoundrel could use his great height to carry them safely to the other side, then he could serve Christ by saving the villagers' lives.

Scoundrel accepted the task and started living in a cave near the river and carrying the villagers across it whenever they needed. From war and killing, he turned his hand to service. After a while, he felt as though he'd been doing it forever.

He worked every day, waiting in his cave till he heard one of the villagers calling, then picking up his staff, stepping outside, putting them on his shoulder and carrying them above the water to the safety of the opposite bank.

One morning, a child's voice called his name.

'Scoundrel?'

He got up and went outside. The breaking day was already warm and bright, promising heat. Scoundrel looked all around, but there was no one there. He went back into his cave. Then he heard the voice again.

'Scoundrel?'

And again he went outside, blinking in the bright light, to see who needed his help, but again there was no one there. He returned to his cave. Then, for a third time, he heard the voice.

'Scoundrel?'

He stepped back out with sharp words ready in his mouth, but forgot them when he saw a small boy, maybe only three years old, waiting beside the river.

'Please will you carry me across?' the child said, wide-eyed.

Scoundrel lifted him onto his shoulder. He weighed less than a leaf and he felt the boy's small, warm fingers sliding into his hair and gripping tight. Then Scoundrel picked up his staff and stepped from the riverbank into the eddying flow.

The river was full and powerful, but this was as it always was. Scoundrel waded with sure feet until the water had risen to his waist. Then, when he and the boy were almost halfway, something started to feel wrong. The water was rising again, but fast, climbing up Scoundrel's stomach and chest, until it was splashing his chin. And now it was pushing against his body so hard he began fearing he was going to be swept away. He held his staff and strengthened his grip on the child's legs.

Christopher: The Wandering Giant

'Hold on,' he called. 'We'll get to the other side. Don't worry. Just hold on.'

But there was no answer.

'Child?' Scoundrel said.

And now a new, disturbing feeling added to the terrifying force of the water. The child's arm was wrapping around Scoundrel's head like a snake. And the small body was getting heavier and heavier, pushing onto Scoundrel's shoulders as if the sky itself were driving him into the earth. But Scoundrel pressed on, one foot in front of the other, hoping they would not slip on the smooth stones of the riverbed. His only hope was to reach the opposite bank.

Never, in all his days as a soldier, had Scoundrel battled so hard. His muscles screamed. His heart beat like hooves on stone. No breath was enough. And just when he thought another step would kill him, he felt the ground rising and his chest coming up out of the water. And the child's grip was loosening and his weight lightening. Scoundrel realised the sky was blue again, though it had seemed black, and the sun was already drying his clothes.

He fell to his knees, his staff sinking into the mud, and he felt the child jump down. When Scoundrel could speak, he said:

'It was like the weight of the world.'

Then he heard the child say:

'It was.'

And as Scoundrel lay there, the little boy crouched down beside the giant and said:

'From now on, your name will be Christopher, because I am Christ and you have carried me. And the weight you bore on your shoulders was the same that I bore on the cross, when I died to redeem all the sins in the world.'

And that was the last Christopher heard before exhaustion overcame him and he fell asleep in the sun. When he came to, it was evening and the little boy was gone. Christopher looked up and saw that his staff was still sticking upright out of the mud and the top had grown leaves and flowers.

❖

Christopher: The Wandering Giant

My own first encounter with a St Christopher wall painting was a surprise. I had decided to walk from Prestbury, a village outside Cheltenham, England, to the nearby hamlet of Hailes. This is the site of a ruined abbey and a rather less dilapidated parish church. It was the kind of English summer weather that tricks you into leaving the house without a coat, then soaks you to the skin, much to the misery of the elderly collie I had with me. But all was still dry when I reached the church and opened the door. Right in front of us was a huge man. He hovered, his feet level with my chest and he was at least three times taller than me. His staff was taller still, a great vertical stripe beside the giant, and the child perched on his shoulder like a parrot. I could only take in the whole view of the giant from the doorway. A few steps into the church and I was craning my neck.

The uninflected Latin spelling of 'Christopher' reads *Cristoferus*. This is an adaptation of the Greek *Christophóros* meaning 'Christ-bearing'. The *-phóros* part of the Greek word comes from the verb *phérō*, to 'bring' or 'carry'. It is related to Latin *fero*, which means the same thing. *Cristofer* is therefore a construction in the same mould as 'conifer' or 'coniferous', for trees that bear cones. Other words in this mould are 'pestiferous' (bearing the plague), 'splendiferous' (bearing splendour) and 'Lucifer' (light bearer). Like Uncumber and like his very name, Christopher is all legend, though his story originated at the dawn of the cult of saints, with those of the early Christian martyrs. He was one of the original canon and he was widely venerated. In Eastern traditions he was sometimes identified as a *cynocephalus*, or dog-headed man, perhaps preserving echoes of Classical and Ancient Egyptian lore. If only that had caught on in the West; those wall paintings would have been a sight to behold.

In churches in Wales and England alone there are over a hundred and thirty surviving medieval wall paintings of St Christopher, and all but a few show him carrying Christ. There is even one in Westminster Abbey, which had in its enormous relic collection a few 'crusts' from Christopher's head.

One of the joys of Christopher is how he subverts a stereotype. Delve into the Bible and giants are the progeny of fallen angels and human women. They are Goliath, the monster wheeled out of the Philistine ranks to fight the shepherd boy, David, forefather of Christ. In medieval histories, giants are Gogmagog of the twelfth-century *Brut* legend, whose name combines Gog and Magog, the cannibalistic tribes that herald the Apocalypse. Giants are the monster of Mont-Saint-Michel who wears a robe made of the beards of his victims and is defeated by King Arthur. Giants are those soldiers in the mythic Muslim armies described in *La Chanson de Roland*, who are, in the world of the text, too grotesque to ever be assimilated into Christianity. In the fifteenth-century Dutch tale of *The Voyage of St Brendan*,

Christopher: The Wandering Giant

the giant is the incorrigible villain who knows himself too well to risk a second damnation. In other words, giants are huge embodiments of evil. But Christopher – formerly known as Scoundrel – comes good and, in the end, joins the ranks of martyrs.

I sense a certain playfulness in medieval wall paintings of Christopher. Parish churches were, of course, *loci* of control and authority, but they were also community buildings and places of celebration and constant relevance. Here people brought their children for baptism. Here they mourned their dead. Here they gathered at high days and holidays for rites to mark the passing of the year in step with the Christian story. The great giant on the wall is benevolent and charming. His size is engaging, even amusing. But that is not to say he wasn't powerful as well, for images of Christopher were steeped in religious magic, often being accompanied by the inscription '*Cristofori faciem die quacunque tueris / Illa nempe die morte mala non morieris*' ('Whoever looks on the face of Christopher shall not that day die an evil death').

In my days researching pilgrim souvenirs, I encountered numerous St Christopher badges. Their function is suggested in Chaucer's *Canterbury Tales*, written between 1387 and 1400, in which the character of the Knight's Yeoman wore 'a medal of St Christopher . . . of shining silver on his breast'. As well as saving those who looked upon him from death that day, Christopher was patron saint of travellers and many of the badges probably pointed to no specific shrine but were worn as amulets to keep their wearers safe on the road. This last practice remains common among modern Catholics.

St Christopher offers an insight into another important function of the medieval cult of saints: the use of amulets and talismans depicting holy figures. One unusual Canterbury souvenir takes the form of St Thomas Becket standing on the back of a peacock. Its base is designed to be fixed to the top of a staff. Thomas wears the garb of an archbishop and has his right hand raised in blessing, while his left holds a processional cross. The chest of the peacock has a hook on it, which might have been designed to suspend one of the thousands of small Canterbury bells sold to pilgrims and inscribed with the name Thomas. There are many dimensions to this modest and rather comical object. The saint's gaze, his blessing hand, and his processional cross would have connoted protection. The peacock, famed for having incorruptible flesh (and therefore representing Christ), for crying out at danger and for the many, watchful eyes on its tail, would have held similar meanings. The ringing of bells likewise has deep-seated historical association with warding off evil and protecting against storms. When set on top of a staff, the Becket-on-a-peacock badge was a Swiss army knife of protective tools.

There are other staff mounts in the shape of cockerels and peacocks, and I wonder if the Becket variation (of which several fragmentary versions survive) is just a spin-off of a popular type. Like peacocks, cockerels were lauded for crowing at danger and they also sounded the morning alarm. In the Gospels, a cock crows when St Peter has thrice denied Christ, leading to their association with penance. To have one on a staff would express the hope that the perils of the road would be detected in good time and that the bearer's soul would be deserving of supernatural defence.

Another badge in the British Museum's collection shows a Christopher carrying Christ and holding his customary staff. However, the top of the staff does not bear the usual sprouting leaves, as per the legend. Instead, it depicts a bird with a crest and curved tail: a cockerel or, at a push, a peacock.

This Christopher badge's moment of iconographic deviance may be explained if we realise that a whole repertoire of protective imagery and objects was available to late medieval travellers. It included images of saints, especially Christopher, as well as cockerels, peacocks, bells and crosses. I wonder if the British Museum badge, which brings Christ and Christopher together with a bird, offered three travel guardians for the price of two.

Of course, ritual words like the Christopher inscription found under wall paintings and totemic images like the Becket-on-a-peacock badge were not strictly orthodox, but they were ubiquitous and beloved. Historian Keith Thomas suggests that, for the most part, Church authorities were disinclined to prohibit them: 'such practices as the worship of relics, the recitation of prayers, or the wearing of talismans and amulets could all be taken to excess, but what did it matter so long as their effect was to bind the people closer to the true Church and the true God?'

What did it matter, indeed.

James: The Unthinkable Penance

Died 44
Feast Day: 25 July

When Gerald set out on pilgrimage he had no notion he would soon mutilate himself. The journey began, like those of previous years, with waving goodbye to his mother. Then he stepped onto the road from Lyons that would take him to the shrine of St James.

All was white by the sunlight and ripe with the odours of the city. On the first night, he stayed alone at his usual inn, his money bag full of coins. When he had drunk and eaten well with the other pilgrims, the usual order of things changed. He blearily made his way behind the inn and up the skirts of a barmaid. The next day, only half remembering what he had done, he had met two friends and continued the journey south.

On the first night with his friends, he left their table to relieve himself outside. While he leaned his forehead against the wall and let the slow stream pool on the roadside, a stranger approached him and watched him as if expecting to be recognised. Gerald willed his body to work faster so that he could return to his friends.

Then the man asked, 'Don't you know who I am?'

'Sorry,' Gerald replied, the stream at last lessening. 'I don't.'

'I am Saint James and you are my faithful pilgrim. You visit my shrine every year and, for that reason, I know everything about you. For instance, I know you fornicated yesterday, and I know you have not done penance, nor gone to confession.'

Gerald put his hand over his eyes and when he drew it away, the man was gone. Gerald fastened his clothes and went inside. There was no sign of his visitor among the pilgrims, merchants and whores. His stomach turned. How had the man known what he had done?

When they went to bed, Gerald lay down on the heaped straw provided on the upper floor for pilgrims. He hardly slept. His mother had raised him to believe in the tortures of Hell. As he lay in the dark, listening to the hot grunts and farts of his fellow travellers, the terror clamped his fingers and toes like burning tongs and encircled his head like a knotted rope. He decided to get up before his companions and ride straight back home. There, he would find a priest, say his confession and do penance for his sin.

But when Gerald left the inn, the man was beside him again.

James: The Unthinkable Penance

'Confession and penance will not win God's forgiveness. You will need to go further to save your soul.'

'What do I have to do?' said Gerald.

'You should cut off your penis and testicles.'

The warm air intensified around his throat. He gasped and said:

'I won't survive.'

'But then you would be a martyr.'

Gerald did not go home. St James had told him what he must do and he could perform that anywhere. He needed to think. He went back to his companions and rode with them further south, the heat of the sun on his head adding to the sickness in his gut. Images of damnation filled his mind. Hell would be hotter than Spain. And the burning would never end.

When night fell, they had reached another village and paid for beds at another inn. This time, they had a room to themselves, but it was no less torturous after the heat of the day. Gerald waited till his companions were asleep, then he unsheathed his knife and, sitting up so that the moonlight was falling across his lap, he exposed the offending parts.

Could he do it?

He thought of St James. He thought of what he would give to go back to when he had kissed his mother goodbye in Lyons and started travelling south. Then, these organs had not felt as they did now, like galls on an oak tree, breeding wasps.

Hardly able to hold the blade in his sweating, shaking hand, he performed the amputation. Then, horrified by what he had done, Gerald stabbed himself in the stomach.

As he died, he convulsed and woke up his friends. They tried to help him, unable to work out how they could save him, realising, when they saw his injuries, they could not.

'Who did this?' said one.

'I don't know, but if we're found here with his corpse, we'll be blamed.'

'Let's go,' they said together.

The next morning, the owners of the inn found Gerald's body and their screams shook through the house and brought the neighbours into the street. He was carried to the entrance of the church and left while a grave was dug. But as news of the corpse spread, people gathered near the steps to the church, watching curiously, sharing figs and speculating about his death. Then Gerald sat up and started speaking.

Of course, on seeing the mutilated corpse revive, the people scattered before they heard what he was saying. They ran to the main street, where they told the crowds, 'A dead man has come to life!'

Now many others followed them back to the church, and there they found the man alive as they had been told, gruesomely wounded, and eager to speak. And they listened, rapt, as Gerald told them what had happened between

James: The Unthinkable Penance

leaving Lyons and his death. And then he told them what had happened to him since he had died.

He explained that, while his friends had stood over his convulsing body, he had felt his naked soul lifted by sharply taloned hands. Then a shrieking swarm of creatures had carried him over a range of snowy mountains, over cypress groves and lakes. And he had realised his penance had failed and he was being borne to Hell. At any moment, he expected to see the mouth of Hell, with its thousand teeth gleaming, with its wet throat and flashing tongue. But then he realised that the shrieks of his abductors, which had been mirthful at first, had now turned fearful. And he realised that the demons were fleeing. Someone was chasing them down.

From where Gerald hung, his wrists grasped by the clawed hands, he could twist his head and look over his shoulder. Though the demons bred a kind of black mist, behind it he could see a man riding on shining clouds, bright as sunlight through a crystal orb.

'Let go of my pilgrim,' called the man. 'I will not let you take him.'

'We deceived him,' cried the demons in return. 'We convinced him. He is ours!'

This time, Gerald recognised the saint as if he had seen him every day of his life. And with this he realised that the man who had called himself St James, who had convinced him to take his own life, had been an imposter.

The true James, the Apostle of Christ, drove the demons on. And then Gerald could see that they had reached the gates of a church, every stone too smooth to have been dressed by human hands. Gerald knew that they were in the heavenly image of Rome and that this was the heavenly basilica of St Peter. And then, even as the talons cut into his wrists, adding to his injuries, his heart swelled with wonder at the sight that met his eyes. The Virgin, small and beautiful as a jewel, sat enthroned in front of the gates, a meadow flowing from under her feet. And her multitudinous court of saints stood in ranks to her left and right, while, before her, James forced the demons, the naked and terrified Gerald among them, into a pen. Then Gerald saw and heard James present his case, with urgent arguments and passionate gestures, to the Virgin. And Gerald understood that he was in the holy tribunal, where the saints pleaded for their pilgrims at Ecclesia's throne.

When James finished, she said:

'Your case is good. You may take him home.'

Then James thrust his hand into the roiling throng of demons and seized Gerald's naked soul. Then he carried him back over the cypress trees and mountains to his body in Spain and lovingly restored him to life.

When Gerald had finished his story, the villagers were agog. Then they praised God and St James. They clothed the mutilated man and gave him food and water, tending him for some weeks until he was strong enough to continue his journey. Gerald reached James' shrine and had a fine wonder to tell its keepers and a fine reason to light a candle, though his lost body parts never did grow back. When the wounds had healed, all that remained was a small protrusion, like a wart, through which he was able to urinate.

❖

In the Bible, James is a disciple of Christ, the brother of John, and the first disciple to die after the traitor Judas. According to James' legend, he was killed in Judea in 44 CE, having first spent time as a missionary in Spain. After his martyrdom, his body is said to have drifted back to Spain in an unmanned boat and found rest in a secret location. This was miraculously revealed in the ninth century, leading to the construction of a church on the gravesite and the beginning of a cult that would bring pilgrims from far and wide.

The story of St James and Gerald comes from a manuscript known as the Codex Calixtinus, compiled in the twelfth century and kept in the Cathedral of St James in Compostela. The Codex Calixtinus (stolen, incidentally, in 2011, and discovered a year later in the garage of the cathedral's former electrician) includes a catalogue of James' miracles. That of Gerald's catastrophic case of mistaken identity offers a helpful insight into what saints could do for their pilgrims. In the text, Gerald calls St James his 'advocate' – a legal term – and the Virgin addresses the demons, highlighting Gerald's proven devotion: 'O you miserable creatures! What were you seeking in a pilgrim of my Lord and Son and of Saint James, his faithful one?' Thus, Gerald's yearly pilgrimage pays off and James comes to his rescue even as demons are dragging his soul to Hell.

According to the Codex Calixtinus, James' pilgrims took to wearing shells, which are among the earliest recorded pilgrim souvenirs and remain a symbol of the Compostela pilgrimage: 'The pilgrims returning from the threshold of the Blessed James sew them on their caps, and they wear them back to their own country with great exultation in honour of the apostle and in his memory and as a sign of such a great journey.' The souvenir is a 'sign' of the eternal benefits of being a pilgrim. It appears on the sculpted Last Judgement scene above the door of the Cathedral of

James: The Unthinkable Penance

St Lazarus in Autun, France; on the side of the blessed is a small knot of hopeful individuals, queuing for heaven with scallop shells on their shoulder bags like VIP labels.

St Andrew, another of Christ's disciples, also travelled west in death. However, his bones' journey occurred after the fourth-century legalisation of Christianity by the Emperor Constantine. According to *The Golden Legend*, a monk called Rule, charged with guarding the saint's relics in the Greek city of Patras, received a vision from an angel telling him to open Andrew's sarcophagus and remove one kneecap, one tooth, three fingers from his right hand and the arm bone between his shoulder and his elbow. Rule was then to take the relics over land and sea to the northern reaches of an island called Britain, where he would use the bones to convert a people called the Picts. Rule obeyed, becoming a middleman for St Andrew's posthumous mission. The story also serves as a foundation legend for the Scottish town of St Andrews and the ruined church dedicated to St Rule that stands there to this day.

Relics were powerful tools for the conversion of non-Christians. Holy bones brought the *virtus* of the saint into regions absent from the Bible and acted as focal points for miracles and wonders. But there are no miracle-working bones in Scripture. They only arrive after the adoption of Christianity by the Emperor Constantine, when missionary work began in earnest, and became, within a few centuries, one of the most important aspects of the popular faith. 'The beliefs promoted by missionaries in the heat of conversion,' as the historian Ralph Finucane puts it, 'were often an embarrassment to later generations of churchmen in a peaceful Christianised Europe when the battle to evangelise had been won; but by then the damage had been done.'

The Seven Sleepers: Into the Cave

DIED 478
FEAST DAY: 27 JULY

Malchus dozed in the warm, wordless contentment that follows a good sleep. He opened his eyes and saw that it was absolutely dark and, apart from his friends' breathing, the air inside the cave was motionless. He was hungry, and wondered whether it was morning and the bakeries would be open. Then his chest tightened. Ephesus, day or night, would be waiting at the bottom of the mountain like a snare. And yet it was their only source of food.

He was lying alongside his six closest friends, whom he had met while working in the court of the Emperor Decius. They were all Christians, and when the war-loving Emperor had outlawed their faith, they had agreed they'd never give in and sacrifice to the Roman gods.

The Emperor, announcing his departure from Ephesus, on matters of state, had decreed that his seven young servants had until his return to cast off their Christianity. But that night, as they had walked home, they had agreed to give all their belongings away and flee to a cave in the mountains. There they would commit themselves to a life of prayer and escape the violent executions dealt to others who had defied their ruler.

They had found the mouth of a cave behind a slender thorn tree, which scratched their necks as they left behind the evening breeze and stepped into the motionless, soundless world beyond. The passageway trailed further underground. Then it had opened out into a cavern. They had huddled in the dark, listening for the shouts of soldiers. But no shouts had come.

Some days had passed and, though they had sneaked into the city for provisions before, Malchus' stomach growled. He heard the others beginning to stir and stood up, stretching and whispering into the darkness that he was going back to Ephesus for bread. It must be morning by now.

Malchus was picking up the ragged cloak they used as a disguise when one of his friends spoke.

'Buy better bread than you did yesterday, won't you? Yesterday there wasn't enough and it was stale.'

Malchus laughed and crept along the passageway to the entrance of the cave, slipping his hand into his pocket and checking for coins. He and his companions had kept enough money to buy bread for themselves for a few months, but it would run out eventually. When he stepped into the light, the air was full of the fresh scents of morning.

His eyes were so blinded that he didn't notice the stump of spiky, sun-bleached wood next to the cave entrance

The Seven Sleepers: Into the Cave

or, beside it, the pile of old stones and broken lumps of mortar.

Reaching the foot of the mountain, he joined the road to Ephesus and made his way up to the city gate. When he reached it he stopped. A symbol hung above the commotion of carts, animals and people. And it was not right. Seeing it there made him nervous. Instead of entering the city, he followed the road around the walls to the opposite gate and saw the same symbol in the same position. He hung back, wondering what to do, but then his hunger urged him on. He entered the city and found a bakery. There he asked for two loaves, brought the coins from his pocket and dropped them into the baker's dusty hand.

Mightsomeness

The man took one look at the coins and grinned up at Malchus. Then he closed his fingers over the gold and began whispering to his apprentice. Malchus, even more nervous than before, made to leave. What had he been thinking? He could gather olives on the hillside and didn't need bread after all. He needed to get back to his friends. But now the baker stepped out from behind his wares and barred the door with his body.

'Where's the hoard?' he said, smiling.

'What?'

'Where did you find this old treasure?'

When Malchus did not answer, the baker repeated his question, then said:

'If you're not going to confess to us, you'll have to tell the whole town.'

The apprentice took Malchus' upper arm and the baker took the other. Malchus protested and struggled against them, but could do nothing to stop them from leading him to the main square where criminals were brought before the judges.

Some hours later, Malchus found himself being tried for theft, surrounded by faces as strange to him as if he were in a foreign city. Two officials had come to hear his case. One was dressed in robes bearing the same symbol as he had seen hanging over the city gates – further mockery – and the other was the city's proconsul.

'Where is the hoard from which you found this money?' they asked him.

Malchus told them earnestly that his parents had given it to him only a few weeks ago. He gave them their names, but neither of the officials nor anyone in the crowd had heard of them.

Malchus, disbelieving and wishing the duplicity would stop, said, 'Where is the Emperor Decius?'

They told him and Malchus laughed, shaking his head.

'But that's impossible,' he said. 'He has only just returned to Ephesus.'

Then Malchus, looking at the symbols on the official's robes, decided to do the only thing that might prove the truth of his words.

'Let me take you to my friends. They will tell you I'm not lying.'

And so Malchus led the officials and a whole throng of citizens out of the city, along the road and up Mount Celion to the entrance of the cave. This time he saw the wide, sun-bleached stump and the pile of stones and it occurred to him that the slender thorn tree had gone. Some way off, he noticed a shepherd building a shelter. Then one of the officials knelt and picked something up from between those stones that remained. It was a piece of ancient parchment.

Reading the text aloud, the official related how, in the midst of his campaign of persecution, the Emperor Decius had come home to find his seven servants gone: those who had refused to renounce their faith. The parchment stated that he had received a vision of where they were hiding and that he had sent his soldiers up the mountain to block them into their cave. It stated that they had died as martyrs. Two Christians had followed the soldiers and witnessed their work. Thus they had written down the story on a leaf of parchment and pushed it between the stones.

Malchus couldn't speak. Feeling more and more as though he were in a dream, he led the officials into the cave. They followed. When they reached the main cavern, he saw his six friends had lit lamps and were sitting up and waiting for their breakfast.

'These are my friends,' said Malchus to the officials. 'Maximian, Marcianus, Denis, John, Serapion, and Constantine. As you can see, they are not dead.'

Then Malchus faced his friends and gestured to the official's robes, which were embroidered with Christian crosses like those that now hung above the city gates.

'This priest tells me that Decius, the usurper and persecutor of Christians, has not reigned for more than a century. Friends, I think Decius sealed us in, intending that we would die of starvation and thirst, but he did not kill us. Can it be that we have been asleep for all those years?'

And now Malchus remembered the shepherd he had just seen outside the cave. The man had unknowingly opened their prison, taking the stone that had blocked them in for

The Seven Sleepers: Into the Cave

his shelter, opening their cave and waking them from their miraculous sleep. And since the days of Decius, Christianity had come to Ephesus and the crosses hung above the gates, proclaiming the people's faith. Malchus laughed aloud. Then he sat down with his friends and explained it all.

The seven young men stayed in the cave until the new emperor, a Christian by the name of Theodosius, had travelled from Constantinople. When he saw them, they appeared to shine in the darkness. Then the one called Maximian said:

'We have been safe in this cave as babes in the womb. But our families are dead and, now, having seen you, our work is done.'

And so the young men lay down together for the last time and, breathing the stone-soft air, died as peacefully as they had slept.

❖

The legendary Seven Sleepers of Ephesus prefigure later fairy-tales like Sleeping Beauty and Snow White. The young men's 'death', being temporary and symbolic, shows how familiar narrative motifs have roots that at least run through medieval Christian soil and may even have had their origins there.

The Seven Sleepers legend is set in modern-day Turkey during the Decian persecution of the Christians (c. 250). The tale existed in Late Antique Christianity, making its way from there into a sixth-century miracle collection by Gregory of Tours, *Glory of the Martyrs*, which brought it into circulation in north-western Europe. After that, it was translated into vernacular languages, including Old English, and was chosen by Jacobus de Voragine for his *Golden Legend*.

I've called on the illustrated *History of Saint Edward the King* by Matthew Paris a few times in the preceding chapters. It relates how, after the death of Earl Godwin (described in January), Edward the Confessor has a vision of the Seven Sleepers of Ephesus rolling over. He interprets it as an ill omen. This is an early example of the use of the Seven Sleepers for prognostication or foretelling of future events, though it is a function they still serve. In German-speaking countries, the Seven Sleepers are weather saints: rain on *Siebenschläfertag* or 'Seven Sleepers Day' (27 June) means rain every day for four weeks. It's the same idea as English sayings around St Swithun, whose feast is celebrated on 15 July and who is said to have asked to be buried beside Winchester's Old Minster, where the rain would fall upon him unimpeded from heaven. If it rains on St Swithun's Day, so they say, four weeks of rain will follow.

The use of saints in prognostication is yet another example of how most people's engagement with the cult of saints tumbled well out of reach of what learned medieval Christians would have judged sound Christian theology.

The Seven Sleepers: Into the Cave

We have seen saints and motifs from their legends giving rise to medicines, travel talismans, incantations and, now, divination.

As a child, I was taken to the main service in our local Anglican church every other Sunday (on the Sundays in between, we attended Catholic Mass). The Anglican building, St Mary's in Great Witcombe, is twelfth-century and much of its furniture post-medieval. And though I had a sense, from the remains of a Roman villa on the hill and the freshwater stream that babbled beside the churchyard, that this might have been a holy site for religions I deemed more interesting than Christianity, it was only when, aged about fifteen, I glimpsed the traces of a pattern of red chevrons on the chancel arch that I wondered if there was more to it than that. What if, the patterns in red, and maybe other colours besides, had extended to every arch between the stone columns dividing the nave in two? I went home that day to read, and the next time I entered St Mary's I imagined the familiar space of pale limestone and magnolia-painted plaster in full technicolour. It was clear now that I had been confusing familiarity with the mundane. But, of course, I still didn't know the half of it. The intervening years of learning have enriched the picture. Which saints might the medieval inhabitants of Great Witcombe have seen on the walls? What beliefs did those images inspire? I had once imagined the church's history like readings from the pale pages of a Stepford wife's diary:

Mightsomeness

all about things well behaved, picturesque and orderly. Now, for me, that history is bright with pigments, set about with cult images, illuminated with candles. It bustles with parishioners who, as the stream flowed beyond the churchyard, carried in their hearts a cornucopia of minor heresies and marvellous stories.

August

Perched in her tempera heavens, a painted image of Virgo oversees a team of workers as they thresh the wheat. Some separate grain from stalk on the barn floor; others use a winnowing fan to shake away the chaff. Beside her, words in red ink tell us that she brings fruitfulness to the season. In earlier ages and in different contexts, she was Demeter, the Roman goddess associated with the harvest and the law. In the tales of Ancient Greece, she was Astraea, who ascended to the stars to escape human wickedness. Medieval readers of the illustrated calendar page might have seen her as the fruitful Virgin Mary, bearer of the Bread of Life, the feast of whose Assumption into Heaven – 'Lady Day in Harvest' – fell on the fifteenth day of August. This month, when the moon was in Virgo, affected ailments to the belly.

In the Gospel of Matthew, John the Baptist uses the image of the wheat being separated from the chaff as a metaphor for the judgement of the virtuous and the sinful. And while the threshing floor could be nothing more than a flat, hard surface on which wheat was struck by flails and shaken by the winnowing fan, it could also be the stage for divine arbitration.

Mightsomeness

At the end of time, each human would join either the ranks of the blessed or the damned. And medieval Catholicism preached the necessity of the sacraments for any hope of salvation, but throughout the Church's history this assertion had seen dissenters. Our August still revels in the cult of saints at the height of its heat, glorying in miracles and heroic martyrdoms. But dissenting voices are on the air, like the first chills of autumn. For some, they forbode winter, for others they promise an end to the madness of high summer.

Germanus: The Resurrection

Died c. 442–448
Feast Day: 31 July (3 August in Wales)

Germanus spread the bones out on the earthen floor in the approximate shape of a cow, while his mind seethed like a stewpot. The heresy still had its adherents, he thought, positioning the pelvis, all chopped up and brown with tatters of cooked meat. Stamping out the false beliefs almost entirely on his first visit to Britain had been a great victory, but there were some in power who still looked to Pelagius. Germanus chewed a scrap of cooked muscle from a thigh bone, then laid it down. The British King was one of them, that was for certain. What other reason could he have for turning Germanus and his followers from his table if he wasn't hankering after the heretic? Germanus spat a lump of gristle into the meagre fire and his hands dealt with a shoulder blade.

He had convinced most of this backwater nobility that their best interests lay in siding with the official doctrine: that all men were indeed born shackled by Original Sin and that the sacraments were the only way to Heaven. He stood up to survey his work. The pile of vertebrae still needed sorting. Dispelling inherited sin, winning eternal life: these were not things humans could manage on their own. They needed guidance. They needed authority. He crouched down and began laying the elements of the spine side by side, seeking order, trying to make them fit as God had ordained. Every tessera in the vast mosaic of Creation had its singular purpose, from the neck bones of the cow to the secrets of the soul. Clearly the crown still needed convincing; the head that ruled all the other members of this fog-muffled island. Germanus put the skull with its stubby horns in place and licked his lips, remembering through his tongue the quality of the brawn.

It was just as well that the King's cowherd had invited them to stay when they had been turned away by the King. The poor man's slaughtering of his only calf for the meal had a certain . . . narrative potential. Germanus unrolled the hide that had been stripped from the carcass. He thought of St Alban, the British martyr whose shrine he himself had restored. Saints drew crowds and the story of Alban was as memorable as it was repugnant. With the cult, Germanus had revived a sense of Rome's relatability: that the rules were beautiful and richly endowed.

He laid the skin over the bones and bent his head to pray. Behind him, the cowherd and his family whispered among themselves, wondering what the priest would do next.

Now, he just needed a miracle.

❖

The 'Pelagian heresy' is named after the fifth-century British teacher Pelagius. It is said to have been suppressed in Britain by St Germanus of Auxerre, who travelled from Gaul with Bishop Lupus of Troyes. Legend has it that, when they were turned away from the British king's household, a local cowherd hosted them instead, slaughtering a calf for the feast. After the feast, Germanus restored the calf to life. Pelagianism, which we have already discussed in relation to David back in March, rejected the idea of Original Sin, which was so important to the way in which medieval Christians understood their relationship to God and the Devil and how to attain salvation.

But Pelagianism was in no way the only 'heresy' of the Middle Ages. There was the Arian heresy from the turn of the fourth century, which contended that God and Jesus had not been 'co-eternally' in existence, but that God had created his son. Then the twelfth and thirteenth centuries saw the rise of the Cathar or Albigensian heresy. This offshoot of medieval Christianity scorned the physical world, which it held to have been created by a malevolent deity, a kind of eternal Satan. The good God had made only the spiritual world, and Jesus was only an angel. To the Cathars, humans themselves were angelic souls without gender or sex and trapped in demonic bodies. Catharism rejected the doctrine of Purgatory, the crucifix, the Eucharistic miracle of transubstantiation (discussed in May) and, most importantly for us, the cult of saints.

The 1209 papal decision to suppress Catharism in the Languedoc region of southern France led to the bloody, twenty-year Albigensian Crusade. While the sect never resurfaced in its original form, some of its tenets helped shape later reform movements, such as Lollardy. The same is true of the roughly contemporary Waldensian movement, founded by Peter Waldo in Lyons, France, in the 1170s. This sect believed in transubstantiation but challenged the need for babies to be baptised to avoid damnation.

As the Middle Ages progressed, the heresies came and went. But the same issues arose time and again: the miracle of the Eucharist, the role of the sacraments, the use of images, the veneration of saints.

Lawrence: 'Turn Me over and Eat'

DIED 258
FEAST DAY: 10 AUGUST

The most ruthless of Decius' torturers had been raised by his violent father, working in the family abattoir and butcher's shop. He associated killing and dismemberment with the one who had so often beaten him and who had come to represent everything a man ought to be.

The butcher's son had grown up to surpass his father in height, width and aggression, and had been sent into the army. When Decius, a brute in his own right, had slit the throat of Emperor Philip and seized the imperial throne, the butcher's son had found a kindred spirit in his ruler and had been raised to the rank of torturer. Under Decius, he had fleshed out his knowledge of the pattern of skin, fluid, organ, sinew and bone which bodies, both human and animal, comprised. Now he also gained the craft of slicing, bleeding, bruising and breaking without causing death or, at least, while keeping death at bay. When the screams simmered on the edge of unconsciousness, he experienced a peace that could be achieved no other way. In this act of controlled domination, he was at last man enough for the great, burly body he had inherited from his father.

Whips that finished in balls of lead and hooks called 'scorpions' flashed in the torturers' hands as they laboured, releasing blood from the convict in arcs of imperial purple. Now the blood poured over broken skin, battered muscle and shattered bones, and all would have been going well were it not for the prisoner's placid smile. Lawrence, the Archdeacon of Rome, was their latest victim, but he was not showing any sign that he was in pain.

The torturer saw the Emperor descending from his seat. Decius had noticed – how couldn't he? – that all was not going to plan.

'Put him under Hippolytus' guard in the prison. We can finish this tomorrow.'

The next day was hotter still. They brought Lawrence out once more and laid a gridiron over glowing coals, transferring the prisoner to it on his back. He gazed up at the sky, looking unconcerned. The butcher's son, adjusting the pitchfork handle in his sweating, calloused hands, felt his temper rise.

It was wrong to see no reaction when pushing fork prongs a finger's depth into a man's thigh. It was wrong that the prisoner's eyes did not cloud over as his skin blistered and hissed on burning coals. It was as corrupt as if one of the pig carcasses in his father's butchery had spoken to him while hanging by its ankle from a hook. The day

Lawrence: 'Turn Me over and Eat'

had just begun and the butcher's son had nothing left with which to torment his victim. He wanted for it to be over. He wanted the order to kill.

But Decius was there and he bent over the man on the coals. But before he could speak, Lawrence turned to look at him with a strange, mournful smile.

'Now that you've roasted this side, why not turn me over and eat?'

In the end, watching Lawrence die brought the torturer no satisfaction. Instead, it kindled within him a confused longing that was in itself torturous. The feeling would press into his heart till he died. And if he had ever been taught to say how he felt, he might have said it came down to a deep envy, even anger, that Lawrence had cheated the contract with pain that was the essence of every human life. Pain had charred every part of his life, after all.

The next morning, Lawrence's burned body was gone. Word reached the torturer that the guard Hippolytus, whom Lawrence had converted from his prison cell the night before, had stolen to the arena that night and taken the dead prisoner away. Hippolytus would suffer, thought the torturer. Hippolytus would pay.

❖

The early Christian martyrs populate the feast days of August. Having fallen foul of earthly judgement, these characters rise after death to the ranks of the righteous and receive the crowns of martyrdom. In their apparent anaesthesia, they are paragons of *virtus*.

Though Lawrence's death is usually dated to the persecution of the Christians under the Emperor Valerian (reigned 253–60), William Caxton's translation of *The Golden Legend* places it in the reign of the Emperor Decius (reigned 249–51). The story goes that Lawrence, the Archdeacon of Rome, offends the Emperor (a violent usurper) by giving away his imperial predecessor's wealth to the poor. This leads to Lawrence's torture and death on the griddle. The manner of his martyrdom would make him a patron saint of the poor and cooks, though it may have originated with a transcription error, reducing *passus est* (he suffered or died) to *assus est* (he was roasted).

According to Caxton's *Golden Legend*, Hippolytus was a Roman soldier converted by St Lawrence while the saint was in his prison. Hippolytus' punishment for taking away Lawrence's body the morning after his death is to be torn apart by wild horses: 'He made Hippolytus to be bound by the feet unto the necks of wild horses, and made him to be drawn among thorns, briars and rocks, till he rendered and gave to God his spirit.' The manner of Hippolytus' death, as well as his name, recalls the Hippolytus of Greek myth and may reflect the circulation of classical sources such as Ovid's *Metamorphoses* in Late Antique and medieval Europe. When reading the legends of the early Christian martyrs, you can't escape their memorable individuality.

Lawrence: 'Turn Me over and Eat'

Lots of them end up dying by decapitation, but each path to death is distinctive.

A panel of twelfth-century stained glass, probably from Canterbury, now in the care of the Metropolitan Museum of Art in New York, shows St Lawrence on a fiery griddle. The red glass makes the flames appear to glow. Later images of Lawrence's martyrdom tend to show him lying down or standing and holding a miniature griddle, but the artists of the Canterbury panel anticipate neither of these conventions. They have shown Lawrence enthroned, as if he is already in heaven, with his feet in the fire. Three further tracts of fire touch his body, though these are colourless. One fiery band crosses his waist, one crosses his shoulders, and the third rains down on his head. They refer to the theory that Lawrence overcame the earthly fire by the spiritual fires of his faith, his love of Christ and his knowledge of God.

It is not, therefore, that he feels nothing during his torture and death, but that he is consumed by burning passions far stronger than anything the world can provoke. It is as a kind of holy furnace that we might imagine *virtus*, blazing from the saint's body and illuminating everything it touches. Images could help depict that invisible power, with translucent coloured glass, or great backgrounds of gold leaf tooled with patterns to reflect the dancing candlelight, or painted stone and mottled marbles that seared the imagination with delight. Even remote villages like that of Morebath in Exmoor, made famous by the historian Eamon Duffy, would come, by the late Middle Ages, to have multiple images of saints before which the parishioners lit candles. In 1488, the church of Stratton Strawless in Norfolk had, as well as depictions of Christ and the Virgin, twelve images of saints. Contemporary paintings on surviving rood screens show that these, even in small rural churches, might not have been muted, inexpert daubings, but works of some skill and vibrancy. And what harm was there in attempting to honour a saint and convey their holiness with the finest craftspeople, forms and materials that patrons could afford?

Bartholomew: Skin on Skin

Died 69/71
Feast Day: 24 August

Now that the artists had done their work, the skin showed a map of the whole world. And not only the world, but the whole of time itself. At the top, Christ oversaw Creation from his seat of Judgement, while walls encircled Eden. Filling in the gaps between the illustrations with neat labels in red and black, Brother Bartholomew's hand moved with the precision of a lifetime's practice, the nib of his pen spreading a little as it landed, then dragging the ink into a plump line, then spreading and springing back together with the release. Each stroke of ink gleamed at first, then dimmed as it dried, but his method was well thought through. By working in strips from the middle to the edge of the map, against the sun, he avoided dragging his arm through the writing he had just finished. In the morning he had started above the walled city of Jerusalem (where the artists had drawn Christ hanging on the cross) and now, as the shadow of a rain cloud crept further across the cloister garden and the hour for vespers approached, he

MIGHTSOMENESS

had reached India, in the easternmost portion of the map, just under Eden.

Brother Bartholomew, who had never travelled further east than Worcester, had a particular interest in India. Over the course of the day, he had unwittingly traced the journey up from the Holy City to that mysterious land that his chosen patron, St Bartholomew, had followed after the Resurrection when he had gone to India to evangelise. The scribe's eyes, tired, dry and webbed with red lines, worked their way over the illustrations that adorned the place labelled INDIA in round, gilded capitals. There he could see a sciapod, lying on its back, its one foot over its head. And there he could see the Indian mountains, populated with heathen tribes, and, above them, the golden mountains, overshadowed by dragons. He saw the altars of Alexander to the south and, to the south of those, an elephant with a castle on its back. What wonders there were in the world.

His quill hovered above the ink horn as his gaze returned to the altars built in ancient times by the old worthy, Alexander. The parchment of the map seemed, to Brother Bartholomew, like a mist over the true appearance of India. If only he could wave the veil aside with his fingers, so he could stand on the banks of the Ganges and see a land glimmering with the gems from the foothills of Paradise.

When St Bartholomew had reached India with Thomas the Apostle, he had discovered temples to the devils

Bartholomew: Skin on Skin

Astaroth and Berith. After he had drawn near the first temple, the demon within had gone out like a candle flame. His worshippers had fled to Berith to ask what had become of their god. Brother Bartholomew imagined Berith's idol looking like those illustrated in the books in the library: a hairy little man, with talons on his hands and feet, a beak like an eagle's and two pointed ears. Thus Berith explained to the worshippers that his kinsman Astaroth had lost his power because of a holy man called Bartholomew.

'How will we know him?' the people had asked the idol.

'You will know him by his black hair, his even nostrils, the flecks of white in his beard and his upright, noble bearing.'

'And what else?'

'You will know him by his white robe and white cloak, hemmed with precious purple stones and others of every colour. For twenty-six years he has worn those clothes and they have never changed.'

'And if we still do not know him? Is there another sign?'

'You will know him because he worships God a hundred times a day and a hundred times a night. You will know him because angels follow him everywhere and ensure that he is never hungry or tired. Bartholomew is always joyful. He knows the future. He speaks all languages and he even knows what I am saying to you now. If he wants you to find him, you will find him. And if you do find him, keep him away from me. I don't want to die like Astaroth.'

But Berith was banished too and St Bartholomew had converted many of the Indian heathens, both high- and low-born. In time, he had angered the King of India, who had ordered Bartholomew's death. It was said that, before he died, Bartholomew had been flayed.

The scent of cold rain on warm stone wafted in through the scriptorium window. Brother Bartholomew sat back from the map. Everything that ever was and ever would be lay before him. Some of it was represented in ink and some of it only implied. Thus he knew, without needing it drawn in ink, that somewhere his saintly patron, Bartholomew, was being skinned alive, while, somewhere else, he was sitting among the blessed awaiting the end of time.

Down in distant Britain too, on the bottom-most edge of the map and far from any of the great events of history, sat Brother Bartholomew, who washed his quill and rose as the bell tolled in the tower. He left the world map lying on its special stand. The parchment was creamy white, the ink pure black and the gilding as brilliant as the raindrops on the grass.

❖

Medieval manuscripts were copied unbound. Mostly, scribes worked on sheets already ruled using a stylus. Then the folded, inscribed sheets would be stacked in groups to form a 'quire' or gathering. These would now be sewn up along the vertical central fold and stacked with many other gatherings and bound, often between heavy timber boards, to form a book. It might finally be bound in leather and decorated with embossed designs or, for high-status manuscripts, a metal sheet, gems and ivory plaques.

Saints' legends survive in books like these. At the time of their writing, they were perceived by most Christians to offer spiritual nourishment. Readers pondered the words, while dwelling on scenes in word and image of horrific torture and death. Of course, some parchment products were not books. The Hereford Mappa Mundi, or World Map, is made from one large single sheet of parchment, almost the same size and shape it was when it was cut from the stretching frame. It has a hole from a compass point in the middle and a great scheme in ink of the world, its wonders and cosmic history within the circle, while, in the upper margin, Christ looks down in Judgement between a happy queue of blessed souls and a rabble of the damned tumbling into the mouth of Hell. The map may have been displayed in Hereford Cathedral for pilgrims visiting the shrine of St Thomas of Cantilupe.

In the Bible, Bartholomew is a disciple of Christ. Tradition holds that he evangelised in India, Ethiopia, modern-day Turkey and Iran, as well as Armenia. He is held to have been flayed before death and many artworks survive of the bare-sinewed saint holding his own skin on his arm.

By the later Middle Ages, Bartholomew's relics would be present among those of other well-known saints in any self-respecting cathedral's collection. A 1383 inventory of relics in Durham Cathedral, the home of Cuthbert's shrine, includes a hair from St Bartholomew, part of one of St Margaret's ribs, St Edward the Confessor's cape, a charred bone of St Lawrence and a bone of St Germanus. And if that sounds a little grisly, then at least many of these would have been encased in gold and rock crystal and adorned with gems and pearls.

Late medieval cathedrals and abbeys were massive buildings, full of sacred treasures, books and natural curios, as well as artworks, altars and chantry chapels. And these institutions held extensive domains, collectively vying with if not exceeding the crown in wealth and influence. I don't think we can overstate the sense of authority exuded by these ecclesiastical buildings, nor their debt to the cult of saints. If anything were to succeed in suppressing it, it would shake them to their very foundations.

September

Medieval calendar pages for September show bare-legged farm labourers ankle-deep in crushed grapes. The juice yielded by their treading feet would be poured into casks and fermented into wine. This was a natural miracle, like turning grain into bread or beer, and it promised warming sustenance through the winter. Now, when the moon is subject to Libra's weighing scales, it is time to consider ailments of the kidneys, hips and buttocks. As the days and nights match each other in length, we arrive at a liminal month between the harvest and the dearth.

In September's stories powerful saps rise, wild beasts roam and celestial surgeons break the skin of the firmament. We will meet Mary again, along with an apple from the Garden of Eden, and Ailbhe will run with the wolves. As autumn sets in, the medieval cult of saints shows itself to serve the body as well as the soul, and fill the map with havens for the faithful. But cracks are snaking over the paint of the holy statues, and a growing faction of dissenters would happily see them burn.

Marymas: From Eden to Golgotha

DIED 48
FEAST DAY: 8 SEPTEMBER

Abraham, ruler of the Israelites, had been walking in his orchard in Jerusalem, when God had appeared to him with a stem cut from the Tree of Knowledge. He asked Abraham to graft it to one of his own trees and guard it because it had a special destiny to fulfil. Abraham agreed, but God didn't tell him everything. He can't have, or the King would have kept a closer eye on his daughter.

Abraham bound the stem, borne from the Garden of Eden, to a strong rootstock and set it into the orchard's soil. There it grew, watched over by an angel.

One misty morning, Abraham's daughter crept down to the orchard and approached the blossoming tree. The guardian let her pass, the many eyes of its wings following her as she took one of the tree's flowers between finger and thumb and broke it off.

Snap.

At once, fragrance filled the air. The girl sniffed the broken stem hungrily until it touched the end of her nose.

Then the smell and the sap soaked into her skin, flowed down her body and conceived a child.

As the months passed, Abraham's courtiers saw that the unmarried girl was pregnant and tried to put her to death. More than once they tied her to a stake, piled wood around it and lit it with burning torches, but powers greater than theirs kept her safe, for the flames only turned into flowers and birds and spun away on the wind. No matter what the courtiers did, Abraham's daughter survived and, in due time, she gave birth to a son called Fanuel.

Years went by and the grafted stem grew into a tree much finer and more beautiful than any of the others in the orchard, and Fanuel grew into a man and inherited Abraham's throne. Each autumn, when the apple tree bore its crop, Fanuel would cut up the fruit and share it among the sick. The apples had healing powers but they had other powers too of which Fanuel was quite unaware.

One day, when Fanuel had finished slicing the apples, he wiped his knife on his thigh and the juice seeped through his robes and into his skin. There it bedded down between the layers of muscle and bone and conceived another child. Weeks passed. Sickness set in. Fanuel's thigh began to swell.

Nine months later, he gave birth to the child that had grown in his leg. When the baby girl appeared, the anguished Fanuel handed her over to one of his most faithful knights with instructions to take her to the forest, kill her and never breathe a word of his shame. And the knight did his best to obey. He took the baby out of the palace and rode towards the wilderness of the forest, but when he was among the trees, a dove appeared to him and told him to stay his hand.

The knight saw an eagle's nest high in a tree. He climbed up to it and laid the infant onto the pile of twigs and feathers, and though he left her there with nothing to nourish her or keep her warm, the little girl somehow survived.

There were times in her adult years when she dreamed of a feathered belly resting on her and the rhythm of steady breaths. Maybe this was the memory of the eagles that had looked after her in her infancy. If so, then they had left while she was still young, because by the time she was old enough to remember, her protector had become a stag with antlers like the spreading branches of a cherry tree. Every day he used his antlers to lift food to her treetop home. Every day, that is, until the arrival of the hounds.

The sight of the hounds was preceded by the sounds of baying and howling. She looked over the edge of the nest and saw her own dear stag running for his life, chased by dogs and followed by men on horseback. She began searching for a way out of the nest, flinging herself from one edge to the other, but finding no way of escape. Terrified for the safety of her friend, she buried her face and screamed into the sticks, feathers and leaves of the nest and the tangles of her own long hair.

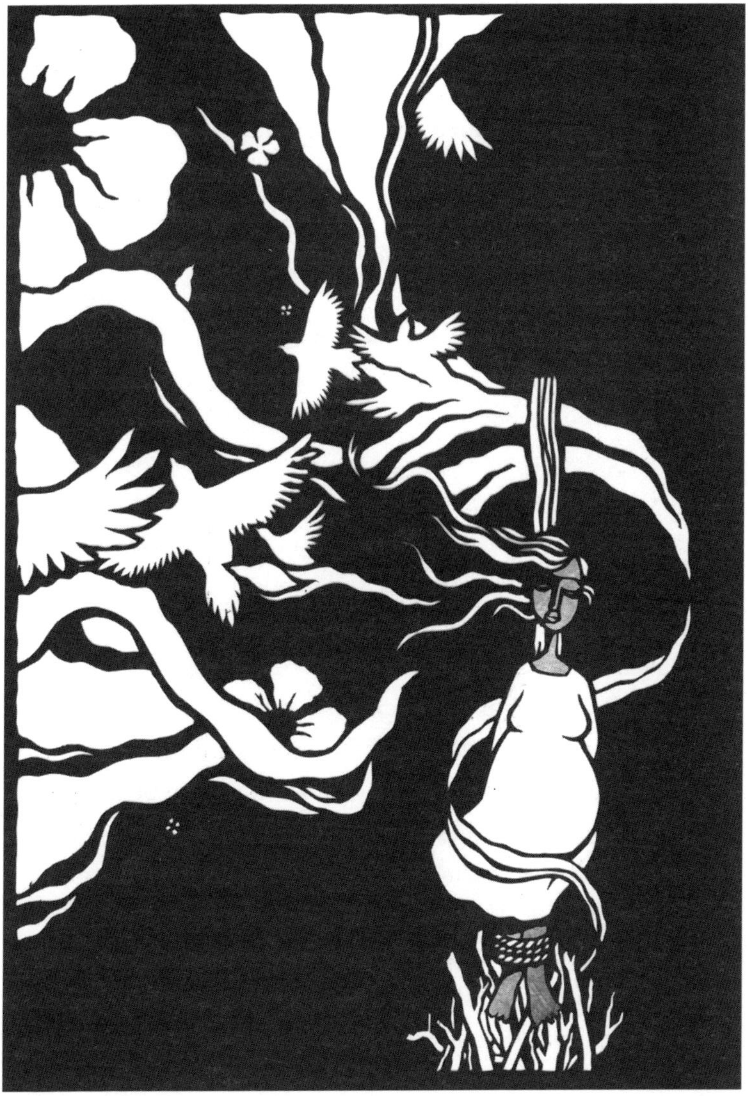

Mightsomeness

When she heard the crash of hooves under her tree, she raised herself to the edge of the nest and looked down again. Her stag was standing with his back to her, his flanks heaving, the horsemen advancing. The hounds had formed an arc of snarling jaws and the nearest of the men had raised his spear. She opened her mouth to let out a wail of anguish and heard herself speak for the first time in her life.

'Don't hurt him!'

'Who are you?' said the man, lowering the spear and looking up at the glaring, wild-looking girl. 'And where did you come from?'

She didn't answer straightaway. She was watching to make sure the stag had fled to safety. As she looked back at the group, her gaze passed over the face of one of the older men at the back. He was familiar.

'I am Anne,' she said, and her own words astonished her, not just because she had not known she could talk, but because until then she had never heard her own name. 'And I don't know who my father is, but my mother's just behind you. Tell him to get me down from this nest.'

The men lowered their weapons as the old man dismounted and walked up to the foot of the tree. She had been right, for he was Fanuel: the one who had gestated Anne in his thigh and sent her away to be killed.

Anne watched him climb with difficulty, but he managed all the same to help her from the nest and reach the forest floor. Then she was lifted up onto one of the horses and taken back to the palace. She would live there for many years and marry the man who had first entered the clearing. His name was Joachim.

When they were very old, God would work a miracle for Anne and Joachim, giving them a daughter whom they would call Mary. She was the last fruit Anne bore, though the child came quite out of season, and Anne would teach Mary how to read, pray and believe in wonders. When she was just old enough, Mary would have a little boy and, like his grandmother and his great-grandfather, he would not be conceived in the usual way.

Mary was the apple. She was the sweetness. In her lay a starburst of life that would show humans back to the Garden, if they did not wander away. But she would have to suffer, and so would her child.

When he was thirty-three years old, soldiers would fell the apple tree in Abraham's orchard. Carpenters would hew the wet timber and joint the beams to make a cross. And her boy's scourged body would be nailed to it in a place called Golgotha and left there till he died. And Mary would cry at the foot of the cross, so that the earth of that place soaked up her tears, along with her son's blood and the ancient sap of the apple tree.

❖

Though Mary is a saint, she seems, in the words of John Shinners, 'almost a fourth member of the Trinity'. And her status as a loving mother who had watched her son die a cruel death only enhanced the sense that she could relate to any human pain and would plead urgently on behalf of her devotees.

Stories sprang up around Mary and her mother, Anne, that had no basis in the Gospels. First, there were stories from the Apocrypha, which never made it into the official Scriptural canon and yet furnished Christians with tales of the life of the Virgin and the infancy of Christ. Then there were romances and miracle tales in vernacular languages, including the story retold above.

The Romance of St Fanuel is a thirteenth-century French story of the Virgin Mary, her mother St Anne and the workings of a grafted shoot from an apple tree in the Garden of Eden. To quote a lecture I attended at Bristol University in 2022 by scholar of medieval French literature, Miranda Griffin, the tale explores 'modes of reproduction that are not fleshly'. And when I discussed the story with Julian Luxford, art historian, he observed the similarity between the manner of Anne's gestation in the leg of Fanuel and that of Bacchus in the leg of Jupiter, according to the much older Classical tradition.

I have decided to offer the story of Fanuel and Anne for Marymas, which marked Mary's birth, because it concerns her genealogy, especially her relationship to her mother.

Marymas: From Eden to Golgotha

St Anne was the patron saint of medieval carpenters, who called the pale mixture of glue and sawdust they used to fill holes in wood 'St Anne's brains'. She was also held to have mothered three daughters – Mary Salome, Mary Cleophas and Mary the Virgin – by three different fathers, and all three Marys are painted side by side on a fifteenth-century altar screen in Ranworth Church, Norfolk, their infant children clambering over their legs. St Mary Cleophas has four sons, including a young St James the Great (whose shrine came to be at Santiago de Compostela) and St John the Evangelist, who would write a Gospel and receive a ring from Edward the Confessor. Another of her sons, Joses, is shown playing with a toy windmill.

Anne conceives the Virgin Mary by Joachim in old age and is often depicted teaching her how to read. This is perhaps how Anne was most widely understood: as the educator and early spiritual guide of Mary, who would, as a young adult, accept the task from the Angel Gabriel of bearing the Son of God. In so doing, she would set in motion a chain of events culminating in her son's death-to-end-all-deaths.

One of the most popular shrines in medieval Britain centred on Gabriel's 'Annunciation' to the Virgin Mary, celebrated on 25 March. Located in Walsingham, Norfolk, it was founded in 1061 when an English noblewoman called Richeldis had a vision of the house in Nazareth where the Annunciation had taken place and the Christ Child had been raised. After the vision, Richeldis replicated in timber the house she had seen. Known as the 'Holy House', it became the centre of an international cult and a major pilgrimage destination. While the Holy House does not survive, later pilgrim badges depict a pitch-roofed building with an Annunciation scene and the cult image of the Virgin and Child (known as Our Lady of Walsingham) inside.

Many symbols were associated with the Virgin Mary. The lily is perhaps chief among them. A very strange story concerning the lily may be found in the 'commonplace book' of a fifteenth-century English yeoman called Robert Reynes. The book is a collection of material Robert thought interesting or useful, including notes about finances, royal edicts, travel tips and many religious preoccupations, not all of which was strictly orthodox. Among these materials, Robert tells the story of a man who had no love of his childhood education. The only thing he retained was the 'Hail Mary' prayer, which quotes the words spoken by the Angel Gabriel in Scripture. The man would speak this prayer incessantly. When he died, Robert writes, the man was buried in the churchyard and a lily grew on his grave. It soon attracted attention, for the words 'Hail Mary' were written on each of its leaves. Of course, this aroused curiosity among the villagers, but this soon turned to suspicion. They decided to dig up the lily and went at the grave with their spades. The lily's root went very deep. The villagers dug down and down, trying to find the end so they could pull up the whole plant. They still hadn't found it when they reached the dead man's head. Then they brushed the earth aside and saw the lily's root was growing from inside his mouth.

Tales like these and *The Romance of St Fanuel* testify to the way in which rogue stories, along with sayings, traditions and beliefs, could sprout from the official rootstock. Mary, as one of the most popular saints, is a prime example of this tendency. The stories' symbolic objects – such as cherries, lilies and apples – shaped people's impressions of her fruitfulness, her purity and her status as a second Eve.

Ailbhe: Wolf Child

Died 528
Feast Day: 12 September

Legend has it that, in the days of Brigid, Patrick and Brendan, King Crónán of Ireland had coveted his servant, whose name was Sant. When she rejected him for another and became pregnant, Crónán had refused to let her raise the child near his own sons. His men had snatched him from her arms and left him under a rocky overhang. Ailbhe's infant hands had been cold when they left him, but the men hadn't noticed the yellow eyes of the wolf watching from further under the stone. Once they had gone, she had squeezed out of her den and wrapped her body around him, helping his pink mouth find her teats and waiting as he began to suck. At last, his fist had clenched on her fur. Hot wolf milk had warmed him and he had not died. She had raised him as one of her own.

Years later, and another she-wolf was in danger. Thorns were tearing at her nose and ears, and the muscles in her shoulders were burning. But the pain did not eclipse the terror forcing her on. Though the wolf was trying to stay close to her pack, she was falling behind. Under her grey fur, her unborn cubs bumped together in watery sacks, draining her energy and weighing her down like a bellyful of stones.

Blasts, baying, hooves crashing ever faster through the rusty sea of bracken, swallowing up her tracks in the black mud and bringing the hunt ever closer, louder and evermore thunderous, with panting breath.

She broke from the forest onto a plain, where she saw the fast-diminishing shapes of her family leaping into copses and hollows. Behind her, the hunt shattered the bank of yellowing hazel and the horsemen singled her out for pursuit.

Had the wolf followed the scent of her pack, she would have died. But now a new scent turned her head. She saw a man walking up from another part of the plain and something told her he had the power to keep her safe. Wheeling round on bog-sodden paws, she raced at him with every last fragment of her strength, while her pursuers wrenched their reins to follow her.

She was a big animal, even without the cubs inside her, but Ailbhe, now a grown man, didn't run away. Raising his staff, he shouted at the horsemen to stay back. They knew him by reputation and obeyed. Then he opened his arms and caught the terrified wolf as if she weighed no more than a cub. He wrapped his arms around her trembling body, making sounds in her ear that she understood. Under his hands, he could feel her pregnant belly.

'A wolf like you saved me when I was a child,' she heard him say. 'Go now, and raise your young not to harm people. You may always eat with us.'

When the wolf was ready, she left him, retreating to a place where she could deliver her cubs. And every day after that, when Ailbhe sat down to eat, she would bring them to see him and they would be fed from his table.

❖

The Irish Latin *Life of Saint Ailbhe of Cashel and Emly* probably dates to the twelfth century. It tells of how wolves raised him in his infancy and how, when he had grown to manhood, St Hilary of Poitiers educated him on the Continent. When they are living in Rome, Ailbhe celebrates his own ordination by bringing a heavenly feast raining down on the citizens that sustains them for three days and nights: 'Namely showers of honey, fish, oil, the whitest bread made of the best wheat and very young wine.' In another episode, apples fill the city all the way to its walls.

Back in Ireland, Ailbhe meets St David's pregnant mother and prophesies that her son will become a bishop and later he even baptises David. The text also relates how, when Brigid sat with Ailbhe on the Curragh of Kildare, she asked for wine to drink and, when he invited her to bring a cup, she said she didn't have one, so a brimming vessel appeared from heaven. Elsewhere in the text, Ailbhe provides St Brigid with a flock of a hundred white sheep and receives permission from St Patrick to convert the inhabitants of Munster, Ireland's southern province. In old age, he leaves the coast of Ireland on a mysterious boat, returning with a fruiting palm branch that he keeps with him till his death three years later.

Ailbhe's life is characterised by travel, wonder-working and a deep sense of spiritual community, both in Ireland and on the Continent. And perhaps this reflects a certain nostalgia on the part of its author for early Irish monasticism. When Irish monks had first left their homeland for missions to Britain and the Continent, led by saints like Aidan, Columba and Columbanus (the last of whom died in 615), they established monastic foundations wherever they went. These included Lindisfarne Priory in modern-day Northumberland, Luxeuil Abbey in eastern France, the Abbey of St Gall in Switzerland and Bobbio Abbey in northern Italy. In the early medieval period, these islands of Celtic Christianity were centres of manuscript production and artistic creation, as well as important stepping stones for pilgrims, especially clerics, travelling from north-western Europe to Rome and Jerusalem.

As the centuries passed, more and more churches and monasteries were built in Britain and the Continent by other missionaries and monastic orders. But these institutions still offered far-reaching networks of communication and travel, often transcending the political boundaries of the age.

Matthew Paris, the thirteenth-century historian of St Albans Abbey, who wrote and illustrated the history of Edward the Confessor and the Life of St Alban discussed in their respective chapters, also compiled a great history known as the *Chronica Maiora*, or 'Great Chronicle', which survives in two volumes in the Parker Library, Corpus Christi College, Cambridge. I first met it as an undergraduate looking for a dissertation topic and I struggled to believe I was allowed to study something so impossibly interesting. Now that it has been digitised, it is the most accessible it has ever been in all its eight centuries. Among the opening pages is an illustrated pilgrimage from London to Jerusalem. As the viewer travels further from home, there are spiky palm trees, volcanoes (with Etna on a fold-out flap for Sicily), camels, Jonah's man-eating whale and even a tortoise labelled *tortue*. And as Matthew's eyes scanned his finished scheme, perhaps he pondered all the books he might have written with a hundred more years to live, even if he confined himself only to illustrating and narrating the legends of all the saints represented by the institutions on each page. But what the illuminated journey also shows is how a man in thirteenth-century Hertfordshire could imagine himself, not without some accuracy, all the way to Jerusalem. The parchment pilgrim glories in the possibility of unimpeded travel within the territories claimed by Christendom, hopping like a child across a stony river from a pen-and-wash St Paul's to a hand-drawn Mont-Saint-Michel, to a Rome shown only as a river among churches, all the way to the Holy City, inland from a bottle-green sea.

Cosmas and Damian: Spiritual Surgery

Died 287/303
Feast Day: 27 September

Two men appeared in a cool, sparsely furnished room with ribbons of mist circling their ankles. It was as if, though the rest of their bodies seemed solid enough, their feet were in another world. The men's eyes passed over the three-legged stool, the pair of silk slippers and the bed enclosed on two sides by silvery drapes, until they came to rest on the man that lay in the bed. He was sleeping on his back, a white cap on his head and two linen-covered pillows under it. His hands lay on his chest, one on top of the other, and his shift was pale as his white skin. He was young, with tawny hair that curled from under his cap.

In all that stillness, his agitated breathing was loud, and no amount of incense could mask the smell of putrefaction.

The men, who had identical olive-skinned features and nimble-fingered hands, went to his bedside, drawing surgical instruments and a beaker of ointment from their shoulder bags and placing the items on the headboard.

Cosmas and Damian: Spiritual Surgery

The man's bedclothes were white, except for the topmost coverlet, which was red as cinnabar. Working together, the men took hold of the coverlet and white sheets and lifted them till they could see, by the blue light of the one high window, the reason why the man, an otherwise faithful devotee of the two saints, had been unable to visit their shrine for weeks.

The infection in his right thigh had set in so severely that much of his leg had turned the purplish green of hellebore. The two men, still supported by wreaths of mist, did not recoil, for they were familiar with such sights. Taking the instruments they needed, they began to cut through the dead flesh, passing each other tools and cloths for cleaning without having to speak. They performed their profession just as they had learned in Syria, many centuries before, and not once did their patient stir.

By the time they had finished, the sky beyond the one high window was red with sunset. They had bandaged the stump and lifted the amputated portion from the bed, wrapping it in cloths. They considered the man. The saint called Cosmas leaned to speak in his brother's ear.

'How should we replace it?'

Damian replied, whispering in return, and Cosmas nodded. Then they drifted from the room, silent as dusk, passing through the house unnoticed by the man's family members, who were sitting down to dinner and praying their kinsman would not die.

The saints travelled out across the empty street to the graveyard of St Peter ad Vincula, where the air was dark and crisp. Had anyone been watching, they would have seen, but not heard, the two men approaching a grave and lifting out a coffin without having to dig the freshly turned earth. They would have seen the men open the coffin and, working with the same swift efficiency as they had in the sick man's room, cut off the leg of the corpse within and replace it with the sick man's leg.

But nobody saw and they returned by the same route to the bedroom. There they attached the corpse's leg to their patient's thigh. When they had finished, there was no scar, not even a ridge, where the living flesh had fused with the dead, and soon the dead pulsed with blood and lost the chill of the grave. The saints drew the sheets over the man's feet and laid the red coverlet back. Then they disappeared, though the ribbons of mist that had hung around their ankles lingered for a moment, like the smoke of an extinguished candle.

A fresh breeze danced over the silvery drapes. After a time, the man in the bed took a deep breath and opened his eyes. He looked around for the first time in many days and sat up. Now he frowned and looked down at the covers. Then he folded back the red and white sheets and saw what lay beneath them. His mouth opened in amazement. He smiled, reaching out and stroking the skin. Then, laughing, he jumped out of bed and ran downstairs to his family.

Cosmas and Damian: Spiritual Surgery

Later that evening, at the advice of a priest, his brothers would take shovels to the graveyard and dig into the freshest grave. Opening the coffin, they would find the newly dead body of a man, who, according to the priest, had come to Rome from Ethiopia. They would see that, not long after his death, his leg, the skin of which was as dark as their brother's skin was pale, had been cut off at the thigh. And they would know where it had gone, for a severed leg lay in its place, white as milk, but for the purplish green flush of rot.

❖

Tradition has it that Saints Cosmas and Damian died as martyrs under Diocletian around 303 and lived in Cilicia in modern-day Turkey. They were brothers, educated in Syria, who became doctors, known as the 'silverless ones' thanks to their practice of never accepting money. One of their posthumous miracles concerns their replacement of a white man's diseased leg with the uninjured leg of a dead black man; a surgical transplant that reflects their professional skills and their posthumous sanctity, as well as lending itself to being depicted in art.

Cosmas and Damian may have been doctors in life, but they are not alone among saints famed for medical miracles. St Eligius (or, in French, Eloi) was a goldsmith from Limoges, in modern-day France, who died around 660. His trade had some bearing on his surgical abilities. He used his craft to cut off the foreleg of a possessed horse, change the shoe and reattach the leg. By the late thirteenth century, pilgrims to Eloi's shrine in Noyon could buy a souvenir in the form of a small square badge with an embossed image of the saint sitting beside an anvil, a hammer in his hand, and the horse standing in front of him. A figure behind the horse holds up a votive taper, or 'trindle', to be offered in thanks at the shrine.

Meanwhile, pilgrims to Thomas Becket's shrine could buy *ampullae* (vessels for carrying small amounts of water, tinged, it was said, with the blood spilled at his martyrdom in 1170. Some of these *ampullae* bear an inscription reading 'Thomas is the best doctor to the worthy sick'). This claim is substantiated by a miracle reported by one Agnes, a Canterbury woman who had suffered from a facial tumour so large it stopped her from eating. She was forced to hold a bowl under her chin to catch the pus dripping from her mouth. But when she drank from a Thomas *ampulla*, a writhing, devil-faced, insect-like creature, 'shaped like a red-hot coal, one and half inches long with a tail like a very sharp awl and crawling on four feet', fell from her lips into the bowl and vanished. Soon the tumour vanished too, and Agnes made a full recovery.

Many pilgrims suffering from mental illnesses sought help from saints. In the Middle Ages, however, their affliction was more likely to be seen as the work of the Devil. A 'demoniac' brought to the shrine of St Hugh of Lincoln on the night of the feast of All Souls spent the hours of darkness screaming so violently that she drowned out the celebration of the Mass. In time she fell asleep and woke up well and sane.

But the ultimate miracle was, of course, revivification – bringing a person back from the dead. A fifteenth-century woman called Alice Newnett, from the Wiltshire village of Mere, reported receiving a vision of the folk saint Henry VI after she had died of the plague. Having come back to life, she walked around in her funerary shroud for several days, perhaps to bear witness to the miracle.

Pilgrims returned to shrines year after year, sometimes day after day, looking for healing in mind and body. Perhaps it's no surprise, given the agonies and expense associated with contemporary physicians. Even if you could afford the bill, surgery was undertaken with limited pain relief, imbalances in the body's humours were addressed with such treatments as bloodletting, and cauterisation (burning) was likewise a method of stopping infection and unwanted bleeding. The efficacy of all these processes would also, it was believed, depend on which figure of the Zodiac was governing the moon. Indeed, when it came to dealing with bodily ailments, the supernatural was, by and large, a gentler and cheaper option. And, if you were lucky, the results might be quite spectacular.

Michael the Archangel: A Hole in the Head

FEAST DAY: 29 SEPTEMBER

The Archangel Michael alighted in the bedroom of the Bishop of Avranches and crossed the floor on shining, feather-shod feet. For the third time that month he approached the Bishop as he slept. The man roused, sensing he was no longer alone. Now he opened one eye.

As the Archangel knelt, his wings reached over them both. Then he began to speak.

'You know, Aubert, what I have to tell you. Twice I have visited you already and yet you fail to obey.'

The Bishop did not answer. He closed his eye and hoped the vision would disappear; not that wishing had worked before. The Archangel went on.

'I am the one with the shield and the sword. The one who sent Lucifer to the pit. I was there when Adam and Eve fled the Garden. I saw Cain murder Abel. I saved Noah as the floodwaters rose.'

The Bishop rolled over and put a pillow on his head. The Archangel kept on talking.

Michael the Archangel: A Hole in the Head

'It was I who guided the patriarchs through hostile lands. In Egypt, I passed over the homes of the Israelites and killed the firstborn Egyptians. I led the Chosen People to the Promised Land, flowing with milk and honey. I ordained the Temple of Solomon. I took the soul of Mary to Heaven and I guide the ship of the blessed over the ocean, overcoming all dangers, bringing it safe to shore.'

Now the Bishop's muffled tones came from under the pillow.

'You're a dream.'

But the Archangel Michael's voice, formed of the same heavenly wind and light that gave him shape, only strengthened over Aubert like a gathering storm.

'I am the sentinel of the New Jerusalem, with diamonds at its gates. I will stamp out the Dragon on Judgement Day. And still you ignore my request!'

Then the gigantic Archangel swept the pillow from the Bishop's head and thrust out a feathered arm, driving the tip of his finger into Aubert's skull, passing through hair, skin, flesh and bone, burning until it had made a deep hole.

'I demand that you build me a church on Mount Tomb, for your people are beset by wolves! Do not dare disobey! I will not ask you again!'

The touch of the Archangel's finger on the back of the Bishop's head made his vision crimson with heat, then white with freezing cold. He lay very still in the dark until he could be sure he was alone.

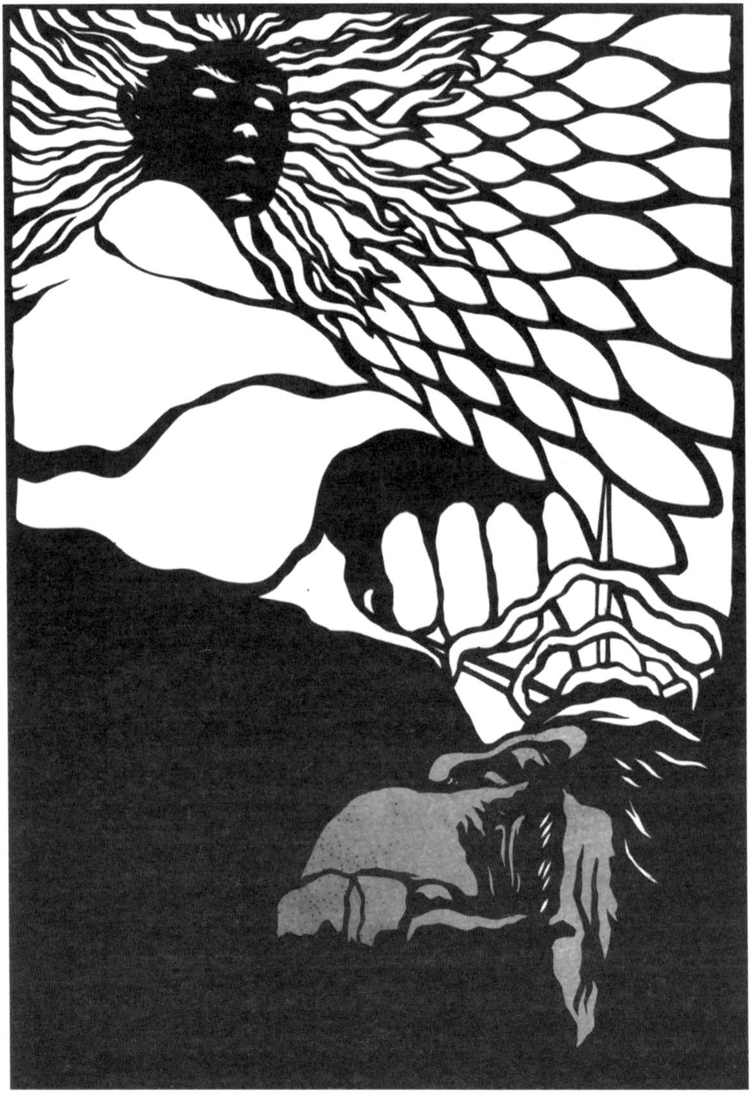

Michael the Archangel: A Hole in the Head

Aubert's usually disciplined mind turned somersaults. He put a hand to the back of his head and felt where the Archangel had pressed his finger. There was a soft patch where a disc of bone seemed to have disappeared from his skull. He could feel the blood pulsing under the skin. Aubert threw off the covers and got out of bed. Forgetting to put on his slippers, he ran downstairs and outside to the stables.

Though the sun had not yet risen, the Bishop threw a coat over his nightclothes, left his palace and travelled to the hill in the sea that they called Mount Tomb. Once it had been the home of a terrible giant, killed by the great King Arthur, but now it was empty. The tide was out, so Aubert crossed the sand and climbed to the summit. He searched, panting and gasping, till he could go no higher. And then, at last, he saw it, glittering as the sunrise charged the horizon: the transient footprint of a great church, blazing in dew, golden as the Archangel's wings. Here the Bishop would build the abbey.

As he committed the shape to memory, Aubert touched the soft part of his skull again. That morning the air tasted not only of the sea, but of something otherworldly too, of something that reached into the past and out into the future. From this day on, the hill would no longer be called the Mountain Tomb, remembered as a haunt of death and demons. Till its rocks crumbled to the sea, till the stars fell from the sky like flaming arrows, till the Archangel filled the heavens and finished what he had started at the beginning of time, driving his sword into Lucifer and destroying him once and for all, it would be called Mont-Saint-Michel.

❖

In the great cosmological epic in which every saint plays a part, St Michael strikes the final blow. In the Apocalypse, or Book of Revelation, he is the bearer of the scales of Judgement, wreathed in blazing plumage, the psychopomp who sails dead souls to the New Jerusalem, the armed angel who tramples the dragon. He became associated with several hill- or mountain-top shrines in medieval Christendom, including on Mount Gargano in Italy, the first to be designated as a holy site, the tidal island of Mont-Saint-Michel on the west coast of Normandy, and St Michael's Mount off the southern coast of Cornwall. Prior to its association with an angelic vision, the second of these had been known as Mount Tomb and long afterwards retained a legendary association with a diabolical giant killed by King Arthur (angels and demons share a taste for high ground). From the eighth century, it became the home of a monastic community, who received the Cornish Mount from Edward the Confessor as a satellite monastery.

The community at Mont-Saint-Michel owed its existence to the legend of the miraculous visitation of the Archangel Michael to Aubert, the Bishop of Avranches. Nevertheless, in fostering the early cult to the Angel, it met

Michael the Archangel: A Hole in the Head

with a problem. Michael, being an angel, had no earthly relics and, especially for the first centuries of the medieval cult of saints, devotees expected relics. When the monks of Mont-Saint-Michel discovered Aubert's bones in a box, complete with a skull bearing a telltale hole in the cranium, their prayers were answered. Historian Katherine Smith has argued that the relics of Aubert provided a 'surrogate body' for Michael, the community's patron saint, and this allowed, in the eleventh and twelfth centuries, the cult of the human saint to give wings to the angelic one. Two distinct characters emerged: the Bishop was the healer; Michael was the avenger.

In 1306, however, a costly gold sculpture of the Archangel was given to Mont-Saint-Michel by King Philip IV. By this time, the emphasis in medieval devotion was shifting away from relics and towards cult images like the one of the Virgin and Child in Walsingham, Norfolk. Smith argues that this new sculpture undermined Aubert's popularity. Hereafter, pilgrims started visiting the hilltop church for Michael alone, though it didn't stop one contemporary Norman grumbling that the Archangel was 'nothing more than a puff of air'.

As a doctoral student, I would often visit Pembroke College Chapel in Cambridge to look at a fourteenth-century English alabaster carving showing the Virgin Mary and the Archangel Michael. It's all on its own now, though it would probably once have been part of a series of devotional images. I have a particular fondness for medieval English alabaster narrative scenes. It might be the way they look like a giant Milkybar. Or it might be the traces of paint and gold leaf that hint at how colourful these objects were before time and cleaning stripped them to a mottled, buttery hue. But I think it's mostly the style of the holy figures, with their overlong fingers and overshort palms, their protuberant eyes and their small, melancholy mouths. I love their attenuated limbs, flowing drapery and docile expressions.

In this alabaster, the Archangel Michael stands with the scales of Judgement grasped in his left hand. He wears a cloak over what looks like a covering of scales or feathers. His legs are thin and sinewy, like the legs of a lanky adolescent. But he has a very grave responsibility. He is weighing a human soul.

A horned demon peers out of the weighing pan to Michael's left, one of its accomplices clinging on, trying to drag the scale down. But it's not working. A much less diabolical face peeps from the pan hanging on Michael's right, its owner small and alone. But their body is somehow heavier than those of both the demons. Look more closely and the reason emerges. A string of beads drapes over the arm of the scale above the little figure. They hang from the hand of the Virgin Mary.

The word 'bead' comes from the Old and Middle English verb *biddan*, meaning 'to pray'. Like Michael, Mary wears a cloak. Her right arm is lifting it up just enough to show that

Michael the Archangel: A Hole in the Head

she is protecting a naked human. The figure, childlike, does not even reach her chest. Here is the soul whose fate will be decided by the tipping of the scale. Mary's prayers, by means of the beads, have made the pan on her side heavier than the one on the side of the demons. For all her delicacy, she is a forceful advocate.

By her gestures, Mary looks to be in dialogue with Michael. He holds up his right hand in a reciprocal sign of acknowledgement. His alabaster fingers are characteristically long and thin, but, like the Virgin, his strength is implicit. In another scene, those fingers could be driving down on the head of a hapless bishop, boring a hole in his skull.

Today, a gold and glass reliquary in the Church of St Gervais in Avranches houses Aubert's skull. From the way the edge of the hole has healed, it looks as though it was made when its owner was still alive. It could be the result of trepanation, but perhaps it was put there by an angel.

In 1693, one Captain Matthias Bird donated a sculpture to the Ashmolean Repository in Oxford. It showed 'a figure in a coat of mail, sculpted from alabaster, which was once covered in gold leaf, holding a sword . . . in its right hand and, in its left, a pair of scales. The right pan of the scales shows a girl's face, the left shows the globe of the Earth.' This image, evidently of St Michael, was found, according to the antiquarian Herman Moll, by 'some labourers digging in a Quarry' near Caerleon. However, Moll can't work out who the image represents, suggesting the goddess Astrea. In the words of art historian Lloyd de Beer, 'parishioners across [pre-reformation] England would have been familiar with [Michael's] image, which abounded in wall paintings, sculpture and on screens in churches great and small. By 1660 this knowledge had been lost, or more accurately, it had been erased.'

The close of the Middle Ages, especially in England, is often dated a century or so earlier, when the populace received a blow to the head forceful enough to bring about a very specific collective amnesia.

Part Four

Clensing

❖

Owls do shriek where the sweetest hymns
Lately were sung;
Toads and serpents hold their dens
Where the palmers did throng,
Weep, weep, O Walsingham,
Whose days are nights,
Blessings turned to blasphemies,
Holy deeds to despite.
Sin is where Our Lady sat,
Heaven turned is to hell.
Satan sits where Our Lord did sway:
Walsingham, O, farewell.

> Attrib. Philip Howard,
> Earl of Arundel (died 1595),
> Bodleian Library, Oxford
> (MS Rawl. Poet. 291 fol. 16)

October

Now oxen drive a plough alongside figures scattering seed from a sling or seed-lip, while Scorpio twitches its sting at the sun. The heavenly body affecting the hips, buttocks, anus and genitals doesn't look much like a scorpion. Artists from north-west Europe, even those who had seen such creatures, had a deep loyalty to convention. When drawing Scorpio, they tended to opt for something like a tailed crab with a pig's face or even a kind of Hydra. Whatever they went for, the result was sinister.

With the October feast of Frideswide we meet a medieval saint whose shrine witnessed a massacre. And with Ursula we find a princess so committed to martyrdom that she will lead an army into death and supply Christendom with an inexhaustible stock of holy bones. The festivities are not over yet, for all the weather is on the turn.

Frideswide: The Hiding Place

DIED 727
FEAST DAY: 19 OCTOBER

Princess Frideswide hid with her companions for three winters in the forests near Binsey. Algar, the King of Leicester, had wanted to marry her, but they had fled down the Thames to escape him. Still, day after day, month after month, year after year, the King persisted in his quest. When he finally found the women, he flushed them out from the trees like sparrows. But God was on their side. Algar chased them all the way back to Oxford, when his horse threw him off and he broke his neck.

Frideswide, now free of her oppressor, lived as she had yearned to, founding a priory in Oxford, where women came together to pray and live in chastity. When she died, her followers laid her body in a shrine. It was still lying in Oxford three hundred years later when a posse of poor young Danes came, in turn, to hide in her church.

It was St Brice's Day, in the Year of Christ 1002, and the Danes had barricaded themselves in the sanctuary of St Frideswide's Church in Oxford. For all they were

Frideswide: The Hiding Place

battle-hardened, nothing had prepared them for this. The people of Oxford had woken in a murderous frenzy – and every town in the land had turned on its Danes. Safety was within that small building. All they could do was hope the people would not destroy their own church.

The building was built with timber and guarded its pale, breathless hideaways as well as the trees that had guarded its namesake. And just as Algar had been determined to flush her out, so too were the people of Oxford determined to flush out the Danes, even if they burned down the church of their princess saint.

Inside their wooden cage, the hostages smelled smoke. Darkness fell around them, plumes rising from pyres built against the exterior walls shadowing the windows. Fire seized the beams and ate up the panels in between.

Messengers came to King Æthelræd with the news that his plan had worked. He had known something had to be done, when Danish mercenaries had begun arriving in England: arrogant youths with their hair worn long on top and shaved at the back, pitching up in towns all over his domains, unable to speak the language and refusing to worship the Christian God. He had feared for his throne, he feared for his people and he feared for the faith. When word had reached him of a Danish plot to unseat him from his throne, he went to his counsellors. With daylight on their faces and righteous anger in their hearts, they had decided what to do.

Some of the Danes died in the church. Some fled on burning legs to beyond the city walls, chased by crazed townspeople with whatever weapons they had been able to lay their hands on. There, the men, most of them young, felt blows fall on the backs of their heads, their necks and their shoulders. They screamed for their mothers as they died.

Later, Æthelræd would give the people of Oxford money to repair the church they had damaged in the service of the King. One day, the bones of Frideswide, their princess saint, would be moved to a shrine on a stone pedestal carved with her face gazing in terror from between woodland leaves. The people would visit her, asking for help and healing for their ills. And, as the centuries passed, the city grew over the graves of the men their ancestors had killed.

❖

The medieval legend of St Frideswide (Friðuswīþ in Old English) enlivens the carvings on her medieval shrine pedestal in Christ Church Cathedral, Oxford. Placid female faces surrounded by carved woodland leaves stare from the stone between the archways; here, the princess and her companions hide in the forest from King Algar, King of Leicester. Look again. Is that fear in the watchful stone eyes?

The tale helps us identify with the women's plight, but it has a bearing on another story relevant to Frideswide, with

Frideswide: The Hiding Place

firmer factual foundations. We know there was a priory, including a church, dedicated to Frideswide in Oxford by at least 1002, and that was when a group of Danes, mostly young men, hid in the church to escape a mob of English townspeople. Their pursuers were even more ruthless than Algar.

At the turn of the first millennium, as part of the second wave of Viking incursions, small groups of Danes had settled in towns all over England. Unlike those who had arrived with the first wave and mostly inhabited the territory known as Danelaw, these new Danes would have been conspicuously foreign. They would also, for the most part, have been young men. On 13 November, 1002, they were rounded up and killed in what has become known as the St Brice's Day Massacre. In the entry for that year in the *Anglo-Saxon Chronicle*, the annalist explains that 'the king gave an order to slay all the Danes that were in England' and who were conspiring to unseat him.

Two years after the massacre, a Royal Charter from 1004 commemorated the renewal of St Frideswide's Priory. It had been destroyed during the 'most just extermination'. The charter records the events in Oxford in some detail. First, it names Frideswide's Priory: 'a certain monastery situated in the town which is called Oxford, where the body of the blessed Frideswide rests'. Then it explains why it needs royal support:

CLENSING

> Those Danes who dwelt in the aforementioned town, striving to escape death, entered this sanctuary of Christ, having broken by force the doors and bolts, and resolved to make refuge and defence for themselves therein against the people of the town and the suburbs; but when all the people in pursuit strove, forced by necessity, to drive them out, and could not, they set fire to the planks and burned, as it seems, this church with its ornaments and its books.

From our perspective, it's sadly ironic that the Danes hid there from agents of an oppressive king, when the dedicatory saint's legend tells of how she and her companions also sought sanctuary from a king. However, had her legend existed in that form at the turn of the eleventh century, holding the massacre on St Brice's Day might have held more meaning among the English than the death of the Danes in Frideswide's church. At least, that was Æthelræd's intention.

Historian Benjamin Savill has argued that Æthelræd and his counsellors chose 13 November, St Brice's Day, for a reason. The legend of St Brice, or St Brictius, was written down by Gregory of Tours around a century after the saint's death in 443. It relates how Brice succeeded St Martin as Bishop of Tours, but only as a curse to punish Brice for his youthful arrogance and vanity, for, as we will discover in November, St Martin's were big boots to fill. The people of

Tours became mutinous, and Brice did penance to cleanse himself of the sins of his youth, but still the citizens rose up to oust him from the bishopric. He fled to Rome, only returning after seven years to reclaim his episcopal throne and rule wisely until his death.

Savill suggests that Æthelræd chose St Brice's Day in the hope it would reflect favourably on himself. In 993, in the wake of prominent Scandinavian attacks, Æthelræd had acknowledged what he called the 'ignorance' of his youth. Later, he had performed public penance. He was likewise operating in the shadow of his predecessor and half-brother, Edward 'the Martyr', who had an active saintly cult. The late tenth century had seen concerted religious reforms, including a 'renewed emphasis on the cult of saints', which had made other saintly feasts more prominent in the collective imagination. When Æthelræd or his advisors got wind of a Danish conspiracy to seize the throne, they might have hoped to take advantage of the parallels between Brice and the English king.

The *sanctorale*, or view of time through the lens of saintly feasts, overlaid the year with holy histories. It would have provided a way of bringing two stories together: one from the Christian past and one from the Christian present. Choosing St Brice's Day might have been an attempt to manage the narrative around the killing of the Danes. At the very least it ensured it wasn't coupled with the feast day of a martyr or, worse, a group of martyrs. Perhaps the government hoped that the killings would be seen by posterity as a necessary measure to protect an anointed servant of God.

If Savill is right, then Æthelræd was unsuccessful in his aim. Eleven years after the massacre of the Danes, Sweyn Forkbeard seized the throne from Æthelræd. He would regain it before his death in 1016 and his son Edmund Ironside would succeed him, only to be killed in the same year and the English throne lost to Cnut. At least, as you will read in late November, some Anglo-Saxon kings could wreak their vengeance on the Vikings from beyond the grave.

Later Norman historians would condemn Æthelræd as a weak, useless and cruel king and his murder of the Danes would be used in support of this portrayal. These histories would also say his son Edmund had been stabbed to death while sitting on the toilet. Indeed, in the thirteenth century, Matthew Paris would even illustrate Edmund in his *History of Saint Edward the King* sitting in a stone privy with a spear through his chest and his hose hanging ignobly round his knees.

However, the Danes killed in the St Brice's Day massacre were not consigned to complete oblivion. In 2008, the bodies of at least thirty-five men and boys, most of them aged between sixteen and twenty-five, were discovered in an excavation in the grounds of St John's College, Oxford. The mass grave lies outside the medieval city walls in a prehistoric henge of the kind often used as execution cemeteries in later Anglo-Saxon England. The skeletons bear wounds consistent with having been brutally murdered from behind. Some bones are even charred. DNA analysis showed the men to have had roots in modern-day Denmark and radiocarbon dated their burial to the turn of the eleventh century.

On St Brice's Day, 2023, I went to St John's College to take part in commemorations of the massacre. The College unveiled a realistic reconstruction of the head and shoulders of one of the young men. Anthropologist and forensic facial reconstruction expert Caroline Wilkinson spoke on the research that underpinned her team's choices for the likeliest forms of non-bony features like lips and ears. The man that emerged from her laboratory has sandy hair and blue eyes, a square jaw and a wide brow. His face is serene. I tried to imagine how he would have looked laughing and joking with his friends. I'd seen him before, I realised, in some bar or lecture hall. Then I felt a pang of sadness, thinking of the same men fighting for their lives in St Frideswide's Priory. The saint's face among the leaves looks just as serene, just as empty of expression. For her and the Danish man alike, the story enlivens the image. It gives it power. You might almost be forgiven for thinking life resided within.

Ursula and Cordula: 11,000 Dead

Died c. 380
Feast Days: 20 and 21 October

The eel vendor squinted at the girls from under the brim of her hat. They had already been assembling in ranks when, in the drizzling dawn, she had heaved her barrow from the Rhine to the marketplace in the heart of Cologne. Now, they were transforming the usually dismal square into a bed of bodies enrobed in close-fitting bodices and skirts, their pale faces serene beneath foreheads domed and white as pork knuckle-bones, their braided hair snaking from their heads and over their pale, bare shoulders.

The crowd was enormous. It spilled out of the main square and down the lanes and alleyways. The eel vendor, minding her heap of silvery wares, had never seen so many people in her life, not least on a single day.

As the crowd swelled, she saw, walking up from the river where their boats had been mooring since dawn, yet more strangers. Many were noble and now the town was teeming with so many shining, carefully groomed faces that she could hardly see a friend among them.

Ursula and Cordula: 11,000 Dead

Her customers were queuing up now. They looked like the servants of the nobility flooding the square, though they were finely enough dressed themselves. Using a board fixed to the back of her barrow, she picked up each eel and drove a nail through its head. Then she cut below the neck and peeled back the skin. The fishes whipped and writhed as, having pulled out the nails, she dropped them into the servants' bags.

But then a peal of trumpets and crashes came from the direction of the city gates, along with shouting, screams and more blasts. The crowd of women and hangers-on trembled like a spider's web. Everywhere, voices called:

'Huns!'

The eel vendor knew about the Huns. They were an invading army pushing west with no care of what or whom it destroyed. They had finally reached Cologne. She began thinking how best to escape. Somewhere nearer than the gates but not yet at the square, horseshoes clattered on stone, bringing more screams and more shouts.

The eel vendor's home was in the direction of the gates. She would not find safety there, but there was another part of the city she knew just as well. When men on horses appeared from one of the lanes, trampling the crowd, raising bows and shooting arrows into it, she abandoned her barrow of eels and fled.

Pushing through the crowds, she saw how, everywhere, the girls had started kneeling down, holding each other's hands and raising their arms, calling to be killed by the soldiers' arrows and swords. And the soldiers were picking them off one by one.

One of the young women, who wore an especially fine dress, had climbed onto a cart and was gazing around at her thousands of companions. The leader of the Huns, who wore a great black helmet, made his way towards her, his mouth open in an ecstatic grin. When she shook her head at him, her chin thrust out, her arms folded, rejecting whatever it was he was saying, he raised his bow. Then she opened her arms and looked up at the sky.

The eel vendor averted her eyes. She had to get away. Struggling between the bleeding, dying bodies of the women and their endless entourage, she made for the lane that would take her to the river.

Blood flowed into the water as the boats of the strangers waved in the current like long brown leaves. The eel vendor reached one and climbed aboard, squeezing into the cabin. She crouched in the dark. The soldiers would not find her here. Then she heard a small voice from the shadows.

'I should be out there.'

The eel vendor gasped. Peering through the gloom, she made out a pale shape curled at the back of the boat. The figure's hair was long, flaxen and arranged in a web of braids, her forehead was domed and her pale shoulders were bare.

'I should be dying with them,' the girl whispered. Then her body jerked towards the outside.

Ursula and Cordula: 11,000 Dead

'No,' said the eel vendor, stopping her with a hand. 'You have escaped. You are safe.'

'Our princess, Ursula; she is showing us the way.'

'I do not think you should follow her. I think you have done the right thing by hiding.'

Outside the boat they could hear a female chorus praising God as the soldiers picked them off one by one.

'How many of you are there?'

'Eleven thousand virgins, led by Princess Ursula. Twenty-six thousand if you count our followers. We were returning to Britain from a pilgrimage to Rome. We would have been home in a few days.'

The eel vendor thought back to the richly clad girl who had been killed by the leader of the Huns.

'Ursula is dead. I saw her.'

'Then she wears a true crown now.'

'And you could go home anyway.'

For a long time, the eel vendor and the girl said nothing, but listened to the massacre and breathed the iron-tinged air. Then the older woman said:

'What's your name?'

'Cordula.'

'Stay here until the soldiers have gone. I'll look after you, Cordula. You're going to be safe.'

She made sure the girl didn't leave the boat for the rest of that day and into the night, while, beyond the boat, the killing seemed never-ending.

Clensing

The eel vendor hadn't meant to fall asleep. When she opened her eyes, it was morning and the girl had gone. Silence lay on Cologne now. The eel vendor went out and scoured the heaped bodies for Cordula's face. It was hard to find her, there were so many and they all looked so alike, but eventually, there she was. The young woman must have died that morning, for her face was not so grey as those of her companions. She lay beside the body of her leader, Ursula. Cordula's mouth was still smiling and raindrops made tiny domes on the whites of her open eyes.

❖

Several versions of the Ursula story survive. *The Golden Legend* tells of a Christian British princess agreeing to marry a pagan prince, but *only* if he receives baptism and *only* if she can prepare herself spiritually for her wedding night with a pilgrimage to Jerusalem via Rome and, then, *only* if she can take ten other virgins like herself, each with a following of a further one thousand virgins. He agrees and the women assemble and set off. The army journeys across Europe, picking up followers along the way, including her betrothed, and their ranks swell to 26,000. They attract the attention of the terrifying Huns, and Ursula receives a prophecy that they will be slaughtered in Cologne. On the return journey, she leads her holy army to the city on the Rhine and there, as divinely promised, they become martyrs. When the leader of the Huns offers to spare Ursula's life if she gives herself to him in marriage, she refuses and he shoots her in the neck. The feast of all but one of the martyred virgins was held on 21 October. The feast of Cordula, however, who, according to legend, hid in one of the company's boats and only emerged to be killed the next day, was celebrated on the twenty-second.

Another version of the story, which was circulating at the same time as *The Golden Legend*, can be found in the popular *Brut* legend, concerning the deep history of Britain. It tells of Ursula and the eleven thousand virgins setting sail from the coast of Britain to become wives for a military colony in Armorica, the future Brittany. When a storm sweeps their ship off course, they end up in Cologne, where the pagan kings Wanis and Melga put them all to death.

In the *Golden Legend* tradition, Ursula amplifies the *virtus*, or manly power, of the holy virgin by becoming a kind of military leader. The text describes the members of her troop as followers of a 'new knighthood'. Their pilgrimage is thus an act of sacred soldiery, ending with their deaths in Cologne.

The cult's origins are unclear. It may have begun with the execution of a smaller number of holy Virgins, according to a fourth- or fifth-century inscription. However, an eighth- or ninth-century text upgrades that number to several thousand and specifies that they were killed by the Emperor Maximian. In 1155, workers unearthed bones probably belonging to a Roman burial ground. These were identified as the skeletons of the virgins, but the many name plaques, which included men and children, may have led to the idea that the virgins amassed a following that swelled their ranks even more.

In 1135, the basilica of St Ursula was built on the site where the bones had been found and the relics stored within the church. While Cologne retained most of the bones, others were taken for veneration elsewhere. This might sound like an authenticity nightmare, but it was said that impostors' bones would be supernaturally ejected if they infiltrated those of the eleven thousand. In churches across Christendom, reliquary busts were made to store the bones, and some churches even displayed them in ranks, the women's blond braids twisting under veils and headdresses, their white faces inclined this way and that, bearing meek expressions of piety. A miracle said to have occurred in Esrum in Denmark tells of how, one Christmas morning, thirteen reliquary heads delighted the monks by bursting into song.

In the November of 1501, England welcomed a Spanish princess called Catherine of Aragon. When her ship had docked at Southampton, she had been accompanied by eleven English women of the upper nobility all dressed alike, along with a larger company of 'knyghts wyves'.

Ursula and Cordula: 11,000 Dead

They were intended to make Catherine look like Ursula with her eleven thousand virgins. On London Bridge, they met another St Ursula tableau. Catherine then processed through the streets of London to her betrothed, Prince Arthur Tudor, the brother of the future King Henry VIII. Thus, embodied by Catherine and Arthur, the legendary British princess would marry the legendary British warlord. The pageantry elevated both figures and made one into an honorary Briton.

The pageantry surrounding Catherine's arrival in England shows yet again how saints' legends could help convey politically important ideas. But Arthur would die young and she would marry his brother, the future King Henry VIII. His marital and dynastic ambitions would, in time, overshadow the political usefulness of the cult of saints. Then the controversies that had existed since its genesis would find expression in reform.

November

November calendar pages show bristling herds of pigs enjoying the fallen beechnuts and acorns on the forest floor. Above, we find Sagittarius, the astral centaur, leaping with his bowstring drawn and his arrow ready to fly. The moon in Sagittarius governed injuries including animal bites and broken bones.

The last day of October, Hallowe'en (All Hallow's Eve), heralded the feast of All Saints or All Hallows on the first day of November. But that night the 'dead-bell' would toll till morning, ringing in the day of All Souls. It was the feast for those who had died without being raised to the sainthood and who might even now be suffering the torments of Purgatory.

It was believed that praying for dead souls could lessen their pain. The wealthy paid for 'chantry' chapels, where priests would say regular masses for their souls. The lowly dead prayed for each other, as suggested by the words of John Mirk, a homilist active at the turn of the fifteenth century. He tells of a man who lived beside a churchyard and would pray fervently for the souls lying in it whenever he passed through that place. Even when he fell foul of a local mob and was being chased through the churchyard, he remembered to kneel and pray: 'And anon therewith all the churchyard rose full of bodies, each one with an instrument of his craft in his hand and drove away his enemies.'

The year is decaying, and with it the cult of saints. With the scurrilous tale chosen for St Martin, we will explore the medieval delight in pairing obscenity with sanctity and differentiate that delight from the subversive intentions of reform. Then we will discover that, though the spiked wheel of legend does not break Catherine, no angel saves her images from iconoclasm in real life. And when at last a royal commissioner arrives in Bury St Edmunds to dismantle its internationally famous shrine, he will laugh at the small box of nail clippings long treasured by the monks.

Martin: Four Wishes

Died 397
Feast Day: 11 November

That morning, the housewife's husband had come running home from the fields early, bearing the news that his incessant prayers, his endless everyday oaths, to St Martin had brought the saint to his side with news that would change their lives. The farmer had hugged his wife, lichenous beard brushing wimple, and told her how he had been rewarded for his devotion with a gift of four wishes.

'Four wishes from Saint Martin, my dove!' he said, with a waft of ditches.

She had not believed him. She had brushed the flour from her hands and played along with his joke.

'Dear husband, haven't I loved you and served you all my life? Haven't I made your food and kept you satisfied? We should share these wishes.'

He gaped. Then he stuck out his chin and said,

'Don't take me for a fool! You'll go wishing for daft things like spools of hemp. Why, for all I know you might turn me into an ass!'

Clensing

'I promise I'll not change your nature by my wish,' she answered.

He thought for a while, then said:

'You may have the first wish, then. But make us proud with it.'

The housewife turned away. *St Martin indeed!* She did not know why her husband was playing this game and assumed he was drunk. If he was, then he deserved no quarter from her. Staring down at the length of dough she had been kneading before he came in, she made her wish.

'Well, my love, what I would like more than anything is for you to be covered from head to toe in cocks: on your head, arms, feet and sides, your belly, your back and your buttocks. I want them sticking out of your face. And I want them hard as pokers. Then, you'll look like the prick you are.'

Behind her came a strangled cry and a burst of popping sounds. She turned back to face him. Her eyes fell to his feet, then wandered up his bowed legs to his belly, then on to his chest, shoulders and face. And wherever her eyes rested she saw that her wish had come true. Her husband of near forty years was transformed almost beyond recognition. Penises split the threadbare fabric of his hose. They poked from under his armpits. They peeped from under the ample flesh of his neck. Penises, pintels and pilcocks, short, long and bent, young, old, pale, bronzed and mottled, adorned his muddy form. From every bit of flesh he had, hung a cock.

The farmer gazed down at his body and ran his misshapen hands over his face and head. His weather-tired eyes filled with tears.

'You've used the first wish for this?'

The housewife, no less aghast, tried to brush off her mistake.

'Why, what a handsome creature you've become,' she said, reaching out to him. Then she added, 'Your one pecker never was enough.'

He pushed her away, stamping his foot with a force that made his new body-parts shake. Then, from a mouth only half visible, he spoke bitter words of vengeance.

'If that's how you want it, wife, then may you be covered all over with fannies back to front, side to side and in between and as many as my willies.'

More popping sounds, and the couple stood gazing at each other in dismay. Now it was the housewife's turn to raise a trembling hand. She touched the skin under her wimple. She fingered a tangle of hair and inner-cheek folds and, within those, an opening like a little mouth. There was nothing else it could be. There was a nether wicket on her head.

And now her floury fingers roamed the rest of her face. They found, where her eyebrows had been, two more, one younger and neater, the other sparsely haired and as loose as if it had delivered eighteen babies. And she knew what each of those felt like. She'd had both in her lifetime.

Clensing

And now, by the strange sensitivity of the skin under her sleeves and shift, she could tell that, wherever there had been a spare stretch of flesh, and her body had much of that, many more of the squirrels had set in.

She glared at her husband and he stared back, forlorn and ridiculous. Loose flesh batted his temples as he shook a head as richly adorned as the head of one of his long-horned cows.

'I wish our privates would go away,' he said, then his wife threw up her hands. Straightaway their third wish came true.

'Oh no,' he said.

The housewife eyed her husband. His cocks had gone, but alarm now stretched his eyes, as his hand moved to his crutch. And even without touching it, she could sense that the place between her legs that had, in her life, brought her rather more pain than pleasure, was smooth as the skin of her knee. And she understood that every prick and purse they ever had between them had now vanished: every single one.

'You have one last wish from your saint,' she said. 'So, husband, what will it be? A lifetime of gold and roast suckling pig? Or your old rod and my tired quim back where they belong?'

❖

Martin: Four Wishes

Nowadays, St Martin of Tours is remembered as France's great evangelist, rather like Patrick for Ireland. Indeed, Patrick's *Life* by Jocelyn of Furness even has the saint educated by Martin. As a historical figure, Martin is held to have been born in modern-day Hungary and served as a soldier in the Roman army. When he converted to Christianity, he evangelised the Baltic peninsula. He then joined St Hilary at Poitiers, Gaul, and subsequently founded a monastery at Ligugé. In 371 he became Bishop of Tours. He is remembered for standing up to heresies, including Priscillianism, which saw all earthly matter as inherently evil, and Arianism, which we touched on in August, in relation to St Germanus.

The details of St Martin's life and miracles were written down at the turn of the fifth century by one of his followers, Sulpicius Severus. This is the source of Martin's most famous miracle, performed when he was still a soldier and not yet baptised. It takes place during a brutally cold winter. Martin passes through the gates of Amiens, wearing nothing but his cloak, because he had been giving away all his clothes to those dying from the cold. Then he sees a homeless man begging for help from passers-by and he does not know, at first, what to do. If he undresses any more, he'll be naked. But then he has an idea. Using his sword, he cuts his cloak in half, giving one half to the suffering man and keeping the other to cover what he can of his body. The narrator describes the shame of the onlookers, who realise 'they could have clothed the poor man without reducing themselves to nakedness'. That night Christ appears to Martin in a dream. The Son of God, wearing the part of the cloak Martin had given away, quotes his own words from Scripture: 'Amen I say to you, as long as you did it to one of these my least brethren, you did it to me' (Matthew 25: 40).

A piece of cloth held to be the half of the cloak retained by Martin was his primary relic in the Middle Ages and resided in his shrine at Tours. Tradition has it that the word 'chapel', as a place to house relics, owes its origins to the transference of the name for Martin's 'little cloak' – or, in Latin, *cappella* – to the small structure built to protect it. In Tours, this holy relic was a stopping-off point for pilgrims travelling to Santiago de Compostela. It was also used as a royal banner in times of war and a holy object on which the kings of France even swore oaths. The feast of St Martin, or Martinmas, remains, in some countries, a day on which to eat roast goose. At the very least this luxurious meat indicates his importance.

So how could such a saint end up granting wishes to a couple with a genital fixation? In seeking an answer to this question, we should note that the story is not unique in medieval Christian culture for combining the sacred and profane. For instance, the carved bosses of Norwich Cathedral depict flagrant nudity, even rape. And in the Rutland Psalter, from *c.* 1260, marginal illustrations of naked men riding dragons bareback and female centaurs nursing their children dance and jig around the holy Psalms. The medieval badge trade also dealt in vulvas in pilgrims' garb, hoods stuffed with phalluses, and women riding penis-ended brooms.

St Martin's Four Wishes is an example of a Continental French *fabliau érotique*, a genre that flourished from the end of the twelfth century to the start of the fourteenth and dealt in lusty priests, gormless husbands and sexually insatiable women. It also featured the odd saint. The *fabliaux* have relatives in Chaucer's *Canterbury Tales* – see the Miller's Tale – and German poems like *Der Rosendorn* in which a vagina leaves its virginal host and begins an argument with her about what men really want.

Fabliaux érotiques, 'the most scandalous and irreverent poetry in Western literature', according to the first, very recent and brilliantly translated compendium by Nathaniel Dubin, often poke fun at more genteel genres, inverting the conventions of courtly literature and fine love espoused by knights and ladies. In the case of *St Martin's Four Wishes*, we might see the poem as a comic response to a miracle reported by a rustic devotee. It does not mock St Martin himself, it mocks the gullible peasant who invokes a saint with every breath and listens too much to his wife. Near the start of the poem, we read:

> The peasant set out on a certain
> Morning, as was his wont, to plow.

He'll not forget Saint Martin now.
'Saint Martin!' he cried out, 'Geeyup!'
And that's when Saint Martin showed up.

When his wife makes her wish, we read:

> Then as soon as the woman spoke,
> Hundreds of pricks began to poke
> Out all over. Penises grew
> Around his nose and mouth, too.
> Some pricks were thick, some oversized,
> Some long, some short, some circumcised,
> Curved pricks, straight pricks, pointed
> And hardy . . .

The list goes on. And the lesson of the story is obvious, isn't it? In case of any doubt, the *fabliau* serves it to us on a plate: when a man lets 'his wife's judgement sway his views / Calamity often ensues'.

Profanity in this context inverts the sacred and laughs at the result, making the peasant and his wife the butt of the joke. Though, as the scholar of medieval literature Ann Marie Rasmussen recently pointed out to me, the moral of the story misses the point, which is so often the case that it might well have a note of irony: the story ridicules the man for being the inversion of the moderate, rational medieval male ideal. Inversion is different from subversion; that comes later, and with considerably less hilarity.

Martin: Four Wishes

The Catholic politician Thomas More wrote the satire *A Dialogue Concerning Heresies* in 1529, six years before being executed at King Henry VIII's orders. More's character the Messenger tells the story of a shrine to St Walery in Picardy, France, famously effective at healing the genitals. He describes how the altar was hung all about with wax votive offerings in the shape of miniature genitalia. The *Dialogue* brushes off criticism of these few follies and harmless abuses; they were not representative of the whole.

A contrary view is offered by the *The Popish Kingdom*, a post-Reformation polemic against what it saw as Catholic follies. In it, the feast of St Martin is set apart as a time of drunkenness:

> To belly cheer yet once again doth Martin
> more incline,
> Whom all the people worshippeth with
> roasted geese and wine:
> Both all the day long and the night, now each
> man open makes
> His vessels all, and of the [grape] oft times the
> last he takes,
> Which holy Martin afterward alloweth to be
> wine,
> Therefore they him unto the skies extol with
> praise divine:

> And drinking deep in tankards large, and
> > bowls of compass wide,
> Yea by these fees the schoolmasters have profit
> > great beside.

Thus, what for one theologian might represent harmless folly, to another represented a gateway into vice. For reformers, the bawdy and comedic – the drunken clergy, superstitious farmers, the nuns hoarding penises and the defecating, farting mob – had become a threatening reflection of a church falling to ruin.

Edmund: Aelwine the Hairdresser

DIED 869
FEAST DAY: 20 NOVEMBER

Wind whistled through the great stone basilica as Aelwine, a lay convert, stepped up to Edmund's tomb. Praying under his breath, he braced his palms against the lid and, with great effort, pushed it aside.

Aelwine gazed down at the body of Edmund. He touched the thin red line on the dead King's neck, the only trace of where the Danes' axe had cut his head from his shoulders. Stooping and studious, Aelwine now drew a comb from the pocket of his cloak. Lifting off the King's crown, he ran its tines through the hair that lay flat against the papery skin. Despite the centuries that had passed since his death, Edmund's locks remained brown as a beechnut. As Aelwine brushed them, the comb lifted and laid the sparse strands in orderly lines. The hairs had grown too long since Aelwine had last been in attendance, so he brought out a small pair of shears and trimmed the hair back to its usual length. Then he did the same for Edmund's moustache and the eyelash-like curls in his cold, oval nostrils. The hairs quivered with the slow breaths of the diligent, devoted Aelwine.

Edmund's martyrdom had occurred over a hundred years ago, when the first Danish invasions had harried the people of Britain. In those days the King had ruled the folk of East Anglia and had refused to pay tribute to the violent Lord of the Danes, whose name was Hingvar. For that, his soldiers had stormed Edmund's royal hall, dragged him from his throne, stripped him of his kingly cloak and bound him to a tree. Then they had shot so many arrows into Edmund's back, thighs, calves, buttocks and neck that the new shafts had dislodged the old and some had even driven right through his body. Finally, one of the soldiers had cut off Edmund's head.

When Aelwine had finished attending to the saint's hair, he held up the comb and removed the little hairs that clung to it. Holding them tight between neat fingers, he put away the comb and shears and withdrew a small box. Using the thumb and index finger of the same hand with which he held the box, he twisted off the lid. Flexing light from the church's triangular windows picked out the curves of more hairs inside. He dropped in the new hairs and twisted the lid back on.

Now Aelwine unlaced Edmund's robe and revealed the body. Though still and cold as a monument, it had suffered no corruption, nor did it smell. Aelwine soaked a cloth in holy water from the font and washed Edmund's skin. He

Edmund: Aelwine the Hairdresser

began with his neck, where the thin red line lay like stitching, and worked down to the milk-white soles of his feet. The wind went on whistling and the attendant's breathing was deep. Now he imagined what it would have been like to have tended Edmund's body, teasing briars from his hair and washing blackberry stains from his temples, on the day it had first been laid in its tomb.

Once the Danes had killed Edmund they had taken off in their boats. But before leaving they had performed one last act of vengeance. When the English came to collect their king's body and give it a Christian burial, they could not find its head. They searched everywhere, calling for their king, spreading out across the fields and fens, guiding their boats down the waterways, determined that his corpse should be buried whole. But the Danes had hidden it well and they thought they might have to give up.

Suddenly the searchers heard King Edmund's voice answering their cries. It was coming to them on the wind blowing from the direction of a spinney thick with brambles and blackthorn:

'I'm here! I'm here! I'm here!'

Running to it, they found the head deep in the thicket, protected by a wolf.

The wolf did not attack them when they lifted the heavy head from between its paws. The great fen beast even followed them to the place where the King's body

CLENSING

lay and watched as they placed the head against the neck. Then the two parts had fused together, leaving a thin red line where the blade had struck, and the wolf had gone back to the wild. Thus the Danes' vengeance had failed.

With the same shears he had used for Edmund's hair, Aelwine trimmed the corpse's nails. *Snip. Snip. Snip.* The clippings went into the box as well. He would return it to the treasury when he had finished: something for the pilgrims to venerate alongside the shrine, not that they came in their old numbers anymore. It was the Year of Christ 1013, the Danes held the English throne, and the taxes were too high for the people to tend to their souls. If the rumours were true, those taxes were set to rise. Aelwine

Edmund: Aelwine the Hairdresser

shook his head, said his prayers of farewell to the corpse, and closed up the tomb.

That night, when Aelwine was back in his chamber, the spirit of Edmund appeared to him. This was a regular and very precious part of his nightly routine and Edmund always came to him in a crown, with gold hemming his tawny robes. Green stockings enclosed his legs, and his beard and nails, Aelwine was always proud to note, were short and neat, his hair evenly trimmed against his neck. That night, Aelwine told Edmund about the rumours that the Danish King, Sweyn Forkbeard, now on the throne of England, would soon be exacting so much tribute from the English that many would face starvation. King Edmund listened gravely and promised to appear to Sweyn and exhort him to withdraw the demand. After all, Edmund himself had not paid tribute to the Dane King Hingvar; why should the English do it now? Some nights later, Edmund appeared to Aelwine again and told him he had done as he had said he would, but that Sweyn had not listened. He would go on taxing the people, Edmund said. He needed Aelwine's help.

Aelwine did not like to leave the body of his beloved saint, but the same saint had given him instructions. In the biting winds and driving rain, he rode north, all the way to Sweyn's court in Gainsborough. Drenched and shivering, Aelwine entered the hall during a feast. It was full of Danes and English sycophants, and they laughed as he shuffled to the dais. Then they went on laughing as he delivered a speech to the King, who sat stiff and tall, his beard shaped with wax into two fierce points. They hardly noticed that Aelwine had written and rehearsed his words well; that his speech was as neat and trim as his fingernails. But they heard him give Sweyn the order of England's beloved saint clearly enough:

'You must stop burdening the people with taxes, or else, Sweyn, you will know their patron's wrath!'

The laughter stopped. Sweyn gestured to his soldiers and they drove Aelwine from the hall. That night, Aelwine found lodging in Lincoln, but left before dawn. Edmund had visited him, saying it would be wise to be well away from Gainsborough before the night was over.

On the second morning of his journey south, Danish soldiers caught up with Aelwine. They were in a tumult, though he could not understand their words. At last, one spoke to him in English.

'Are you the priest who threatened King Sweyn?'

'I am,' he said.

The Dane told him what had happened and he pictured it all in silent triumph. King Sweyn had been lying drunk in his bed, still clothed, still crowned, a richly woven blanket gathered about his legs. His eyes had opened as a figure in tawny robes had materialised in the air above him. The ghost of a king had wielded a money bag in one hand and in the other he had grasped a spear. Then the Dane had uttered a cry of horror as, eyes ablaze, the spirit of Edmund

Edmund: Aelwine the Hairdresser

had thrust the spear into Sweyn's chest, piercing the fine clothing and rupturing the body within. Sweyn had been dead before his servants had drawn back the hangings from his bed, but they had come soon enough to see the apparition before it disappeared.

And so it was that, as surely as the seasons passed beyond the church of Bury St Edmunds, so surely could Aelwine be found inside each month, tending to his beloved Martyr King, gathering clippings and trimmings for his little box and whispering his devotions. And even now the shrine and relics have been gone many hundreds of years, if you sit for long enough in the church when all the visitors and clergy have gone, you might hear the *snip* of his shears.

❖

The young Richard II kneels down, his hands raised in supplication. He wears a red cloak, embroidered with his insignia, the golden stag, encircled by the seedpods of the broom plant, representing the Plantagenet royal line. On his chest he wears a great gold badge, also showing the stag. Its body is white, as if it has been enamelled, and each tine of spreading antlers is tipped with a pearl of white. More Plantagenet broom-pods in gold hang around his neck, embellished with pearls and, perhaps, a sapphire. His delicate crown is just as luxurious. Richard's well-groomed hair, beardless face and regal finery stand out against the figure behind him, whose hand proffers him forward with a touch to his shoulders. The hand and the arm of the man are laced with veins, his cloak is of rough animal hide and his hair is wild and long. From this and from his halo and the small symbolic lamb he holds in his other hand, the figure is recognisable as St John the Baptist, the cousin of Christ, who lived in the desert foretelling the coming of the Messiah. John the Baptist who wore nothing but camel-skins and ate only locusts and honey.

Behind the King and the biblical prophet stand two more figures. Like Richard, they are wearing crowns, and like John, they have haloes. They are kings, as well as saints, and they reach their right hands towards Richard as though presenting him. The King immediately behind Richard is old and hoary. His left hand holds a ring set with a large gem. The King behind him is younger and carries an arrow. They are Edward the Confessor and Edmund the Martyr.

A frame encloses all these figures and forms one half of a diptych: a pair of panel paintings joined by a hinge to form a sort of precious birthday card with the main image on the inside. The other half of the diptych shows the Virgin Mary with the Christ Child on her lap, surrounded by a host of angels. All the angels are wearing Richard II's stag badge and one is waving a banner of a red cross on a white ground. By the late fourteenth century, when this diptych was made, the red cross would have been firmly associated with St George. The orb terminating the handle of the banner contains a minute image of a white castle and a boat in full sail: Richard's kingdom in miniature.

The Wilton Diptych is believed to have been the portable altarpiece of Richard II. It shows Edmund and Edward, the patrons saints of England, though they had lived hundreds of years before Richard came to the throne and before English identity had coalesced into anything like what it was by the late fourteenth century, when the diptych was made.

Edmund the Martyr was born around 841 and died in 869, either in battle against an invading Viking army or, as the story goes, as a martyr refusing to forfeit his kingdom to the Danes and pay tribute to their king. The story that a wolf guarded Edmund's severed head is also legend, first attested in an account of his martyrdom by the French Benedictine monk Abbo of Fleury (died 1004). He also writes of a female attendant at the saint's grave who trimmed the saint's hair and nails:

> A certain widow named Oswyn lived near the holy tomb, and prayed and fasted there many years. She would cut the hair of the saint each year and trim his nails, chastely, with love, and place those holy relics in the shrine on the altar.

The shrine would have included offerings in gold, silver, wax and wood from grateful pilgrims, and when, according to Abbo, thieves stole into the cathedral to make away with the costlier votive offerings and to break into the shrine, Edmund freezes them motionless: one on a ladder, one digging.

Some decades after Abbo, a monk at Bury St Edmunds, known as Herman the Archdeacon, wrote up a collection of miracles about his community's saint. Oswyn the widow becomes Aelwine the lay convert, who facilitates Edmund's ghost in ending Sweyn Forkbeard's tyranny. But both Oswyn and Aelwine are fastidious in collecting the trimmings of Edmund's body.

The Abbey of Bury St Edmunds was dissolved in 1539. Its relics were removed by John ap Rice, a commissioner working under Thomas Cromwell and Henry VIII. John reported his findings at the shrine of St Edmund, which included 'much vanity and superstition, [such] as the coals St Lawrence was toasted withal, the paring of St Edmund's nails, St Thomas of Canterbury['s] pen-knife'. Thus, relics that had been described with great solemnity in medieval texts resurface in the reformers' writings as objects of scorn and ridicule.

Catherine: The Scholar and the Wheel

Died 305
Feast Day: 25 November

As persecution swept through the Empire, it had been important to Catherine's father that she learn all she could and be strengthened by her learning. Thanks to him, she had been trained in astronomy, logic, arithmetic, grammar, music, geometry and rhetoric – the art of spoken argument. Together, these disciplines had taught her not only to see the world in all its wonder, but how to argue well. For that reason, when she saw all her fellow Christians giving up their faith before Emperor Maxentius, she went to him and put forward her case for setting them free.

Maxentius had made a show of astonishment, then he had laughed without humour, and said, 'Young lady, my apologies, but I did not listen properly. I will listen tonight, when you explain it all to me again.'

Later that day, he had invited her to a debate. She accepted. And the longer they sparred, the clearer it became that she was winning. Catherine was the superior scholar. The Emperor accused her of sophistry and sent for the best philosophers in the Empire: masters of rhetoric and logic, scholars who would put Catherine in her place.

When they arrived, they scorned Maxentius for summoning them from their homes for the sake of an argument with a girl, but, standing on a stage before the people of Alexandria, she defeated them all soundly. The philosophers at once rescinded their old beliefs and accepted Christianity, and Maxentius burned them for treason.

The Emperor's next offer was to give Catherine riches in exchange for her submission. When she refused, he put her in the dungeon and went away for twelve days. But even there, angels had visited her, illuminating the dungeon and feeding her hot bread rolls fresh from the ovens of Heaven. Thus sustained, she converted his wife and the imperial guard.

When the twelve days were over, soldiers led Catherine out of the prison. Feeling refreshed, she stood at the edge of the crowded arena and considered what she saw. Metal saw blades and sharp iron nails thrust from the rims of the four wheels in its centre. Their hubs connected to a device that brought them together and made them turn in opposite directions.

The Emperor's scheme, Catherine deduced, was to make her lie between the wheels and set the mechanism turning. They would tear her to pieces and kill her. As Catherine looked down at the instrument made of wheels, she understood that the Liberal Arts would only take her so far. Faith, true faith, was beyond reason.

Catherine: The Scholar and the Wheel

The wheel machine squatted in the centre of the arena, newly oiled and grim. All attention was turned towards it and the small figure of Catherine behind. And all minds anticipated the carnage of metal meeting flesh.

But then an angel, massive as the city itself, ruptured the fabric of the visible world. It struck the heavy timber and the instrument burst apart.

Later that day, Maxentius would have his wife's breasts cut off and then her head. Then, when Catherine refused to marry him and would still not give up her faith, he had beheaded her as well, milk poured from her neck.

❖

According to legend, St Catherine of Alexandria died at the orders of the Emperor Maxentius in around 305. In the sixth century, the Byzantine emperor Justinian I founded a monastery at the base of Mount Sinai in Egypt. In the ninth century, it became the home of Catherine's body, carried to Sinai, legend has it, by angels. Her remains were steeped in saintly power: they exuded holy oil and her hair continued to grow. The monastery was dedicated to St Catherine and, being an important stopping point for European pilgrims travelling to Jerusalem, this further boosted her fame. In the eleventh century, her relics were acquired by the Church of the Holy Trinity in Rouen, France, and her cult flourished in north-western Europe. In England, it took hold more surely after the Norman Conquest, probably encouraged by the new ruling classes. By the eve of the Protestant Reformation, she was a household name, patron to countless trades and disciplines, as well as to unwed girls. In Britain she was widely chosen as patron by guilds, churches, confraternities and places of education, and there are many surviving badges in the shape of her characteristic wheel.

Scholar of the Reformation Eamon Duffy notes how saints with the most spectacular, miracle-rich and suffering-laden legends tended to have the strongest cults in late medieval England. 'Pierced flesh and exploding torture machines' were common to the martyrdoms of Sebastian and George, as well as Catherine. And she was also revered

Catherine: The Scholar and the Wheel

alongside Margaret, the two of them being depicted either side of the shrine image of Our Lady of Walsingham. They also featured frequently with other virgin martyrs, as attested by the surviving rood screens of East Anglia and Devon.

But Catherine's popularity begs certain questions. Was this brilliant young rhetorician, who defied authority and brought proud men low, a medieval feminist icon? Did girls look up from their prayers in village churches and resolve to be 'more Catherine'? The answer is probably a 'no' in both cases. In later medieval England, at least, saints' legends were not so much examples to follow as catalogues of their protagonists' extraordinary power. Catherine's scholarship is one aspect of her particular *virtus*. If you're after a holy advocate, then she will argue the Devil out of the room.

I have already touched on the shift in emphasis in the medieval cult of saints from relic veneration to the veneration of cult images. Catherine was no exception. Her image appeared not only on rood screens, but on panel and wall paintings, in alabaster carvings and in metalwork. She is generally easy to spot, with her wheel held in her hand or glimpsed behind her legs like a shy child hiding behind their mother.

In January we looked at Gregory the Great's letter to Bishop Serenus, exhorting him not to destroy images of saints, because 'to adore a picture is one thing, but to learn through the story of a picture what is to be adored is another'. By the early fifteenth century, reformers were claiming that the holy pictures themselves were being adored. This was, in their view, idolatry.

The start of the Protestant Reformation is usually dated to 1517, when Martin Luther published his *Ninety-Five Theses*. These primarily concerned the Church's selling of indulgences to reduce the buyer's time in Purgatory, but Reformist feeling soon took hold in Britain, absorbing tenets of earlier 'heresies' like Lollardy. In 1532, the English preacher Hugh Latimer whipped the people of Bristol into a frenzy by preaching against venerating, decorating and lighting candles before holy images. He even condemned the invocation of saints more generally. Such was his influence that a prominent conservative preacher declared all the people of that city 'eretykes'. Fearing religious images, iconoclasts had already been at work in the 1520s and very early 1530s, casting out images from churches and even pricking the figures with bodkins to see if they would bleed. And, while Henry VIII initially opposed reform, by 1533 he saw its advantages. Breaking with Rome allowed him to divorce Catherine of Aragon and marry Anne Boleyn. In 1534, he had installed himself as the head of the Church of England and put the weight of the crown behind the English Protestant Reformation.

By the mid-sixteenth century, iconoclasm was no longer the practice of a zealous minority. Even to possess a religious image had become treachery. The King's Injunction of 1547 makes that clear enough, specifying the removal of all 'shrines, covering of shrines, all tables, candlesticks, trindles or rolls of wax, pictures, paintings, and all other feigned miracles, pilgrimages, idolatry and superstition: so that no memory of the same remains in walls, glass windows or elsewhere within their churches or houses'. Its purpose was to eradicate the cult of saints and the images that kept their memory alive.

The extent of the destruction is hard to quantify, but the odd remnant can help us imagine what was lost. An especially magnificent survival is an altarpiece dating to the fourteenth century and measuring nearly four metres long. Its painted figures lean this way and that on their embossed gold backdrop with quintessential Gothic elegance, their pigment, though somewhat faded, still glowing with azurite blue and translucent red lake. As well as a Crucifixion flanked by the Virgin Mary and John the Evangelist, the panel shows Saints Dominic, Catherine, John the Baptist, Peter, Paul, Edmund, Margaret and Peter the Martyr. It was found in a barn in the 1920s and is believed to have been made for the Dominican Priory in Thetford, Norfolk. At some point in its history, presumably during the Reformation, an iconoclast crossed out St Catherine's face, gouging through the paint with two hard lines.

Back in May, I mentioned a fifteenth-century panel painting showing the Virgin Mary holding a fruiting cherry branch. It is believed to have come from another Dominican

Priory, this time in Dartford, Kent. By 1863 it was in nearby Battel Hall House. Here, six saints flank the Virgin Mary, including St Agatha, with a dagger skewering her exposed breasts. To Mary's immediate right stands St Catherine, wheel in one hand and sword in the other. Her face has also been completely scratched away; probably in 1539, the year of Dartford Priory's dissolution by the government, along with numerous other foundations.

Some survival stories show determination to preserve the outlawed tradition, even at great personal risk. Art historian Lloyd de Beer recently identified that seven surviving alabaster scenes of the legend of Catherine once belonged to the same altarpiece. He showed that they were made at the behest of a noble couple, Laurence and Catherine Ireland, in the later fifteenth century, to be housed in a new chapel dedicated to St Catherine on their estate in Lydiate, then in Lancashire. Exactly what happened to the large narrative sequence during the Reformation is a mystery; while it was certainly broken up into smaller panels, perhaps to make it easier to hide, it suffered no drastic iconoclasm. However, we do know that, by the nineteenth century, the panels were on display in Lydiate Hall. They had been kept safe since the Reformation and brought out when it was no longer treachery to do so, presumably after the Catholic Relief Act of 1791.

Two of the alabaster Catherine panels now reside in the Society of Antiquaries, London, and the rest are in the

Catherine: The Scholar and the Wheel

Catholic Church of Our Lady, Lydiate. They have never been reunited physically, but we can imagine them together. They show the legend in full: Maxentius having the philosophers burned, Catherine's imprisonment, the exploding wheel, Catherine in prayer, her beheading, her burial by angels at Sinai and a fragment of a free-standing figure of the saint to oversee it all. Each scene is an exquisite example of contemporary alabaster craftsmanship, with its predilection for long limbs and faces as thin and ovaloid as grains of barley.

December

The sow's carcass melts the snow as a man kneels on her belly, holding her legs to keep them from kicking. She is only just dead or maybe she is still dying. A warmly dressed woman collects the blood.

Men peer from the windows of a tavern while, on the path outside, another woman stares in shock, her hands covering her mouth. Snow covers the landscape and the trees are bare and darkly vivid. Startled birds take flight in a white sky. Everything is rigid with cold and shock, but for the soft, hot body lying in the snow.

Moments ago, the sow was squealing in terror, but now, with her death, there will be a supply of meat, bones and blood to take the onlookers into January.

This calendar illustration comes from an early sixteenth-century manuscript from Ghent, Belgium (now in New York's Pierpont Morgan Library, Ms. M.399), but versions of the 'killing of the pig' labour for December appear in manuscripts from across medieval Europe. Often, the pig is being 'pole-axed' or hit with the back of an axe-head. Watched over by a moon in Capricorn, December is the month for attending to injuries to the knees and tendons.

Clensing

It is the month for Advent and, with Christmas, the feast of Christ's birth, an important new beginning in the Christian liturgical year. However, for us, it is also an ending. Perhaps Janus can see it coming from where he sits at the feast. His world is about to change irrevocably. In the countries affected by the Protestant Reformation, the calendar of feast days, with its vignettes of agricultural labours and Zodiac symbols, will lose its relevance, becoming an archaic curiosity in books from a bygone age.

In December, we will meet Saints Nicholas and Thomas Becket. Memory of the first remains strong, even in the secular West, having travelled with popular traditions to territories unknown, but half-dreamt of, by medieval Christians. Today St Thomas Becket has fallen a long way from his once meteoric fame and we will discover why when we see him come to blows with yet another king called Henry. At last, as the year draws to a close, the candles will be extinguished, and the images and offerings taken away to be burned.

Nicholas: The Mistake

Died: 4th century
Feast Day: 6 December

The cathedral at the heart of Myra was already full of people. They had come to celebrate the ordination of Nicholas. His landlady was with them, squeezing to the front so that she would see the man in whose presence she found herself – usually so confident – shy as a child. She had known he was holy. She had known he was special. She had seen it in her own behaviour when he was in the room: how her hands would forget how to do whatever they were doing, whether making pastry, working at her tapestries or tying the bows on her baby's boots. When Nicholas came into the room, she would forget the niceties of everyday conversation, and her tongue would stumble over familiar words. It was the sense of utter calm that he emanated, as well as wisdom, for all he was just a young man. When Nicholas was nearby, she felt she was in the company of one older, even, than her father, with all the authority of a sage.

That morning, Nicholas had not joined them for breakfast. As she had looked after her other guests and seen to the needs of her children, a neighbour had called through the window that a new bishop had been found for the city. People were claiming, she had said, that an angel had appeared to the churchmen who had assembled to make the appointment and it had told them that their chosen candidate would be the next man to walk into the cathedral. It had been someone called Nicholas. And the landlady had felt no doubt that it was *her* Nicholas. The consecration, it was said, would be happening that very day, and she had hurried to complete her domestic duties so that she could be there. Her mind had been in a daydream as she had fed and washed the children and readied herself for the ceremony. Now, having run across the city and into the cathedral, she had reached the carved screen in front of the sanctuary and was peering through it. She could see the profiles of monks singing and she could see Nicholas encircled by priests. He was beautiful to her eyes and distant as a star.

She felt tears spill down her face and she lifted her fingers to her lips and prayed. One priest was placing a mitre on Nicholas' head, while another was anointing his forehead with oil. The silk met the hair and the oil met the skin and her heart swelled. She felt a thousand miles away from the household that occupied her time; she felt next to Heaven. And then Nicholas' eyes met hers.

It's not unusual for parents to have nightmares that, in a moment of distraction, they have left their children in danger. The landlady had experienced such nightmares, but she had never been diverted enough from her duties for anything like that to occur in real life. At least, she had not been so diverted until she had found out that her favourite tenant, the one she looked at with awe and wonder, was being made Bishop of Myra.

Her bliss turned to dread. She realised she had to get home as fast as she could, for it might already be too late. She turned and pushed her way back through the crowd, out of the cathedral and through the town towards home, running and calling. By the time she turned onto her street, her voice was hoarse.

When she got to her front door, her hands were shaking so much that they fumbled the handle. She tried again, now calling her son's name so loudly that people were stopping and staring. She managed this time, and threw herself into the house. As her eyes adjusted to the dark interior, she saw the fire and clay bath resting on top of it. And in the bath, she saw the water had risen to a boil and that, just as she had dreaded, her dear baby son was still sitting in it. She seized the child from the water and ran with him into the light. She had to see what could be done to save him, if there was anything that could be done.

The landlady clasped the child to her breast with one hand and ran the other over his fat thighs, calves and buttocks and all those tender parts that had been submerged in the boiling bath. But they felt as they always did: not blistered and burned, but perfect, whole and smooth.

And now he started to laugh. She held him out in front of her, confused and relieved. And as her breathing slowed, she was able to see again the scene that had met her eyes as she had burst back into her house. Her son had been splashing in the boiling bubbles as if they had been cool to the touch and his eyes and two white teeth had been shining in his plump face as he grinned. By some miracle, her baby was unharmed.

The landlady said her son's name, quietly this time, kissed his temple and smelled his damp hair. Then she shut her eyes and gave thanks, for she knew that Nicholas had sent her back to her child and protected her child from death.

❖

While Nicholas, the fourth-century Bishop of Myra, is one of the great child-helping saints, votive offerings to other saints show a widespread belief in their general efficacy in helping the young. In 1307, twenty-five years after the saint's death, examiners recorded votives left at the shrine of Bishop Thomas Cantilupe in Hereford Cathedral. They counted ninety-five children's shifts. Similarly, when, in 1942, the tomb of Edmund de Lacy (died 1455) in Exeter Cathedral was damaged by a bomb, the clear-up team found numerous small wax body parts, including the complete figure of a girl with long braided hair, a heart-shaped face and her hands raised in prayer. She wears a full-skirted dress, laced at the front from chest to hips in a style that is probably fifteenth-century. She looks out of large, round eyes, their surface clouded by age. The material is hollow-cast wax, dark as a ginger nut. She is a votive offering left to the dead bishop in thanks for a miracle, perhaps the girl's recovery from accident or disease.

In many countries in Continental Europe, 6 December is a day for receiving presents from the original St Nicholas. This same figure, whose story is set in modern-day Turkey, was imported to America as *Sinterklaas* by Dutch migrants, becoming 'Santa Claus'. However, both St Nicholas and Santa Claus are associated with secret gift giving and children. These traditions may be traced to the medieval legends that grew up around his cult, the former being found in *The Golden Legend*, in which, under cover of darkness, Nicholas leaves an impoverished father three sackfuls of gold with which to pay his three daughters' dowries. His connection to children may owe much to a story popular in late medieval England known as *The Three Clerks*, in which three boys are murdered by a butcher and pickled in a barrel. When Nicholas refuses to buy meat from the butcher's counter, but only from the grisly barrel, the remorseful butcher and his wife open it and the saint brings the boys back to life. It may also derive from the story of the miracle of the baby in the boiling bath, which comes from an Anglo-Norman *Life of St Nicholas* by the twelfth-century author known as Wace.

Clensing

In England, St Nicholas' association with children led to the 'boy bishop' custom, which had begun by at least the thirteenth century. There are records from cities across the country of a boy being chosen from among the cathedral choristers and dressed up as a miniature bishop from the feast of St Nicholas to 'Childermass', which fell on the fourth day of Christmas and marked King Herod's massacre of innocent children in his attempt to kill the infant Christ. That the boy bishop should give a sermon on Childermass was even written into the statutes of St Paul's Cathedral in 1518.

The Popish Kingdom, published in 1570, describes familiar St Nicholas traditions, especially for readers with Continental European connections. Its assessment of the practices, however, suggests the author would be disappointed by their longevity, since it describes how:

> The mothers all their children on the eve do
>   cause to fast,
> And when they, every one, at night in
>   senseless sleep are cast,
> Both apples, nuts and pears they bring, and
>   other things beside,
> As caps, and shoes, and petticoats, which
>   secretly they hide,
> And in the morning found, they say that this
>   St Nicholas brought:
> Thus tender minds to worship saints and
>   wicked things are taught.

Nicholas: The Mistake

We may never know why some folk traditions originating from the cult of saints endured to the present while others did not. Maybe, in the case of old Saint Nick and his nighttime largesse, the children just refused to stop believing.

Thomas Becket: The Rose and the Lily

Died 1170
Feast Day: 29 December

Snow whitened the stones of Christ Church as William sat turning the leaves of the book he and Benedict had written. Between its heavy oak boards nestled a collection of wonder-tales that would long outlive their writers. The work paid homage to their murdered archbishop, Thomas of Canterbury, whose relics lay close enough to radiate warmth even as winter draughts raced and rattled through the cloister.

William, a deacon, had witnessed the murder, which had taken place on the fifth day of Christmas, in the Year of Christ 1170. He had been filing to vespers with his brethren, when four of King Henry's knights had stormed the cathedral, their swords held aloft like paschal candles, and the noise and shouting had frozen the monks' chant in their throats. All but a few of the brothers had run at once to the enclosed safety of the choir.

Trouble between the King and the Archbishop had been brewing for years. Henry wanted all clergy accused of crime to be tried by the crown. Thomas, his former friend, called it a tyrannical bid for divine authority. Tonight was a reckoning and all the brothers knew it. Tonight, blood would be spilled.

As the altercation between the knights and the Archbishop had intensified – Thomas refusing to revoke the excommunication of officials siding with Henry, and the knights growing evermore violent – William had crouched behind a bench in the choir. In his terrified paralysis, he had not been alone. Brother John, Archbishop Thomas' secretary and a famous scholar in his own right, was curled behind an altar like a snail behind a leaf. For all their seniority, they hadn't been as brave as the young, strapping Edward

CLENSING

Grim. He had stood firm beside Thomas as the knights had flicked the Archbishop's cap from his head with a sword-point and tried to drag him from the cathedral. Edward Grim still had a scar on his freckled forearm from when he had defended Thomas from another fall of the sword. No, that kind of heroism had been beyond William, as it had been beyond Brother John. But they would have their part to play.

Once the knights had fled from the cathedral, leaving the Archbishop dead in a pool of blood and shredded brains, the older monks had known what to do as if they had been rehearsing for it for their whole lives. They had emerged from their hiding places and, taking in the carnage of the scene, they had set to work.

The Archbishop had not been murdered. No. He had been martyred, which meant he was now one of a heavenly elite whose earthly commemoration needed expert management. The first thing to be done was to have the body taken from where it lay at the top of the stairs and carried down into the vaulted crypt. With it should go the fragment of blade that had sheared from one of the knights' swords and the disc of skull that had been sliced from Thomas' head, killing him on the spot. Cupped in the hands of one of the novices, the bone looked like an ivory bowl, only the rim of blood-reddened hair showing what it really was. Then the senior monks had sent for cloths to soak up the mottled mess. They would be needed later on.

Thomas Becket: The Rose and the Lily

Thanks to years of learning and teaching in the Cathedral school, the older brothers at the scene had beheld the situation, not as it appeared to earthly eyes, but as it really was. The disc of skull was not the crown of Thomas' head, but the Crown of Martyrdom. The sword had not been wielded by a knight, but by Anger herself, whose weapons would always shatter on Virtue's immovable brow. The blood and the brains were not the effusions of a mortal man, but the red and white of the rose and the lily, of sacrifice and purity.

In rejecting the demands of the King, Thomas had refused to hand the Church over to tyranny. He had accepted death like a martyr under Decius or Diocletian or in heathen lands as an apostolic missionary. He was a second Thomas the Apostle. And when the truth escaped, devotion would bloom from Ireland to Byzantium. The people did not trust their kings; the people trusted their saints.

In the years that followed Thomas' martyrdom, stories of his miracles pierced the soils of Christendom like the first flowers of spring. William gathered them faithfully.

The snow cloud had stained the light in Christ Church library the pale tan of old parchment as William turned the leaves of the book to one of his favourite stories, collected not by himself but by his collaborator, Benedict, now Abbot of Peterborough. He remembered how the man called Eilward, a native of Weston in Bedfordshire, had stood in

CLENSING

front of Benedict, bright-eyed and chirpy as a robin, while pilgrims had moaned and wept beside the shrine. Smelling strongly of beer, he had told the priest how it had all started when he had got into a fight with a neighbour who owed him money and, when he hadn't been paid back, how he had stolen his neighbour's grindstone and a pair of work gloves. But his neighbour had caught him, struck him on the head with the grindstone and accused him of stealing much more than he had really taken.

'I was put to trial by the ordeal of being plunged into water, Father,' Eilward had explained. 'In this way they found me guilty and sentenced me to blinding and castration. Thanks be to God and the Holy Martyr Thomas! They mutilated me. And they did a thorough job of it, Father, removing one eyeball whole and chopping the other to pieces in its socket. Then they cut off my testicles, Father, and buried them.'

William, stationed a little closer to the shrine, had glanced over to his colleague, who was starting to take notes. Then he had looked at Eilward. William knew something of medicine, but no expertise was needed to ascertain that Eilward's eyes were whole and in his head. As to whether he had testicles, that was harder to tell.

Eilward had survived, he said, despite much bleeding, and his daughter had guided him back to Bedford. There they were taken in by a friend. For ten days Eilward had sat in the dark, but on the tenth night . . .

'I saw Saint Thomas, Father, with the eyes of my spirit! He wore white robes and held a bishop's staff, which he used to draw crosses where my eyes had been. And he told me to make offerings in the church. And the next day, when I had done as he said, my eye sockets began to itch so terribly I peeled off the wax laid over them, wanting to scratch the flesh with my fingers. But when the wax was gone, I could see a bright light. My host waved a hand in front of my face and I told him what he was doing. I was able to see, even though I still had no eyeballs! After that, the people of Bedford came to me in crowds. They told me that if they looked deep into the sockets, they could see pupils in the scarred flesh, small as the eyes of a sparrow. My eyeballs grew back, Father, by Thomas' prayers and the Grace of God. Because of that, I promised to make a pilgrimage here.'

He related how the streets of Bedford had filled to send him on his way. But four miles down the road he had felt another itch a long way from his eyes. He had put his hand between his legs to scratch it and felt two growths, small as peas. In the coming days these had grown bigger, just as his eyes had done, and – praise be to Holy Thomas, the best doctor to the worthy sick – his dear testicles had returned. He had shared the good news with anyone who would listen.

'And they always wanted to feel the place and I always let them, for we should never hide the power of Thomas and the Grace of God.'

Eilward had laughed heartily and Benedict and William had laughed with him, thanking him for his testimony. Then they had done the necessary checks and, in time, included his story in their collection. William hoped it would be chosen for the glaziers to render in coloured glass for the windows that would surround the new site of the shrine. There had recently been a fire in the cathedral and building work was underway to renew the east end and magnify it enough to receive the body of St Thomas from where it now lay entombed in the crypt.

Somewhere the sun was setting and William's eyes were tired. He shut his life's work and, returning it to one of the many book chests, left it lying in the dark. The library was gloomy now, silent, draughty and cold. And yet, as he turned towards the place where the body of Thomas lay, William felt heat on his face.

❖

Thomas Becket was born around 1120 to a merchant family in London's Cheapside. One later *South English Legendary* (or verse hagiography) would claim that his father 'Gilbert beket of London' had served in the Holy Land as a crusader soldier. It would spin a tale of how the daughter of the Emir had seen him among her father's prisoners and converted at once to the Christian faith. After his escape, she had made a solo journey to London to find him, though she spoke not a word of English and had attracted much attention from the citizenry by her beauty. Eventually word would reach Gilbert of the woman who sought him by name and he would be advised by the bishops of St Paul's to bring her for baptism and marry her. Thanks to his time as prisoner, he could speak her language. She would conceive Thomas on their wedding night.

The legend of Thomas' Middle Eastern heritage has no known historical basis, but it does tap into a tendency in medieval European literature to attribute a certain hotheadedness and wild determination to women from Islamic kingdoms. Perhaps the temperament of his legendary mother helped account for Thomas Becket's changeability in adulthood.

Historically speaking, Thomas rose to become Royal Chancellor and close friend of King Henry II of England after a string of clerical jobs. This led to his elevation in 1162 to Archbishop of Canterbury, head of the English Church. Henry probably hoped the appointment would give him an ally among the elite clergy, but, if so, his hopes were dashed. Thomas Becket changed, embracing his new role with a religious zeal he had not exhibited before, and when Henry sought to pass laws compelling priests accused of crimes to be tried by the State rather than the Church, Thomas not only defied him, but excommunicated the King's allies, denying them the promise of salvation.

On 29 December 1170, four of Henry's knights – including one 'Reginald Fitzurse' – confronted Thomas Becket in

Canterbury Cathedral. According to eyewitness accounts, Thomas refused to be cowed by the knights' aggression and stood firm until they had killed him with a blow that cut off the top of his head.

Once the knights had fled, the monks emerged from their hiding places, moved Becket's body to the crypt, saved the fragment of his skull, scooped up the red blood and white brains, and set aside the shard of metal blade that had broken on the cathedral floor from one of the knights' swords. These would become his primary relics. Then the monks took Thomas' body away and removed the vestments from his corpse. Contemporary accounts claim they discovered that he was not only wearing a hair shirt, but hair breeches. This captured the imagination of later preachers like John Mirk, who wrote that the garments 'bred so much vermin on him that it was a horrible sight to see'.

As the news of the murder spread, miracles were reported across Christendom and pilgrims began flocking to Thomas' tomb in the cathedral crypt. He was soon seen as a holy champion against royal oppression; Thomas was Catherine, refusing to submit to the Emperor. He was Margaret, steadfast in her resistance to the Roman governor. He was a good, old-fashioned martyr. By 1173, Becket had been declared a saint by the papacy. In 1174, Henry II performed public penance, processing barefoot into Canterbury, lying face down before Becket's tomb and receiving lashes from the monks.

Thomas Becket: The Rose and the Lily

In the same year, a fire destroyed the east end of Canterbury Cathedral. In the refurbishments, a new east end was constructed, specially illuminated with a programme of stained glass that narrated the miracle reports collected at the shrine-side by two monks called William and Benedict. The cathedral was also extended to the east with the new 'Corona' chapel for Becket's ornate reliquary bust. The chapel's Latin name alluded not only to the fragment of the crown of Becket's skull enclosed in the reliquary, but also to the crown of martyrdom, which it was believed he had received upon his death. Around the high altar, the monks installed a crescent of variegated white and rust-red columns of imported marble and had the walls painted red. These colours alluded to the lily and the rose, purity and sacrifice, brains and blood.

Metaphors like these helped medieval spin doctors elevate a messy political murder to a martyrdom. One of the aspects of the event that they took advantage of was the name 'Fitzurse', which means 'son of a bear'. In the accounts of the murder written by eyewitnesses like Edward Grim, the 'bear' knight helps give expression to the notion that the knights were frenzied predators and the Archbishop an innocent lamb. Distilled to its allegorical essence, the bear becomes an embodiment of Anger.

When I was working at the British Library, I was given the job of checking digital images of an illustrated manuscript of Prudentius' *Psychomachia*, a fourth-century poem describing an epic and very gory battle between the Virtues and Vices. It became a popular classroom text for teaching Latin (a sort of moral *Horrible Histories*) and had a conventional cycle of illustrations. They include an image of Anger breaking her sword on the head of Patience.

Now, in the early textual accounts of Becket's martyrdom, the knight who kills Becket is called Richard le Bret, and his sword breaks on the floor of the cathedral. Fitzurse only delivers blows earlier in the conflict. However, in the earliest known depiction of the martyrdom, from a very large collection of Becket's letter correspondences collated around 1180 by a monk called Alan of Tewkesbury, the killer blow is delivered by Fitzurse, identifiable by the bear heads on his shield, and his sword shatters on Becket's head. The readers for which it was intended are likely to have learned their Latin from texts like Prudentius' *Psychomachia* (there is a surviving copy from Christ Church) and would have known the image of Anger breaking her sword on the head of steadfast Patience, so it would be a mistake to dismiss this as inaccuracy. To its makers, it may have done a better job of expressing the moral truth of the event than an image that stuck closer to the textual description. Art is not literal, and why should it be?

In 1220, fifty years after his death, the first ever jubilee was celebrated with the translation of Thomas Becket's body from its tomb in the crypt to a spectacular golden shrine raised high on a pedestal in front of the high altar. The shrine was set with a great ruby that King Louis VII of France had presented to the Canterbury community in 1179. Later royal pilgrims enriched the saint's remains yet more. Two miniature golden ships were donated by Edward I in 1285, along with four golden statuettes and brooches set with precious stones. Edward likewise donated the royal crown of Scotland after seizing it during his campaigns for Scottish overlordship. What with gifts from kings, queens and nobility, as well as its own opulence, the shrine would have been an overwhelmingly luxurious sight.

The theatre that pilgrims encountered when visiting Becket's shrine is described by the humanist Desiderius Erasmus, in his 1526 colloquy *A Pilgrimage for Religion's Sake*, which takes the form of a dialogue:

> OGYGIUS Gold was the basest Part. Every Thing sparkled and shined with very large and scarce Jewels, some of them bigger than a Goose's Egg. There some Monks stood about with the greatest Veneration. The Cover being taken off, we all worshipp'd. The Prior, with a white Wand, touch'd every Stone one by one, telling us the Name in *French*, the Value of it, and who was the Donor of it. The Principal of them were the Presents of Kings.
>
> MENEDEMUS He had Need to have a good Memory.

CLENSING

OGYGIUS You guess right, and yet Practice goes a
great Way, for he does this frequently.

The donations of non-elite pilgrims were beneath being listed aloud by the Prior but may be inferred from the evidence of other shrines that were heavy with miniature wax body parts, tapers or trindles, gold rings, cloths, chains from freed prisoners and weapons. Even the votive offerings decorating the shrines of less famous saints, like Thomas of Cantilupe in Hereford, could number in the thousands. And as well as models and other artificial objects, there were bodily 'ejections'; one Canterbury devotee wanted to take a miraculously sneezed-up cherry stone home, rather than contribute it to Canterbury's collection.

All this helps us imagine Thomas Becket's shrine, but we should remember to combine its own richness and adornments with the sounds of Mass being sung and the prayers and pleadings of pilgrims, the sight of flickering candles and coloured shafts of sunlight, the smells of incense and bodies and the thaumaturgic aura of the whole sacred space. These would have made visiting Canterbury and destinations like it an experience of knockout visual, auditory, spiritual and olfactory force. Whether rich or poor, medieval or modern, it's hard to imagine anyone not being overwhelmed by the experience of these sites.

The sensory onslaught wouldn't have ended with leaving the cathedral. In the fifteenth-century sequel to the

Thomas Becket: The Rose and the Lily

Canterbury Tales by an author called Beryn, the narrator describes pilgrims venerating relics, then leaving the cathedral to buy (or steal) souvenirs:

> They prayed to Saint Thomas in the ways they knew.
> And then, while a good monk told and taught them
>   the names,
> Each man kissed the holy relics with his mouth.
> And then they went to other holy places
> And performed their devotions,
> And left for dinner, as it was nearly noon.
> Then, according to custom they bought signs [souvenirs]
> So that others should know who had their part.
> Each man set his silver to whatever he liked
> And, in the meanwhile, the Miller pilfered
> A bosom-full of Canterbury brooches.

Newly cast, silver-bright and arranged on market stalls, these signs included *ampullae* full of blood-tinged water, as well as playful badges in the shape of swords that slid into tiny scabbards, Becket on horseback or in a ship returning from exile in France or, one of the most common badge types, the bejewelled reliquary bust that stood in the Corona Chapel. A great deal of creativity went into the design of Canterbury souvenirs and it is little wonder. In the view of his pilgrims, Becket was a champion of the people, a defender of faith and a challenger of tyrants, and they flocked to Canterbury in droves.

Clensing

For over four centuries, it seemed there was nothing for the Crown to do but go along with it. Even when Becket's cult had passed its heyday, it was still a major presence in the Christian spiritual landscape. Only a seismic shift like the Protestant Reformation would have the power to change that. Across north-western Europe, the popularity of major cult centres began to dwindle. The changes to the shrine of St James are described, albeit, perhaps, with some hyperbole, in Erasmus' *Pilgrimage for Religion's Sake*:

> MENEDEMUS Prithee tell me, how does the good Man St *James* do? and what was he doing?
>
> OGYGIUS Why truly, not so well by far as he used to be.
>
> MENEDEMUS What's the Matter, is he grown old?
>
> OGYGIUS Trifler! You know Saints never grow old. No, but it is this new Opinion that has been spread abroad thro' the World, is the Occasion, that he has not so many Visits made to him as he used to have; this great Apostle, that used to glitter with Gold and Jewels, now is brought to the very Block that he is made of, and has scarce a Tallow Candle.

In England, the waning popularity of the cult of saints compounded with Henry VIII's abhorrence of the precedent set by Thomas Becket's legendary defiance towards the crown. Henry VIII had been threatened with excommunication by the Pope in 1533, but that didn't stop him. As the self-appointed head of the new English Church, Henry would no longer be listening to senior ecclesiastics, dead or alive, or accepting their judgements. In 1538, the King's commissioners dismantled Thomas Becket's shrine, filling twenty carts. They annihilated the various holy stations within the cathedral and destroyed the reliquary bust in the Corona Chapel. Becket's bones were, it is said, burned. In the same year, images of and services to Thomas Becket were outlawed. His name was struck from calendar pages and his liturgies obscured with rough rubbings of red ink. In Bury St Edmunds, parishioners refused to join in with a parson who, in singing a service to St Thomas, defied the royal proclamation. Across the kingdom, images were destroyed or, in the case of the community of Ashford in Kent, turned into St Blaise by swapping the cross in his statue's hand with a wool comb.

Still, some things lay beyond the reach of Henry's commissioners and the grassroots iconoclasts. There are over five hundred surviving Thomas Becket pilgrim souvenirs. These are probably not testaments to rebellion. While some must have been illicitly treasured for a time, most were probably forgotten about, lost from a hat or bag or thrown away to end up buried in the old waterways and pilgrim routes during the centuries of Becket's active cult. This is where we find them today, with pilgrim souvenirs showing other saints and secular badges of heraldic animals and genitals and whatever else could be cast in pewter. The forbidden images of saints in this form were just too numerous, too cheap and too disposable to be worth anyone's trouble. They slipped through the Reformation nets and one can't help loving them for it.

Thomas Becket reveals the strength of popular devotion that saints inspired, as well as the administrative heft needed to suppress it. But what should we do about the age-old censorship of legends that have not only much to reveal about our heritage, but are complex and compelling in their own right? Well, I say we tell them anew, and see what they tell us in return. This is a starter for ten. I've barely scratched the surface.

Testament

Then Mary plucked a cherry,
as red as the blood,
Then Mary went home
with her heavy load.

Then Mary took her babe,
and sat him on her knee,
Saying, My dear son, tell me
what this world will be.

'O I shall be as dead, mother,
as the stones in the wall;
O the stones in the streets, mother,
shall mourn for me all.

'Upon Easter-day, mother,
my uprising shall be;
O the sun and the moon, mother,
shall both rise with me.'

'The Cherry Tree Carol' (Child Ballad 54A),
The English and Scottish Popular Ballads,
ed. Francis James Child (1882–98)

Epilogue

Patrick's Staff of Jesus – the Bachal Isu – was publicly burned in Dublin in 1538. At roughly the same time, the great ruby from Thomas Becket's shrine became the centrepiece of a ring for King Henry VIII, though its whereabouts are a mystery today. In the 1560s and 1570s the reform government warily but effectively suppressed England's popular mystery plays, while, in 1571, the Church of England laid out its doctrines in a document called the *Thirty-Nine Articles of Religion*. Still conscious of the early heresies, it accepted infant baptism as a necessity for salvation, but rejected the authority of the Pope and codified the status of the English monarch as its supreme leader on earth. It also rejected the miracle of transubstantiation, alongside belief in Purgatory, the use of indulgences and the veneration of saints and their images. English Protestantism scorned the rituals and prayers that people had for centuries spoken in the hope of gaining supernatural protection, seeing them, at best, as vacuous vanities and at worst diabolical. And, of course, it followed that saints' legendary *virtus* was irrelevant. This new order disempowered saints and threw away their bones.

Over the course of this book, we have met many objects and legends that escaped annihilation and the dangers of the subsequent centuries by sheer luck, but there are some treasures that survive to this day *thanks* to the Reformation. In January, we met the thirteenth-century Black Book of Carmarthen, the earliest surviving manuscript entirely in Welsh. It contains the story of Scoithín's terrifying alter ego, Yscolan, and is a unique testament to the shared cultural roots of Brittany and Wales. The Black Book was taken from the treasurer of St David's Cathedral by Sir John Prise of Brecon (died 1555), the King's principal registrar in ecclesiastical matters. John Prise collected and studied medieval manuscripts and he was eager to understand the literary heritage of Wales. No wonder the Black Book caught his eye. To this day, Prise's manuscripts may be found in major collections, including the National Library of Wales and the Bodleian Library.

In England, books written in Old English received similarly special treatment. Many were gathered by the reformer Archbishop Matthew Parker (died 1575), who sought to show that an original, purer English Church had existed before its fall into perceived idolatry and vice. It is said to be thanks to Matthew Parker's exhaustive pillaging that we have the saying 'nosey parker', though there is little evidence for this. And it is also thanks to Parker, former master of Corpus Christi College, Cambridge, that the Gospels of St Augustine still reside in the College's library and are used in the consecration of the Archbishops of Canterbury. Its shelf-fellows include a ninth-century copy of Bede's *Life of Cuthbert* and many hundreds of medieval manuscripts besides, wrested from the fires of reform.

And, of course, the Reformation gave rise to its own legends, with its own saints and monsters. King Henry VIII's former chancellor Thomas More had initially stood beside the King in his defence of orthodox Catholicism. But, as Henry's views shifted with his personal and political aims, More did not follow. He went on opposing the Reformation until he was executed in 1535. The sixteenth-century Welsh Chronicler Elis Gruffydd offers a story of how Thomas More turned his garden into an anti-Eden: 'the Garden of Pain', with trees bearing such names as 'the Tree of Suffering', 'the Tree of Conscience', 'the Tree of Truth' and 'the Tree of Punishment'. There, it says, he would tie 'heretics' to the trees and force confession from them by making them wear burning boots, knotted ropes around their heads and iron presses on their thumbs. In this Protestant legend, the antagonists of medieval lore come back to life as Catholics clinging to an outworn creed.

But, even in Protestant kingdoms, legends and their legacies endured, and some popular habits died either hard or not at all. *Sinterklaas* – St Nicholas – travelled from Holland with colonists to New Amsterdam, the future New York City, and merged with a magician of Nordic folklore who punished naughty children and gave gifts to the good. In

Protestant Germany, edible dormice are still called *Siebenschläfer* (or 'seven sleepers'), as they were in some dialects of English until recent decades. The name preserves their place among *Hausgeister*, or 'house spirits', who protected the home or at least functioned as an omen if discovered snoozing in the eaves.

In England, St George had become such a powerful military symbol that his legend endured without need of shrines or cult images, though these were often spared by iconoclasts anyway. Even as late as 1536, a church in Reading was paying for materials to make an image of St George, including three calf-skins, two horse-skins, a platform for the figure to stand on, iron for the horse, St George's 'coat' and roses, bells, a girdle and a dagger. In the Denbighshire village that bears his name, a tale endured of the hoof prints of St George's horse in the churchyard wall, while the diary of Henry Machyn (died 1563) records that the knights of the Order of the Garter processed singing in Westminster Great Hall on St George's Day morning, 1559, and elected new knights in the afternoon. Today, of course, St George's flag is England's flag.

The tale of Uncumber and the minstrel was tenacious enough to make its way, under the title 'Die heilige Frau Kümmerniß', into the first collection of tales published in 1812 by the Brothers Grimm. Meanwhile, Catherine, patron saint of spinsters and young women, endured in 'Catherning', recorded in eighteenth-century Worcester-

Epilogue

shire as a gathering of young women on 25 November to make merry. On St Catherine's day in Peterborough in 1854, female children from the workhouse dressed in white with scarlet ribbons and, led by a 'queen', processed through the town singing and begging for alms. And, of course, we still explode her wheel on Bonfire Night when we light our fireworks.

The Marian legends of the bowing cherry tree or date palm lived on in folk ballads, surviving as 'The Cherry Tree Carol'. A version collected by Francis Child in the nineteenth century implies a connection between the red juice of the fruit and the blood her child will shed at His death. The memory of the date palm version of the same story also lived on in England till the nineteenth century, when an old Christian told the folklorist John Brand:

> the letter O remained upon the stone of the date for a remembrance that our Blessed Lady, the Virgin, with her divine Babe in her arms, resting herself at the foot of a palm-tree (which inclined her branches and offered a cluster of dates to her Creator) . . . cried out in amazement 'O how sweet they are!' This exclamation engraved the letter O . . . upon the date stone, which being very hard, better preserved it.

And other saints' legends and motifs live on in folklore, as testified by a tale of St Eloi recorded in 1963 from a carter living in Wincanton, Somerset (a village now famed for its horse racecourse). Alterations to the church in 1735 had yielded a carving buried in the wall of the saint with his forge. The carter told the collector, Ruth Tongue (a controversial figure, but let's give her the benefit of the doubt), a version of the same story that I gave in synopsis in September – of the horse reshod by having its leg removed and reattached by the saint. However, his is given from the perspective of another carter who takes his horse, not to Eloi's shrine in Noyon, France, but to the village of Wincanton, where the saint has his smithy. Meeting the carter outside, he gives him cider, bread and cheese and sets about working on the horse:

> Carter, 'e took a look and then took another look, and 'e gollops down 'is zider . . . and Saint were busy in the smithy, and old 'oss were standing there wi' three legs! . . . ''Ere we are, then,' says the Saint, coming out and he brings out fourth leg, and 'e claps it on, and old 'oss stands there . . . Ah! That was St Aloys, that was, down to Wincanton. Proper fine smith!

This retelling by the carter (whose name was not written down) fizzes with a familiar affection, awe and personal ownership; St Aloys, the West Country blacksmith, looked out for his own with skill and a generous lunch.

Finally, the antisemitic blood libel initiated in the legend of William of Norwich finds new expression in ballads from early modern protestant England and Scotland, so that

Epilogue

Little St Hugh of Lincoln, becomes Little *Sir* Hugh, but the murderers' identity is the same.

But whatever we can say of all that has survived the fire, it remains that the Protestant Reformation removed a panoply of protectors from the collective Christian imagination. And it did this without offering an equally vivid replacement or removing its corresponding threats. Under Protestant skies, the Devil still wandered abroad. He could still impersonate a friend. Sulphur could still rise from cracks in the earth. And illness and accident remained. As the sun set on the sixteenth century, reports of infernal doings multiplied, and fear of witches bloomed. Gone were the saints who had once driven demons from pilgrims at their shrines. The defensive weapons needed casting anew.

Today, evil and fear endure. The dragon, the devouring giant, the rapacious emperor, the broken torturer, the enemy in disguise, the spectre on the road, the terrors of displacement, exclusion, illness and death: the bombs fall, the innocent die, the waters rise and the threats strike over and over again.

We still need stories of strength and miracles, for if they cannot offer safety, they can demand better. And if we can tell them for love of peace, for love of empathy, and for each other, if we can sing them to the rhythm of the seasons, like the sweeping of the scythe, and narrate as we go the world's untold, untellable wonders, then the *virtus* will be ours, over and over again.

I was walking on a meadow,
I was walking on the turf;
Under one foot – soil,
Under the other foot – earth,

I saw a boat on the meadow,
Ploughing a trench through the lea,
And when it came closer
The boatman called to me,

'How do you walk on water?
How do you walk on the sea?
How do you walk on water?
Tell me, please, tell me.'

I picked a flower from the meadow,
Put it into his hand,
Saying, 'You are not seeing reality.
I am, though. I am.

'How do you sail on the meadow?
How do you sail on the lea?
How do you sail on the meadow?
Tell me, please, tell me.'

He plucked a fish from the meadow,
Put it into my hand,
Saying, 'You are not seeing reality.
I am, though. I am.'

Acknowledgements

Two surprises lay inside my second-hand (but beautifully dark green and gold-embossed) copy of Dr Pádraig Ó Riain's translation of the Latin *Life of St Ailbhe*. When it arrived, I found it contained a commemorative *ex libris* identifying it as one of the books owned by the late Professor Richard Sharpe (1954–2020). He translated, among many other medieval texts, Adomnán's *Life of St Columba* and this book has benefited from his work. The translated *Life of Ailbhe* must have been in his library before its dispersion and it seemed to me a lovely thing that the book's inside cover had been so carefully labelled. But the *ex libris* was not the only discovery. A University of Cork postcard of an ogham stone and another of several Irish monuments slipped from among the pages. The first contained a friendly note from Dr Ó Riain to Professor Sharpe, and the second identified the book as a review copy for Professor Sharpe to consider. I wish all books bore such provenance information and I hope readers of this one write notes to their friends in the flyleaves and label them up for posterity. But my purpose in relating this anecdote is to extend my first thanks to the sociable, quiet, rigorous work of the scholarly community. May it live forever.

Acknowledgements

Jasmine Palmer and Jon Riley are the gentlest, steeliest editors in the world and more kind than I can say. In this, they are representative of the whole team at Quercus. Thank you for honing, designing and publishing my books.

Much is owed to encounters that took place long before this book was underway, in a world of medieval badges, manuscripts and reliquaries, as well as people full of passion and knowledge. Thank you especially to Dr Lloyd de Beer and Dr Naomi Speakman for inviting me to work with the British Museum's collection of pilgrim souvenirs and secular badges.

For their focused advice since this project began in earnest, I thank Dr Jordan Pullicino, Dr Dustin Aaron, Professor Paul Binski, Dr Seán Hewitt, Dr Mary Wellesley, Dr Ann Marie Rasmussen and Annie Raff. For his close reading of the text and scholarly insights, I thank Professor Julian Luxford. For guidance on medieval methods for preparing live eels, I thank Dr John Wyatt. Geraldine Fowler, I owe you much for giving my daughter a book illustrated with paper cut-out – thank you. And for scanning my paper cut-outs so patiently and well, my thanks go to Jasmine Willow Steel at Postscript in Frome. And there have been a host more guides along the way, including Danielle Elwick, Chris Pig, Joumana Medlej, Grace Pengelly, Violet Venables-Ziminski, Stella Reilly, Alex Mirza, Stephen Wilkinson and Max Porter. Thank you for taking the time to walk, listen and debate.

Acknowledgements

And, finally, thank you to my family and to Will for everything. And thank you to dear 'Trog', who began this book with me as an embryo and who, with your new name, is now big enough to sit on our shoulders. I have treasured our journey. You and your sister are all *virtus*.

Further Reading

For readers looking to delve deeper into the heyday of the medieval cult of saints, I would recommend *Medieval Popular Religion, 1000–1500: A Reader*, ed. John Shinners (second edition, University of Toronto Press, 2008); Robert Bartlett's *Why Can the Dead Do Such Great Things? Saints and Worshippers from the Martyrs to the Reformation* (Princeton University Press, 2013); André Vauchez's *Sainthood in the Later Middle Ages* (Cambridge University Press, 1997); and Ronald Finucane, *Miracles and Pilgrims: Popular Beliefs in Medieval England* (J. M. Dent, 1977). Together, they have offered me a wide-ranging, deeply absorbing context to such medieval legend compendia as Jacobus de Voragine's *The Golden Legend* (I have used the 1998 Penguin edition) and *Legends of Scottish Saints: Readings, Hymns and Prayers for the Commemorations of Scottish Saints in the Aberdeen Breviary*, ed. Alan Macquarrie (Four Courts Press, 2012).

As for the English Reformation, no student can do without Eamon Duffy's *The Stripping of the Altars: Traditional Religion in England, 1400–1580* (second edition, Yale University Press, 1992), nor his *The Voices of Morebath: Reformation and Rebellion in an English Village* (Yale University Press, 2003).

Further Reading

And a hefty but very readable exploration of religious magic and popular spirituality of the post-Reformation period is provided by Keith Thomas' *Religion and the Decline of Magic: Studies in Popular Beliefs in Sixteenth- and Seventeenth-Century England* (Penguin; Weidenfeld and Nicolson, 1971).

I mention many pilgrim souvenirs and secular badges in this book. An important volume for anyone interested in this subject, especially in terms of English finds, is Brian Spencer's *Pilgrim Souvenirs and Secular Badges* (Museum of London, 1998). More recent work has been undertaken by Ann Marie Rasmussen, who has spearheaded the creation of a Medieval Badges resource site, with embedded articles and images: www.medievalbadges.ca. The Kunera database is another wonderful resource, created by Radboud University, for exploring 26,000 pilgrim souvenir and secular badge-finds: https://database.kunera.nl/. And for anyone interested in scrutinising these objects at close, if virtual, quarters, I direct you to the annotated interactive 3D models of badges we made for the Digital Pilgrim Project at the British Museum and uploaded to its page on Sketchfab.

Time in the Medieval World: Occupations of the Months and Signs of the Zodiac in the Index of Christian Art, ed. Colum Hourihane (Penn State University Press, 2007), is a profusely illustrated introduction to the medieval Zodiac symbols and Labours of the Months. If any readers are looking to grow their expertise on this subject beyond the wealth of online resources (including Wikipedia), this is an excellent place to start. It is also worth searching online for the digital facsimiles of manuscripts in public collections. The British Library, the Bodleian Library and the Bibliothèque nationale de France (see gallica.bnf.fr) are among the many libraries that now have platforms offering digitised manuscripts. Psalters with the kinds of calendars I have been describing include the Luttrell and Queen Mary Psalters (British Library, Add. MS 42130 and Royal MS 2 B VII) and the Ormesby Psalter (Bodleian Library, MS Douce 366).

Many traditional practices for saintly feast days are found in the two newly reprinted volumes of *Brand's Popular Antiquities of Great Britain: Faiths and Folklore*, ed. W. Carew Hazlitt (Reeves and Turner, 1905; Alpha Editions, 2019). These are astonishing books.

Below, I offer various primary and secondary sources I found helpful and which may prove likewise for others. While some must be purchased, some cheaply, some less so, others are available as open access online. I have sought to indicate the reading that falls into the latter category.

January

1. Scoithín

William Forbes Skene, *The Four Ancient Books of Wales: Containing the Cymric Poems Attributed to the Bards of the Sixth Century* (Edmonston and Douglas, 1868), p. 318.

A Celtic Miscellany: Translations from the Celtic Literature, ed. and trans. Kenneth Hurlstone Jackson (Penguin Classics, 1972).

Further Reading

Michael McCaughan, 'Voyagers in the Vault of Heaven: The Phenomenon of Ships in the Sky in Medieval Ireland and Beyond', *Material Culture Review* 48 (Fall 1998), 170–80.

The Black Book of Camarthen (National Library of Wales, Aberystwyth: Peniarth MS 1).

2. Edward the Confessor

David J. Bernstein, *The Mystery of the Bayeux Tapestry* (Weidenfeld and Nicolson, 1986).

Paul Binski, 'Reflections on *La estoire de Seint Aedward le rei*: Hagiography and Kingship in Thirteenth-Century England', *Journal of Medieval History* 16 (1990), 333–50.

Nicole Leapley, 'The Eyes Have It: Blindness and Vision in Matthew Paris' *Estoire de seint Aedward le rei*', *Mirator* 12 (2011), 30–52.

H. R. Luard, *Lives of Edward the Confessor* (Longman, Brown, 1858), freely available via archive.org.

Le Estoire de Seint Aedward le Rei (Cambridge University Library, Cambridge: Ee.III.59).

3. Mungo

Robert Bartlett, *The Natural and the Supernatural in the Middle Ages* (Cambridge University Press, 2008).

Cynthia Whidden Green, 'Saint Kentigern, Apostle to Strathclyde: A Critical Analysis of a Northern Saint' (master's thesis, University of Houston, 1998); her translation of Jocelyn of Furness' *Life of Kentigern* is available online, open access, via the Internet History Sourcebooks Project.

Alex Woolf, 'A Classical Source for the Conception of Kentigern', *Pictish Arts Society Newsletter* (2002).

I have also used Caesarius of Heisterbach, *The Dialogue on Miracles*, Vol. 1, trans. H. von E. Scott and C. C. Swinton Bland (Harcourt, Brace and Company, 1929): for the story of the contracts with the Devil, see Book V, Chapter XVIII. A 2023 translation by Ronald Pepin is now available from the Liturgical Press.

4. Smaragdus

Robin Norris, 'Genre Trouble: Reading the Old English Vita of Saint Euphrosyne', in *Writing Women Saints in Anglo-Saxon England*,

ed. Paul E. Szarmach (University of Toronto Press, 2013),
pp. 121–39.
Anonymous Old English Lives of Saints, ed. and trans. Johanna
Kramer, Hugh Magennis and Robin Norris (Harvard University
Press, 2020), pp. 27–53.

5. Agnes

*The Golden Legend or Lives of the Saints, compiled by Jacobus de
Voragine, Archbishop of Genoa, 1275. First Edition Published
1470. Englished by William Caxton, First Edition 1483*, ed. F. S.
Ellis (Temple Classics, 1900), Chapter 24 ('Agnes'); digital text
freely available online via www.christianiconography.info/
goldenLegend.

Gawain and the Green Knight, trans. W. A. Neilson (Middle English
Series: Cambridge, Ontario, 1999). Shortly before the lines cited,
this poem also describes the exchange of New Year's gifts, or
'handsel'.

February

6. Brigid

Maeve B. Callan, 'Of Vanishing Fetuses and Maidens Made-Again:
Abortion, Restored Virginity, and Similar Scenarios in Medieval
Irish Hagiography and Penitentials', *Journal of the History of
Sexuality* 21 (May 2012), 282–96.

Sanas Cormaic ('Cormac's Glossary'). For the original Latin, see
the transcription of the Yellow Book of Lecan (Trinity College,
Dublin, MS 1318, H.2.16), now digitised on the Early Irish
Glossaries Database (www.asnc.cam.ac.uk). My translation is
adapted from Whitley Stokes, *Three Irish Glossaries: Cormac's
Glossary, O'Davoren's Glossary and a Glossary to the Calendar of
Oengus the Culdee* (Williams and Norgate, 1862).

'Cogitosus's Life of St Brigid the Virgin', in *Saint Patrick's World:
The Christian Culture of Ireland's Apostolic Age*, translations and
commentaries by Liam De Paor (University of Notre Dame Press,
1993), pp. 207–24.

Further Reading

For the story of the 'Nun of Watton', see *Aelred of Rievaulx: The Lives of the Northern Saints*, trans. Jane Patricia Freeland, ed. Marsha L. Dutton (Cistercian Publications, 2006).

7. Werburgh
Goscelin of Saint-Bertin: The Hagiography of the Female Saints of Ely, ed. and trans. Rosalind C. Love (Oxford University Press, 2024).
The Life of Saint Audrey: A Text by Marie de France, ed. and trans. June Hall McCash and Judith Clark Barban (McFarland and Co, 2006).

8. Ia
Caitlin Green, 'St Ia of St Ives: A Byzantine Saint in Early Medieval Cornwall?', blog post (17 January 2018).
K. A. Hemer, Jane Evans, Carolyn Chenery and Angela L. Lamb, 'Evidence of Early Medieval Trade and Migration between Wales and the Mediterranean Sea Region', *Journal of Archaeological Science* 40 (2013), 2352–9.
Charles Thomas, 'The Context of Tintagel: A New Model for the Diffusion of Post-Roman Mediterranean Imports', *Cornish Archaeology* 27 (1988), 7–25.

March

9. David
Rhygyfarch, *Life of St David*, trans. Arthur Wade-Evans (Society for Promoting Christian Knowledge, 1923), available online, open access, via archive.org.
Beatha Bharra, Saint Finbarr of Cork: The Complete Life, ed. and trans. Pádraig Ó Riain (Irish Texts Society, 1994).

10. Patrick
My Name is Patrick: St Patrick's 'Confessio', trans. Pádraig McCarthy (2011). The translation of the *Confessio* and *Patrick's Letter to the Soldiers of Coroticus* is also available to read online via www.confessio.ie.
'Sir Owain', in *Three Purgatory Poems: The Gast of Gy, Sir Owain,*

Further Reading

The Vision of Tundale, ed. Edward E. Foster (Medieval Institute Publications, 2004).

Roy Flechner, *Saint Patrick Retold: The Legend and History of Ireland's Patron Saint* (Princeton University Press, 2019).

Froissart, *Chronicles,* ed. and trans. Geoffrey Brereton (Penguin, 1968).

11. Cuthbert

The Voyage of St Brendan: Representative Versions of the Legend in English Translation, ed. W. R. J. Barron and Glyn S. Burgess (University of Exeter Press, 2002).

Bede, *Ecclesiastical History of the English People,* trans. D. H. Farmer, R. E. Latham and Leo Sherley-Price (Penguin, 1990).

Bede, *Life and Miracles of St Cuthbert*, in *Ecclesiastical History of the English Nation,* trans. J. A. Giles (1910), pp. 286–349: digital text freely available online via the Internet History Sourcebooks Project.

St Cuthbert Gospel (British Library, London: Add. MS 89000).

12. William of Norwich

Christians and Jews in Angevin England: The York Massacre of 1190. Narratives and Contexts, ed. Sarah Rees Jones and Sethina Claire Watson (York Medieval Press, 2013).

Thomas of Monmouth, *The Life and Passion of William of Norwich,* trans. Miri Rubin (Penguin, 2014).

The Abingdon Apocalypse (British Library, London: Add. MS 23555).

Debra Higgs Strickland, *Saracens, Demons, and Jews: Making Monsters in Medieval Art* (Princeton University Press, 2003).

April

13. George

Jonathan Good, *The Cult of St George in Medieval England* (Boydell Press, 2009).

Michael Michael, 'The Iconography of Kingship in the Walter of Milemete Treatise', *Journal of the Warburg and Courtauld Institutes* 57 (1994), 35–47.

Further Reading

Michael Prestwich, *The Three Edwards: War and State in England, 1272–1377* (Routledge, 1981).

Samantha Riches, *St George: A Saint for All* (Reaktion Books, 2015).

The Walter Milemete Treatise (Bodleian Library, Oxford: Christ Church MS 92).

14. Mellitus

Paul Binski, 'The Cult of St Edward the Confessor', *History Today* 55, No. 11 (November 2005).

For Gregory the Great's 'Letter to Mellitus', see Bede, *Ecclesiastical History*, trans. Farmer *et al.*, Chapter 30.

For the salmon legend, see Luard, *Lives of Edward the Confessor*.

15. Erkenwald

Saint Erkenwald, ed. Clifford Peterson (University of Pennsylvania Press, 1977).

The sources that may have influenced *St Erkenwald* are discussed in *Middle English Saints' Legends*, ed. John Scahill and Margaret Rogerson (D. S. Brewer, 2005).

May

16. Brendan

The Voyage of St Brendan, ed. Barron and Burgess, Introduction.

17. Mary

Selections from English Wycliffite Writings, ed. Anne Hudson (University of Toronto Press, 1997).

Three Late Medieval Morality Plays: 'Everyman', 'Mankind' and 'Mundus et Infans', ed. G. A. Lester (New Mermaids: Bloomsbury, 2014).

How the Wise Man Taught His Son, in *Codex Ashmole 61: A Compilation of Popular Middle English Verse*, ed. George Shuffleton (Kalamazoo, 2008): available online via the TEAMS Middle English Texts Series at https://d.lib.rochester.edu.

The Luttrell Psalter (British Library, London: Add. MS 42130).

Marian badge with acorns: Museum of London (object number 90.244/2).

Further Reading

Hood of cherries badge: British Museum, London (object number 1856,0923.7).

June

18. Boniface
Willibald's *Life of St Boniface*, in *Soldiers of Christ: Saints and Saints' Lives from Late Antiquity and the Early Middle Ages*, ed. Thomas Noble and Thomas Head (Pennsylvania State University Press, 1995); digital text also freely available online via the Internet History Sourcebooks project.

The Ragyndrudis Codex (Hochschul- und Landesbibliothek, Fulda: 100 Bonifatianus 2).

19. Columba
Adomnán of Iona, *Life of St Columba*, trans. Richard Sharpe (Penguin, 1995).

Michael Herity and Aidan Breen, *The Cathach of Colum Cille: An Introduction* (Royal Irish Academy, 2002).

The Cathach of St Columba (Royal Irish Academy, Dublin: MS 12 R 33).

20. Alban
For the story of Alban's martyrdom, see Bede, *Ecclesiastical History*, trans. Farmer *et al.*, Chapter VII.

Gildas, *On the Ruin of Britain*, trans. J. A. Giles (1841; In Parenthesis, 2000); for St Alban, see Chapter II, §11.

Book of St Alban (Trinity College Dublin: IE TCD MS 177).

July

21. Veronica
The Golden Legend, trans. Caxton, ed. Ellis, Chapter 53 ('The Passion of Our Lord').

22. Uncumber
'A Dialogue Concerning Heresies', in The Complete Works of St. Thomas More, edited by Mary Gottschalk, Vol. 6. (Yale University Press, 1963), freely available online via https://thomasmorestudies.org.

Further Reading

Lewis Wallace, 'Bearded Woman, Female Christ: Gendered Transformations in the Legends and Cult of Saint Wilgefortis', *Journal of Feminist Studies in Religion* 30 (Spring 2014), 43–63.

23. Margaret

Róisín Donohoe, '"Unbynde her Anoone": The Lives of St Margaret of Antioch and the Lying-in Space in Late Medieval England', in *Gender in Medieval Places, Spaces and Thresholds*, ed. Victoria Blud, Diane Heath and Einat Klafter (University of London Press, 2019), pp. 139–56.

Martha G. Blalock and Wendy R. Larson, 'Margaret of Antioch', in *Middle English Legends of Women Saints*, ed. Sherry L. Reames (Medieval Institute Publications, 2003), pp. 111–248; the digital text of the *Stanzaic Life of Margaret* is freely available online via the TEAMS Middle English Texts Series, https://d.lib.rochester.edu.

Sarah Fiddyment *et al*, 'Girding the loins? Direct evidence of the use of a medieval English parchment birthing girdle from biomolecular analysis,' in *Royal Society Open Science* (2021). Freely available online.

C. Rawcliffe, 'Women, childbirth, and religion in later medieval England' in *Women and religion in medieval England*, ed. D. Wood (Oxbow Books, 2003), pp. 91–117.

D. C. Skemer, *Binding words: textual amulets in the Middle Ages* (Penn State Press, 2006).

24. Christopher

Julian Luxford, 'Recording and Curating Relics at Westminster Abbey in the Late Middle Ages', *Journal of Medieval History* 45 (2019), 204–30.

Roger Rosewell, *Medieval Wall Paintings in English and Welsh Churches* (Boydell Press, 2008).

Jacobus de Voragine, 'St Christopher' (Chapter 39), in *The Golden Legend*, trans. Christopher Stace, ed. Richard Hamer (Penguin, 1998).

Badge with cockerel staff: British Museum, London (object number 1884,0305.2).

Further Reading

25. James

The Colloquies of Erasmus, trans. Nathan Bailey, ed. E. Johnson (Reeves and Turner, 1878), Vol. 2; freely available online via resources.warburg.sas.ac.uk/pdf/nah7374b2324315A.

The Miracles of St James: Translations from the Liber Sancti Jacobi, ed. Thomas Coffey, Linda Kay Davidson and Maryjane Dunn (Italica Press, 1996).

Codex Calixtinus (Cathedral Archives, Santiago de Compostela).

26. The Seven Sleepers

Anonymous Old English Lives of Saints, ed. and trans. Kramer *et al.*, pp. 587–651.

H. R. Luard, *Lives of Edward the Confessor* (1858).

August

27. Germanus

The Golden Legend, trans. Caxton, ed. Ellis, Chapter 107 ('Germain').

Malcolm Barber, *The Cathars: Dualist Heretics in Languedoc in the High Middle Ages* (Routledge, 2000).

Heresy and Authority in Medieval Europe: Documents in Translation, ed. Edward Peters (University of Pennsylvania Press, 1980).

28. Lawrence

Eamon Duffy, *The Stripping of the Altars: Traditional Religion in England, 1400–1580* (Yale University Press, 1992).

———, *The Voices of Morebath: Reformation and Rebellion in an English Village* (Yale University Press, 2003).

The Golden Legend, trans. Caxton, ed. Ellis, Chapter 117 ('Laurence').

'The Martyrdom of St Lawrence' (stained glass, *c.* 1180): Cloisters Collection, Metropolitan Museum of Art (accession no. 1984.232).

29. Bartholomew

The Golden Legend, trans. Caxton, ed. Ellis, Chapter 123 ('Bartholomew').

Medieval Popular Religion, 1000–1500: A Reader, ed. John Shinners (University of Toronto Press, 2008).

The Hereford Mappa Mundi, *c.* 1300 (Hereford Cathedral).

Further Reading

September

30. Marymas

Medieval Popular Religion, ed. Shinners.

Maureen Barry McCann Boulton, *Sacred Fictions of Medieval France: Narrative Theology in the Lives of Christ and the Virgin, 1150–1500* (Boydell & Brewer, 2015).

Le Romanz de Saint Fanuel et de Sainte Anne et de Nostre Dame et de Nostre Segnor et de Ses Apostres, ed. Camille Chabaneau (Maisonneuve et Charles Leclerc, 1889).

Blake Gutt, 'Medieval Trans Lives in Anamorphosis: Looking Back and Seeing Differently (Pregnant Men and Backward Birth)', *Medieval Feminist Forum: A Journal of Gender and Sexuality* 55 (2019), 174–206.

31. Ailbhe

Beatha Ailbhe: The Life of Saint Ailbhe of Cashel and Emly, ed. Pádraig Ó Riain (Irish Texts Society, 2017).

The Commonplace Book of Robert Reynes of Acle: An Edition of Tanner MS 407, ed. Cameron Lewis (Garland, 1980).

32. Cosmas and Damian

The Golden Legend, trans. Caxton, ed. Ellis, Chapter 143 ('Cosmas and Damian').

33. Michael the Archangel

Katherine Allen Smith, 'An Angel's Power in a Bishop's Body: The Making of the Cult of Aubert of Avranches at Mont-Saint-Michel', *Journal of Medieval History* 29 (2003), 347–60.

Christopher Lee Pipkin, 'Monster Relics: the Giant, the Archangel, and Mont-Saint-Michel in the Alliterative *Morte Arthure*', *Arthuriana* 27 (Spring 2017), 95–113.

October

34. Frideswide

Martha G. Blalock and Wendy R. Larson, 'The Legend of St Frideswide of Oxford, an Anglo-Saxon Royal Abbess', in *Middle English Legends of Women Saints*, ed. Sherry L. Reames (Medieval Institute Publications, 2003), pp. 23–50.

Further Reading

Benjamin Savill, 'Remembering St Brictius: Conspiracy, Violence and Liturgical Time in the Danish Massacre of 1002', *Journal of Ecclesiastical History* 73 (July 2022), 480–504.

35. Ursula and Cordula
The Cult of St Ursula and the 11,000 Virgins, ed. Jane Cartwright (University of Wales Press, 2016).

Catherine Sanok, *New Legends of England: Forms of Community in Late Medieval Saints' Lives* (University of Pennsylvania Press, 2018).

Jacobus de Voragine, 'The Eleven Thousand Virgins' (Chapter 59), in *The Golden Legend,* trans. Stace, ed. Hamer.

November

36. Martin
The Golden Legend, trans. Caxton, ed. Ellis, Chapter 166 ('Martin').

The Fabliaux: A New Verse Translation, trans. Nathaniel E. Dubin (Liveright, 2013), pp. 741–5.

Michael Camille, *Image on the Edge: The Margins of Medieval Art* (Reaktion, 1992).

Noel Malcolm, *The Origins of English Nonsense* (HarperCollins, 1997).

Ann Marie Rasmussen, *Wandering Genitalia: Sexuality and the Body in German Culture between the Late Middle Ages and Early Modernity* (King's College London, 2009).

Thomas More, *A Dialogue Concerning Heresies*.

The Popish Kingdome, or reigne of Antichrist: written in Latin Verse by Thomas Naogeorgus and Englyshed by Barnabe Googe (1570), ed. Robert Charles Hope (Chiswick Press, 1880), [p. 53v], freely available via archive.org.

37. Catherine
The Golden Legend, trans. Caxton, ed. Ellis, Chapter 172 ('Catherine').

Eamon Duffy, *The Stripping of the Altars*.

38. Edmund
Rebecca Pinner, *The Cult of St Edmund in Medieval East Anglia* (Boydell & Brewer, 2015).

Further Reading

Abbo of Fleury, 'The Martyrdom of St Edmund', trans. K. Cutler, in *Sweet's Anglo-Saxon Primer*, ninth edition (Oxford University Press, 1961), pp. 81–8.

Herman the Archdeacon and Goscelin of Saint-Bertin: Miracles of St Edmund, ed. and trans. Tom Licence (Oxford University Press, 2014).

December

39. Nicholas

Otto E. Albrecht, *Four Latin Plays of St Nicholas from the Twelfth-Century Fleury Play-Book* (1935; University of Pennsylvania Press, 2016).

For more on votive offerings at shrines see Ronald Finucane, *Miracles and Pilgrims: Popular Beliefs in Medieval England* (J. M. Dent, 1977).

For the 'Boy Bishop' tradition, see *Brand's Popular Antiquities of Great Britain: Faiths and Folklore*, ed. W. Carew Hazlitt, Vol. 1 (1905; Alpha Editions, 2019).

Joel Fredell, 'The Three Clerks and St Nicholas in Medieval England', *Studies in Philology* 92 (Spring 1995), 181–202.

Jacobus de Voragine, 'St Nicholas' (Chapter 2), in *The Golden Legend*, trans. Stace, ed. Hamer.

Wace, *The Hagiographical Works: The 'Conception Nostre Dame' and the Lives of St Margaret and St Nicholas*, ed. and trans. Jean Blacker, Glyn S. Burgess and Amy V. Ogden (Brill, 2013); for the story of the baby in the boiling bath, see the *Life of St Nicholas*, lines 121–94.

The Popish Kingdome, or reigne of Antichrist, ed. Hope.

40. Thomas Becket

Lloyd de Beer and Naomi Speakman, *Thomas Becket: Murder and the Making of a Saint* (British Museum Press, 2021).

The Colloquies of Erasmus, trans. Bailey, ed. Johnson.

The Tale of Beryn, with A Prologue of the merry Adventure of the Pardoner with a Tapster at Canterbury, ed. F. J. Furnivall and W. G. Stone (N. Trübner, 1887), lines 165–75; digital text freely available online via archive.org.

Further Reading

For the legend of Thomas Becket's mother, see Chapter 27 ('St Thomas of Caunterbury'), *The Early South-English Legendary, or Lives of Saints: Vol. 1: MS. Laud 108, in the Bodleian Library*, ed. Carl Horstmann (Early English Text Society, 1887; reprinted Forgotten Books, 2018).

Amy Jeffs, 'Anger's Broken Sword: Prudentius' *Psychomachia* and the Iconography of Becket's Martyrdom', *Journal of the British Archaeological Association* 173 (2020), 26–38.

Alec Ryrie, 'How to Erase a Saint: Thomas Becket and Henry VIII', British Museum Blog (5 July 2021).

Prudentius, *Psychomachia* (British Library, London: Cotton MS Cleopatra C VIII).

41. Testament

For the 'date stone' and the afterlife of Saints George and Catherine, see *Brand's Popular Antiquities of Great Britain*.

For the story of 'St Aloys and the Lame Nag', see Katharine Briggs, *British Folk-Tales and Legends: A Sampler* (1977; Routledge, 2002), p. 300.

Francis James Child, *English and Scottish Popular Ballads*, Vol. 1 (Dover Publications, 1965), for The Cherry Tree Carol, see no. 54.

The Original Folk and Fairy Tales of the Brothers Grimm: The Complete First Edition, trans. and ed. Jack Zipes (Princeton University Press, 2016), Chapter 66 ('Saint Solicitous').

For the story of 'Thomas More and the Garden of Pain', see Elis Gruffydd, *Tales of Merlin, Arthur, and the Magic Arts: From the Welsh Chronicle of the Six Ages of the World*, trans. Patrick K. Ford (University of California Press, 2023), pp. 145–6.

Timeline of Feast Days

Unknown
Uncumber: 20 July

Immortal
Michael: 29 September

First century
Veronica: 12 July
44   James the Great: 25 July
48   Mary the Virgin (multiple feast days)
69/71   Bartholomew: 24 August

Third century
251   Christopher: 25 July
258   Lawrence: 10 August
287/303   Cosmas and Damian: 27 September

Fourth century
Nicholas: 6 December
303   George: 23 April
304   Agnes: 21 January

Timeline of Feast Days

304	Alban: 22 June
304	Margaret of Antioch: 20 July
305	Catherine of Alexandria: 25 November
380	Ursula and Cordula: 20 and 21 October
397	Martin: 11 November

Fifth century

442–448	Germanus of Auxerre: 31 July
460–490	Patrick: 17 March
470	Smaragdus (formerly Euphrosyne): 16 January
478	The Seven Sleepers: 27 July

Sixth century

Scoithín: 2 January

Ia: 3 February

525	Brigid: 1 February
528	Ailbhe: 12 September
575	Brendan: 16 May
589	David: 1 March
597	Columba: 9 June

Seventh century

614	Mungo (or Kentigern): 13 January
624	Mellitus: 24 April
687	Cuthbert: 20 March
693	Erkenwald: 30 April

Timeline of Feast Days

Eighth century
700 Werburgh: 3 February
727 Frideswide: 19 October
754 Boniface: 5 June

Ninth century
869 Edmund the Martyr: 20 November

Eleventh century
1066 Edward the Confessor: 5 January

Twelfth century
1144 William of Norwich: 26 March
1170 Thomas Becket: 29 December

Index

Aachen (Germany) 200–1
Abbo of Fleury 343–4
Abingdon Apocalypse (manuscript) 108
Adomnán (bishop of Iona) 164, 178–9
Aelwine 335–44
Æthelberht (king of Kent) 130
Æthelræd (king of England) 307–12
Africa xiv, 42, 70, 87, 114–15, 150
Alan of Tewkesbury 374
al-Balkhi, Abu Ma'shar xvii
Albertus Magnus 29
Albigensian heresy, *see* Catharism
Alexander the Great (king of Macedon) 41, 266
Alexandria (Egypt) 32, 35, 346, 348
Alfred Atheling 12–15, 17–20
Algar (king of Leicester) 306–9
Anatolia (Turkey) 122
Anglo-Saxon Chronicle 309
antisemitism, *see* Jews and Jewry
ap Rice, John 344
Arabia and Arabic xvii, 25, 122
Arianism 257, 329
Armenia xix, 9, 122, 269
Armorica 319; *see also* Brittany and Breton
Arthur (king of Britain) 41, 124, 228, 297–8

Arthur (prince of Wales) 321–2
Ashford (Kent) 379
Asia xiv, 114–15
Aubert (bishop of Avranches), *see* St Aubert
Augustinian Order 108, 218; *see also* St Augustine of Canterbury
Avranches (France) 294, 298, 301
Bacchus (Roman god) 135, 278
Barra of Cork, *see* St Finbarr
Bartlett, Robert 29
Battell Hall (Kent) 159, 352
Becket, Gilbert 370–1
Becket, Thomas (archbishop of Canterbury), *see* St Thomas Becket
Bede, the Venerable, *see* St Bede
Belinus 136–7, 140, 143
Benedict (abbot of Peterborough) 364, 367–70, 373
Benedictine Order 165, 343; *see also* St Benedict
Besançon (France) 29
Bhagavad Gita xiii–xiv
Bible xiv, 9, 28, 29, 87–8, 100, 107–8, 155, 160–1, 180, 205, 228, 231, 239, 241, 269, 278, 342, 384–5; Genesis 73–4; John 99–100, 279; Jonah 286; Mark 87–8; Matthew 253, 329–30;

Bible (*cont.*)
  Psalms xvi, 33, 97, 150, 157, 173, 179–80, 330–1; Pseudo-Matthew 158; Revelation 121–2, 298
Bird, Matthias 301
Black Book of Carmarthen 11, 384
Bobbio Abbey (Italy) 285
Bodleian Bowl (Ashmolean Museum) 109
Boleyn, Anne (queen of England) 350
Boniface VIII (pope) 91
Book of Durrow 179
Book of Kells 179
Brand, John 387
Brennius 136–7, 140, 143
Bristol (Somerset) xviii, 113, 350
Bristol University 278
British Library (London) xviii, 99–100, 373–4
British Museum (London) xviii, 43, 156, 198, 231
Brittany and Breton xix, 11, 69–70, 80, 319, 384
Brut (chronicles) 143, 228, 319
Brutus (supposed king of Britain) 136–7, 140
Bubwith, Nicholas (bishop of Bath and Wells) 3
Burchard (bishop of Worms) 90–1
Burgess, Glyn 151
Burton-on-Trent (Staffordshire) 218
Bury St Edmunds (Suffolk) 106–7, 324, 341, 344, 379
Byzantium, *see* Constantinople
Caerleon (Wales) 301
Caesarius of Heisterbach 29
Cairo (Egypt) 35
Callan, Maeve 55

Cambridge University xviii, 18; Corpus Christi College 286, 384–5; Pembroke College 299–300
Candlemas 47–8
Canterbury Cathedral 73–4, 130–1, 174, 200, 230, 263, 371–7, 383
Cantilupe, Thomas (bishop of Hereford), *see* St Thomas of Cantilupe
Carthage 42
Catharism 257–8
Catherine of Aragon (queen of Engand) 320–2, 350
Caxton, William 199, 262
Ceredigion (Wales) 80–1
Chad (bishop of Lichfield), *see* St Chad
Chanson de Roland, La 228
Charlemagne (emperor) 41
Charles VI (king of France) 43–4
Chaucer, Geoffrey 229–30, 331, 376–7
Chester Cathedral (formerly St Werburgh's Abbey) 63–5, 70, 101
Chester-le-Street (Durham) 98
Child, Francis James 382, 387
Christ Church Cathedral (Oxford) 123–4, 305–13, 364, 367, 374
Christmas 3, 47, 73, 155–6, 159, 320, 356, 362, 364
Church of the Holy Trinity (Rouen) 348
Clement VII (pope) 379
Cnut (king of England and Denmark) 312
Codex Calixtinus 240
Cologne (Germany) 199–200, 314–20

Index

Constantine (emperor of Rome) 10, 43, 241
Constantinople 70–1, 122, 249, 348, 367
Conwenna 137, 143
Cormac Cuilennáin (bishop of Munster) 52–3
Coroticus (Brittonic chieftain) 83, 86, 88
Cowley, William xx
Cromwell, Thomas 344
Crónán (king of Ireland) 282
Crossybrennan (Kilkenny) 77
Culross (Fife) 23–8
Dartford Priory (Kent) 351–2
de Beer, Lloyd 302, 352
de Bridport, Giles (bishop of Salisbury) 108
de Lacy, Sir Edmund 360–1
de Voragine, Jacobus 43, 123, 250
Decius (emperor of Rome) 243–4, 247–9, 259–62, 367
Denmark and the Danes 12–13, 19–20, 137, 306–13, 320, 335–40, 343
Diocletian (emperor of Rome) 42, 291, 367
Dives and Pauper 48
Dominican Order 209, 351–2; *see also* St Dominic
Dryhthelm (monk of Melrose) 97
Dubin, Nathaniel 331–2
Dublin (Ireland) 383
Duffy, Eamon 47, 263–4, 348
Dumnonia (Brittonic kingdom) 70–1, 80
Dunbar (East Lothian) 96
Durham Cathedral (formerly Abbey) 64, 98, 100–1, 270
Eadbald (king of Kent) 130–1

Easter 14, 73, 75, 106, 113, 150, 159–60, 382
Eata (bishop of Lindisfarne), *see* St Eata
Edith (queen of England) 12–19
Edmund Ironside (king of England) 312
Edward I (king of England) 21, 108, 124, 133, 375
Edward II (king of England) 124
Edward III (king of England) 123–5
Edward the Confessor (king of England), *see* St Edward the Confessor
Edward the Martyr (king of England), *see* St Edward the Martyr
Edwin (king of Northumbria), *see* St Edwin
Egypt xix, 4, 10, 65, 70, 79, 228, 295, 348
Eilward of Weston 367–70
Eleanor of Castile (queen of England) 21
Ely Cathedral (Cambridgeshire) 12–15, 19, 63–4
Ephesus (Greece), *see* Seven Sleepers of Ephesus
Erasmus, Desiderius 112, 375–6, 378
Erkenwald (bishop of London), *see* St Erkenwald
Esrum (Denmark) 320
Ethiopia xix, 123, 291
Eton (Berkshire) 200
Exeter Cathedral (Devon) 360–1
fabliaux érotiques 331–2
Faddan More Psalter 173
Farne Islands (Northumberland) 93–7; *see also* Lindisfarne
Finbarra, *see* St Finbarr

Index

Finucane, Ralph 43, 241–2
Fitzurse, Sir Reginald 371–4
France, French and the French xviii, xix, 12, 18, 29, 43–4, 89, 91, 107, 109, 124, 207–9, 217, 240–1, 258, 278, 285, 291, 329–33, 343, 348, 375, 377, 388
Franks Casket (British Museum) 100
Frigg (Norse god) 126
Froissart, Jean 91–2
Gainsborough (Lincolnshire) 339–40
Gaul 131, 257, 329; *see also* France and the French
Gawain and the Green Knight 41, 163
Geoffrey of Monmouth 143
Georgia 123
Germany, German and the Germans xix, 29, 107, 109, 130–1, 150–1, 171–4, 188, 200, 208, 250, 331, 385–6
Ghent (Belgium) 355
Gilbertine Order 55–6
Gildas, *see* St Gildas
Glasgow (Scotland) 28, 30
Glastonbury Abbey (Somerset) 53
Godwin (earl of Wessex) 12–22, 250
Godwin (priest) 102–3
Golden Legend, The 43, 123, 195, 199, 216, 241, 250, 262, 318–19, 361
Goscelin of Saint-Bertin 65
Greece, Greek and the Greeks 70, 79, 100, 129, 199, 227, 241, 253, 262
Green, Caitlin 71
Gregory I (pope), *see* St Gregory the Great
Gregory II (pope) 171
Gregory of Tours 249–50, 310–11
Griffin, Miranda 278
Grim, Edward 365–6, 373

Grimm, Jacob and Wilhelm 386
Gruffydd, Elis 385
Gutenberg, Johannes 200–1
Hailes (Gloucestershire) 227
Hanbury (Gloucestershire) 64
Harold Godwinson (king of England) 12, 16–17, 20
Harthacnut (king of Denmark and England) 12–15, 19
Hastings (battle) 16, 20
Heisterbach (Germany) 29,
Hengist (king) 130
Henry I (king of England) 20
Henry II (king of England) 174, 356, 364–7, 371–2
Henry III (king of England) 133–4
Henry VI (king of England) 293
Henry VIII (king of England) 321–2, 333, 344, 350–1, 378–9, 383, 384–5
Herbert, Bishop of Norwich 106
Hereford Cathedral 150, 269, 360, 376
Herman the Archdeacon 344
Herod I (king of Judea) 362
Hildesheim (Germany) 188
Hingvar (king of the Danes) 336, 339
Holland and the Dutch, *see* Low Countries
Holy Island (Northumbria), *see* Lindisfarne
How the Wise Man Taught His Son 159
Howard, Philip (earl of Arundel) 304
Hugh of Avalon, *see* St Hugh of Lincoln
Hungary 329
Iasconius (sea creature) 78
Imbolc (festival) 52–3
Immraim Bran ('Voyage of Bran') 10

Index

India 9, 265–9
Iona (Scotland) 178–9
Ireland, Laurence and Catherine 352
Ireland and the Irish xiv, xix, 4, 9–11, 17, 28, 49, 52–5, 64–5, 69, 71–2, 75–9, 83, 86–92, 96, 137, 149, 156, 171–9, 282–5, 329, 367, 383
Isabel (countess of Arundel) 21
Isabella (queen of England) 124
Islam 43, 228, 371
Italy and the Italians xix, 17, 137, 184, 199, 207, 285, 298
Janus (Roman god) 3, 356
Jean, Duc de Berry 36–7, 43–4
Jerusalem xiv, 13, 76, 196, 265–6, 272, 285–7, 318, 348
Jews and Jewry 43, 103–9, 388
Jocelyn of Furness 28–31, 88, 97–8, 329
John of Salisbury 365–6
Jupiter (Roman god) 278
Justinian I (emperor of Byzantium) 70–1, 348
Kelham (Nottinghamshire) 218
Kildare (Ireland) 49, 284
King's Lynn (Norfolk) xviii
Languedoc (France) 258
Latimer, Hugh 350
Latin xvi, 11, 28, 37, 86–7, 89–90, 100, 149, 179, 186, 227, 284, 330, 373–4
le Bret, Sir Richard 374
Lent 73, 113
Lichfield (Staffordshire) 64
Ligugé Abbey (France) 329
Limoges (France) 291
Lincoln Cathedral 98–9, 107, 292–3
Lindisfarne (Northumbria) 93–101, 285
Lindisfarne Gospels 100
Lisle, Sir William 91–2
Little St Hugh of Lincoln 107, 389
Lithuania 123
Llyfr Du Caerfyrddin, see Black Book of Carmarthen
Lollardy 143–4, 160–1, 258, 350
Lough Derg (Ireland) 91
Louis VII (king of France) 375
Low Countries xix, 71, 151, 171, 208, 228–9, 361, 385
Lucca (Italy) 199, 207
Lupus (bishop of Troyes), see St Lupus of Troyes
Luther, Martin 350
Luttrell Psalter 157
Luxeuil Abbey (France) 285
Luxford, Julian 278
Lydgate, John 217
Lydiate Hall (Lancashire) 352–3
Lyons (France) 209, 233–7, 258
Machyn, Henry 386
McClure, Nikki xx
Mankind 158–9
Manannân Mac Lir (Irish god) 10
Marie de France 89
Martinmas 330; see also St Martin
Marymas 272–8
Maxentius (emperor of Rome) 345–8, 353, 372
Maximian (emperor of Rome) 319–20
Melrose (Northumbria) 96–7
Mellitus (archbishop of Canterbury), see St Mellitus
Mere (Wiltshire) 293
Michaelmas xvi
Milemete, Walter 124
Mirk, John 218, 323–4, 372
Moll, Herman 301–2

Index

Monkwearmouth Jarrow (Northumberland) 96
Mont-Saint-Michel (Normandy) 228, 286–7, 297–9
More, Sir Thomas, *see* St Thomas More
Morebath (Devon) 263–4
Mortimer, Sir Roger 124
Mount Gargano (Italy) 298
Mount Sinai (Egypt) 348, 353
Munich (Germany) 200
Munster (Ireland) 52, 284–5
Mynyw, *see* St Davids (Pembrokeshire)
Myra (Turkey)] 357–60
Naogerg, Thomas 192
Netherlands, *see* Low Countries
Newnett, Alice 293
Nicholas (bishop of Myra), *see* St Nicholas
Normandy and the Normans 16–19, 81, 89, 95–6, 103, 107–8, 149, 298–9, 312, 348, 361; *see also* France, French and the French
Norwich Cathedral (Norfolk) 74, 102–9, 330
Noyon (France) 292, 388
N-Town Plays 158
Olybrius (Roman governor) 212, 216
Oswyn, *see* Aelwine
Our Lady's Church, Lydiate 352–3
Ovid (Publius Ovidius Naso) 262
Oxford 306–8; Ashmolean Museum 301; Bodleian Library 304; Christ Church College 123–4, 305–13, 364, 367, 374; St John's College 312–13
Paphnutius, *see* St Paphnutius
Paris, Matthew 17–22, 107, 133–4, 186–8, 250, 286–7, 312

Parker, Matthew (archbishop of Canterbury) 286, 384–5
Patras (Greece) 241
Patrick (bishop of Ireland), *see* St Patrick
Paul the Hermit 95–6, 150
Pelagius 80, 143–4, 255, 257
Persia 71–2
Peterborough (Cambridgeshire) 367, 387
Philip (emperor of Rome) 259
Philip IV (king of France) 299
Picardy (France) 333
Picts 86, 179, 241; *see also* Scotland, Scotic and the Scots
Poitiers (France) 284, 329
Popish Kingdom, The 192, 333–4, 362–3
Portugal 123, 204
Priscillianism 329
Prise, Sir John 384
Procopius 70
Prudentius (Aurelius Prudentius Clemens) 99, 186, 373–4
Ragyndrudis Codex 174, 180
Rasmussen, Ann Marie 332
Reynes, Robert 280–1
Rhygyfarch (clerk of St Davids) 80–1
Richard I (king of England) 108
Richard II (king of England) 341–3
Richeldis de Faverches 279
Riches, Samantha 123
Ripon (Yorkshire) 64
Rocamadour (France) 200
Romance of St Fanuel, The 278, 281
Rome and the Roman Empire xiv, 3–4, 10, 40, 42, 70, 86–7, 91, 97, 100, 122, 130–2, 142–3, 171, 181, 184–7, 216, 238, 243, 251, 253, 256, 260, 262, 284–7,

Index

291, 311, 317–20, 329, 345, 350, 372
Ronwen (daughter of Hengist) 130
Rosendorn, Der 331
Rouen (France) 348
Royal Gold Cup (British Museum) 43–5
Rubin, Miri 106
Rutland Psalter 330–1
Sæberht (king of Essex) 130
St Áed 54
St Agatha 352
St Agnes 4, 39–45, 181, 185, 208, 216
St Aidan 75, 96–7, 285
St Ailbhe 271, 282–7
St Alban 21, 164, 181–9, 256, 286
St Albans (Hertfordshire) 17–18, 133, 181–9
St Albans Cathedral (formerly Abbey) 186–9, 286
St Aloys, *see* St Eligius
St Amphibalus 186–8
St Andrew 10, 241
St Andrews (Scotland) 241
St Anne 273–9
St Apollonia 42
St Asaph 28
St Aubert 294–302
St Audrey, *see* St Etheldreda
St Augustine of Canterbury 130–3, 137, 173, 384–5
St Augustine of Hippo 72
St Barbara 192
St Bartholomew 42, 265–70
St Bede 64, 96–7, 130–1, 144, 173, 185–7, 385
St Benedict 79
St Blaise 379
St Boniface 164, 165–74, 178, 180

St Brendan 71–2, 77–82, 95–6, 145–51, 176, 228–9, 282
St Brice 306, 309–13
St Brigid xvi, 47, 49–56, 64–5, 79, 282, 284–5
St Cainnach 54
St Catherine of Alexandria 192, 324, 345–53, 372, 386–7
St Catherine's Chapel, Lydiate (Lancashire) 352
St Chad 64
St Chelidonius 99, 186
St Christopher xiii, 192, 220–32
St Ciarán 54
St Columba 28, 64, 126, 164, 175–80, 285
St Columbanus 285
St Cordula 314–19
St Cormac 175–8
St Cosmas 288–91
St Cuthbert 64, 74, 93–101, 270, 385
St Damian 288–91
St David 10–11, 28, 64, 74–82, 143, 257, 284
St David's Cathedral (Pembrokeshire) 384
St Davids (Pembrokeshire) 75–6, 80–1
St Dominic 351
St Eadburg 173
St Eata 95
St Edmund the Martyr 21, 99, 106, 124–5, 324, 335–44, 351
St Edward the Confessor 4, 12–22, 124–5, 129, 133–4, 250, 270, 279, 286, 298, 312, 342–3
St Edward the Martyr 311
St Edwin 96
St Eligius 291–2, 387–8
St Elizabeth 155

Index

St Eloi, *see* St Eligius
St Emeterius 99, 186
St Erkenwald 136–44
St Erkenwald (poem) 142–4
St Ermenilda 63
St Etheldreda 61, 63–4, 89
St Euphrosyne 4, 32–8
St Fanuel 273–8, 281
St Felicity 42
St Finbarr 5–11, 75–9
St Frideswide 305–13
St Gabriel the Archangel xiv, 279–80
St Gall's Abbey (Switzerland) 285
St George 114–25, 181, 185, 192, 216, 342–3, 348, 386
St George (Denbighshire) 386
St Germanus of Auxerre 187, 255–8, 270, 329
Saint-Gervais d'Avranches (France) 301
St Gildas 185
St Godehard 188
St Gregory the Great 44, 130–2, 135, 142, 349–50
St Guinefort 208–10
St Gwinear 67–9
St Harold of Gloucester 107
St Helen's, Ranworth (Norfolk) 279
St Hilary of Poitiers 10, 284, 329
St Hippolytus of Rome 260–3
St Hugh of Lincoln 41, 98–9, 107, 292–3; *see also* Little St Hugh of Lincoln
St Ia 47, 67–72
St Ive (Cornwall) 69
St Ives (Cambridge) 69
St Ives (Cornwall) 69–71
St Ivo 69
St James 10, 233–42, 279, 378

St James' Cathedral (Spain), *see* Santiago de Compostela
St Jerome 36–7, 43–4, 65
St Joachim 276–9
St John the Baptist 155, 188, 253, 342, 351
St John the Evangelist 99–100, 134, 239, 279, 351
St Joseph 153–5, 158
St Joseph of Arimathea 199
St Julitta 217
St Kentigern, *see* St Mungo
St Lawrence 42, 259–64, 270, 344
St Lazarus' Cathedral (Autun, France) 240–1
St Luke 100, 199
St Lupus of Troyes 257
St Margaret of Antioch 181, 211–19, 270, 348–9, 351, 372
St Margaret's, Stratton Strawless (Norfolk) 264
St Mark 100
St Martin of Tours 10, 310, 324–34
St Martin's Four Wishes 331–2
St Mary Cleophas 279
St Mary of Egypt 65
St Mary Redcliffe, Bristol (Somerset) 113
St Mary Salome 279
St Mary the Virgin xiv, 47, 100, 145, 152–61, 188, 199–200, 238–40, 253, 264, 271, 272–81, 295, 299–301, 342, 349, 351–2, 382
St Mary the Virgin, Little Dunmow (Essex) 159
St Mary's, Great Witcombe (Gloucestershire) 251–2
St Matthew 100, 253, 330
St Mellitus 13, 126–35, 144, 173
St Menas 65, 70

424

Index

St Michael the Archangel xiv–xv, 121–3, 294–302
St Michael's Mount (Cornwall) 298
St Michael's Tower, Glastonbury (Somerset) 53
St Modwenna 218
St Mungo xvii, 4, 23–31, 64, 88, 97–8
St Nicholas xvi, 356–63, 385
St Nicodemus 199
St Non 81
St Paphnutius 32–6
St Patrick 10, 53, 55, 64, 74, 83–92, 178, 282, 284–5, 329, 383
St Patrick's Purgatory (Lough Derg, Ireland) 89–92
St Paul 129, 173, 351
St Paul's Cathedral (London) 126, 129, 131, 136–44, 286–7, 362, 371
St Perpetua 42
St Peter 13, 127–9, 133–4, 231, 351
St Peter the Martyr 351
St Peter's Abbey, *see* Westminster Abbey
St Peter's Basilica (Rome) 91, 238
St Rule 241
St Quiricus 217
St Samthann 53–4
St Scoithín 4–11, 17, 75–6, 384
St Seaxburh 63
St Sebastian 42, 192, 348
St Serenus 44, 349–50
St Serf 23–8, 64
St Stephen xvi, 42, 218
St Swithun xvi, 250
St Thomas of Cantilupe 269, 360, 376
St Thomas the Apostle 266–7, 367
St Thomas Becket 21, 174, 200, 230–1, 292, 344, 356, 364–80, 383
St Thomas More 208, 333, 385
St Uncumber xix, 9, 202–10, 227–8, 386
St Ursula 192, 305, 314–22
St Ursula's Basilica (Cologne) 320
St Valentine 42
St Veronica xvii, 195–201
St Walery 333
St Werburgh 47, 57–66, 79, 101
St Werburgh's Abbey, *see* Chester Cathedral
St Wilfrid 64
St Wilgefortis, *see* St Uncumber
St William of Norwich 74, 102–9, 388
Salisbury (Wiltshire) xviii, 108
Sanchia of Provence (countess of Cornwall) 21
Santiago de Compostella (Spain) 112, 239–40, 279, 330, 378
Savill, Benjamin 310–12
Scotland, Scotic and the Scots 23–8, 30, 86, 96, 124, 178–9, 241, 375, 388
Serenus (bishop of Marseilles), *see* St Serenus
Seven Sleepers of Ephesus 16, 243–52, 385–6
Severus, Sulpicius 329–30
Shapur II (emperor of Persia) 71
Shinners, John 278
Sicily (Italy) 286
Sir Cleges 159
Sir Owein 89–90
Smaragdus, *see* St Euphrosyne
Smith, Katherine 299

Index

South English Legendary 149, 370
Spain and the Spanish xix, 99, 186, 235, 239–40, 320–1
Stanzaic Life of Margaret 216
Stephen of Bourbon 209
Strickland, Debra Higgs 105
Sweyn Forkbeard (King of Denmark and England) 312, 339–41, 344
Syria 122, 136, 289, 291
Theodosius (emperor of Rome) 249
Thetford (Norfolk) 351
Thomas of Monmouth 105–9
Thomas, Keith 231–2
Thor (Norse god) 126, 130–1, 166, 172
Thorney Island 13, 126–8, 131; *see also* Westminster Abbey
Tintagel (Cornwall) 70
Tipperary (Ireland) 173
Tongue, Ruth 388
Tostig Godwinson 12
Tours (France) 10, 249–50, 310–11, 329–30
Trajan (emperor of Rome) 142
Tunisia 42
Turin (Italy) 198
Turkey xiv, xix, 122, 249, 269, 291, 361
Valerian (emperor of Rome) 262
Vienna Palimpsest 122–3
Vikings 64, 98, 101, 309, 312, 343
Vortigern (king) 130

Voyage of St Brendan, The 71–2, 149–51, 228–9
Wace (poet) 361
Waldensianism 258
Waldo, Peter 258
Wales and the Welsh xix, 11, 28, 70–1, 75–6, 80–1, 143, 228, 255, 301, 384–5
Wallace, Lewis 208
Walsingham (Norfolk) 112, 279–80, 299, 304, 348–9
Weedon Bec (Northamptonshire) 60
Weston (Bedfordshire) 367–8
Westminster Abbey 18, 20–2, 126–34, 228, 386
Wilfrid (bishop of York), *see* St Wilfrid
Wilkinson, Caroline 313
William I (king of England) 16–7
William of Canterbury 364–70, 373
William of Newburgh 108
Willibald of Mainz 172–3
Wilton Diptych 341–3
Wincanton (Somerset) 387–8
Winchester Cathedral (Hampshire) 250
Windsor (Berkshire) 124
Woden (Norse god) 126, 130–1
Wulfar (king of Mercia) 63
Wycliffe, John 160–1
Wynfrith, *see* St Boniface
York 55, 108